Trade Names

Rose Doyle is a Dublin writer and journalist. She is the author of thirteen novels, two of them for younger children and one for teenagers. She has also written radio plays, short stories and more journalism than she cares to remember. When not writing, she enjoys the company of friends, goes to films, walks, talks and compulsively reads.

Trade Names

TRADITIONAL TRADERS AND SHOPKEEPERS OF DUBLIN

ROSE DOYLE

Foreword by Peter Sheridan

NEW ISLAND

TRADE NAMES
First published 2004
by New Island
2 Brookside
Dundrum Road
Dublin 14
www.newisland.ie

Copyright text © Rose Doyle
All photographs by *Irish Times* photographers

The author has asserted her moral rights.

ISBN 1 904301 65 7

British Library Cataloguing in Publication Data. A CIP catalogue record for
this book is available from the British Library.

Typeset by New Island
Cover photograph © Keith Pointing / Virginie Amant
Design by Fidelma Slattery @ New Island
Printed in Spain by Edelvives

10 9 8 7 6 5 4 3 2 1

Contents

To everyone in the Property Department of The Irish Times

Foreword

I've never had a problem with nostalgia. It has become a dirty word and I don't understand why. Yearning for the good things of the past has become tarnished, somehow. Well, I have to confess that memories of my childhood fill me with incredible warmth and make me misty-eyed into the bargain. When I go back there, it touches me in a way that contemplation of the future never does.

The world seemed permanent through my ten-year-old eyes. That's how it should be when you are that age – immutable, unchanging, familiar. We need cornerstones in order to grow. Coming as I did from the North Wall, the survival of the docks and the community that served it seemed as certain then as the properties of an isosceles triangle. What would my little brain have done had I been told that dockers would not be needed in the future; that they would be replaced by steel containers; that their homes would be razed to the ground; that a financial services empire would be built on their reservation. They might as well have told me that the laws governing geometry were being suspended forthwith.

The relationship of the city to the river is symbiotic: Baile Átha Cliath, the town of the ford of the hurdles, was established because the river provided the means of survival – water and food. As Dublin developed from town to city, its dependence on the river deepened. Not alone did the inhabitants fish its depths, but from it one genius, Arthur Guinness, created a drink so famous that it became synonymous with Dublin itself. Once brewed, the wooden barrels were carried in barges down the river Liffey from Usher's Island to the waiting ships docked beside the Custom House.

There always seemed to be a Guinness ship waiting to sail, the *Lady Patricia* or the *Lady Miranda*. As a kid, a great thrill was to run up the gangplank and board the vessel without being caught by one of the charge hands. The docks were a wonderful playground and the river activity meant we were spoiled for choice. Crossing on the ferry was a particular thrill – it went from the steps at Guild Street, on the north side, to Erne Street on the opposite bank – and in summer it wasn't uncommon to dive off halfway across and swim back to shore.

On dry land, the horse and cart still ruled. All day long, convoys carried imported goods from the port to destinations around the city. It was part of our education to learn the timing so that we could "hop up on the back". Coal lorries were predominant but to be avoided at all costs if you didn't want a clatter from your ma. A particular favourite of mine were the CIÉ carts that went from the Midlands Depot (where my father worked as a clerical officer, grade two), because they were generally clean and their route took them right past my house in Seville Place (number 44). They went as far as the stables on Portland Row and thus halved the walk to O'Connell's School on the North Circular Road, a welcome respite.

Yes, I do pine for those days when the river was spectacular, visually and commercially. It is a quieter place these days and seems like it has lost its zest, feels disconnected from its hinterland. The traffic daily queues along the north and south quays, but the shouts of men at work have gone: each driver seems cocooned and intent solely on getting away from there as quickly as possible. No one seems to belong any more. The sense of place has disappeared. No one feels connected to the river.

This transformation happened in the rush to modernity. It happened in the name of progress. But it happened at a price and for the most part we are discouraged from counting it. In the days when the horse and cart ruled, goods got to their destinations faster than they do now. We won't bring back four-legged transport but that's a fact. A study undertaken in London made a comparison on journey times in 1896 and 1996 and the horses came out on top by a long way. They are also better for the environment. But we can't stand in the way of progress now, can we?

There are so many areas of life where a disimprovement in services and quality of life have been sold to us as the opposite. I have my own long list and I won't bore you with it all — but indulge me on the subject of meat. God be with the days when there was a butcher's shop on every corner and you could complain about the Sunday roast if it wasn't up to standard. Along came the supermarket (progress, don't you know) and it put the small family butcher out of business. In the area of Dublin where I live we had two local butchers but they've both packed up and gone. It is a difficult task now to buy meat from a human being. Or just to ask a question when you're not sure. Everything is pre-packed, making the whole thing an awful experience. It has nothing to do with consumer needs and all to do with commercial expediency. Bob Dylan was right when he said that "money doesn't talk, it screams".

So thank God for Rose Doyle and her timely homage to old-fashioned common sense. In a world where illusion is sold as reality, we need someone to unmask the trickery and show us true craft. This she has done in great spadesful. Her technique is simple but brilliant — she plays listener and lets the voices of her subjects speak without intrusion. And what do we find: not a balance sheet or a mention of profit and loss anywhere. Just the voices of individuals who speak with great love and pride in what they do and what their ancestors did before them. Their stories are full of humour, humility, warmth and insight. And there's lots of nostalgia there, too, but I'm not complaining and neither should you.

Peter Sheridan

Brendan Crowe of Crowe & Co., Thomas Street. *Photograph: David Sleator*

Crowe & Co.

Monumental Sculptors,
9 Thomas Street, Dublin 8

Brendan Crowe is a man of philosophical commitment. A lifetime of dealing with death in stone has taught him the uselessness of planning, the value of living in the present, the acceptance of death's inevitability and to marvel, always, at the resilience of people in tragedy.

Stone itself is the other marvel in Mr Crowe's life. "It's the weathering and agelessness that gets to me," he says. "Put your hand on an old, warm stone in a cemetery or lean on a boulder jutting out of a hill and you feel yourself as nothing. You'll be gone and it'll still be there.

"Think too of the people who for centuries have brushed in and out the doorways of old stone houses. They're gone and the doorway's still waiting for people to come in and out and make fools of themselves." All of which might make him sound a tad melancholy. He's nothing of the sort. Mr Crowe, of Crowe & Co. Monumental Sculptors in Thomas Street, is a wiry, humorous, 70-year-old life enthusiast.

Stone carving, the making of grave and tomb stones such as memorial Celtic crosses, is a family thing. His father and a dead brother, Eamon, were in the business and he works today with his other brother, Paddy, and Paddy's son, David.

Business is good. "The Celtic Tiger never impinged on us," he says. "How could it?" Indeed. People will always die, always need gravestones.

A man who deals in fundamentals, Mr Crowe begins his story with a wry: "In the beginning was the word. My father, Patrick Crowe, was in business from the 1930s. He was based in Harold's Cross and was a very fussy, old-style craftsman. There are different kinds of stoneworkers — cutters, carvers, masons. I'm a mason first; I became a stone carver. In the sixties and seventies stone-carving skills began to die but they're well on the way back now.

"The stone trade was a closed one in years gone by. You had to have a son and a line back to Brian Boru before you could get in. It's all opened up now. I taught for 10 years in the NCAD [National College of Art and Design] and the girl students were great. They tried harder, working away all the time. The boys wanted immediate results."

He himself served a seven-year apprenticeship, a large part of it in Earleys Studios in Camden Street working on "high-class church carvings. I worked on Galway Cathedral, a place much maligned at the time.

"I was in Earleys when my father died. I left there and went out on my own. My father's customers came with me, people who'd been with him since 1940. He'd worked for Joe McGrath of the Sweeps — made his wife's stone. We did a stone for Jack B. Yeats out in Taney in Churchtown, for his sisters' grave. He was a very nice man. He died in 1957, same year as my father."

So — what did his father have carved on his grave stone? "He just had a Celtic cross with Patrick Crowe on it. Very simple. On my own I'll just have my name and date of death, that I was married and had one daughter."

He's admiring and warm about the community in Thomas Street. "They're great. Only thing killing us is the traffic. We've an excellent site but they've put a bus lane at our gate. This was a stone place before us, called Courtneys. So there's a line here!"

He thinks aloud, half-heartedly, about retiring. About his brother Paddy retiring. "We should have planned and walked out a certain day and gone to the South of France, or something. To me being retired is not being idle. I'd like to cycle around the city and see all the changes to it. In some ways it's been improved, in others degraded."

He sees people, daily, at their most vulnerable. "I marvel at their resilience in tragedy. In some families you see death following death, young and old dying. I have to say young deaths are increasingly related to drugs and suicide. You get a picture of a lovely young man of 21 and find out it's a suicide.

"But life goes on. You get up in the morning and the rest of your life is waiting."

He sees death as "something we're all confronted with in our own way" and enjoys listening to people because "I'm fascinated by their lives. It's all drama, from beginning to end. You hear such stories of bravery and forbearance. Most people are very businesslike about the stone they want but others, women usually, I have to say, expand a little. If you listen they'll talk." Life, he thinks, "is about treading water in the hopes of something else — and enjoying it".

He's never travelled much, never wanted to. He used to play the clarinet and is an avid reader; Evelyn Waugh is his favourite writer. He'd like these days to be "more optimistic about trends in Ireland. But I'm a bit pessimistic about it. There's a lack of tolerance, especially towards immigrants coming here."

What about changes in the business? Cremation hasn't affected things much, not yet. The importation of foreign granites, especially Chinese, has made a difference. "Stone has had a renaissance. There's new machinery, new technology. It'll become more of an industrial thing and less of a craft but there will always be a strong craft element. People will always want crosses and the like. David will probably keep things going here. He's very good with stone."

Christmas is the busiest time for monuments and headstones. "It's dreadful. Everyone wants stones for Christmas. I'm only beginning to realise there's life after Christmas, that there will be another Christmas, and another."

He laments the current trend for the "trivia" of teddy bears and football crests carved on head stones.

"Religion is still there but secular intrusions are increasing. A stone should be a story about the family, names and dates and relationships. They're grave markers, that's all. I ask people how they'd like their grave to be perceived in 200 years' time."

He's proud of the Crowe speciality in Celtic crosses. Like the one they made for the poet Seán Pleimeann, who died in 1899. And another for John Keegan, who died in 1847 and was described by Mr Crowe as a "hack journalist and humanitarian". His grave in Glasnevin is marked by a Crowe cross. A 24 feet high Celtic Cross by Crowe marks the year 2000 in Carrickmore, Co. Tyrone. The list goes on.

He muses that he's probably passed his prime, says he's wondering if it's worth hanging on, if he should make his bow to the hereafter.

"It's death. You're confronted by the damn thing creeping up on you. We never really acquire the ability to live in the present. If we did we'd be in heaven. I'm constantly harking back myself. Afraid to confront the future. Maybe it's death I'm afraid of — but it's something we have to think about, we have to. You reach a day when there's a relieving clause in the contract. Death is not all horror. You just step away from earthly things and you're ready, after all the suffering and joy, and it's time to shut the door."

Charles Byrne and his daughter Geraldine at Musik Instrumente, Stephen Street. *Photograph: Matt Kavanagh*

Charles Byrne Musik Instrumente

21–22 Lower Stephen Street, Dublin 2

Music, for Charles Byrne, is "the life of the soul". A piece of music can haunt people, he says, bring them together, make friends of strangers. He plays several instruments, most especially the violin, which he came to at an early age.

He remembers the first time he held one in his hand, how he listened to it then started to play. He's in his seventies now, his feelings undiluted. "It's like a voice," he says. "The violin talks to me. I can feel it."

He also restores, repairs and sells violins and string instruments. He's been doing it for a lifetime, says it's in the blood as well as the soul and that he doesn't know how to, and couldn't, do anything else. He's a peaceful man, filled with passion for music, for life, for the care of instruments and, always, for his family. A happy man.

His workrooms and shop, Charles Byrne Musik Instrumente, 21–22 Lower Stephen Street, Dublin 2, is hallowed ground for musicians and music lovers. Has been since 1920. An earlier shop, at 39 Annesley Avenue, North Strand, helped build the family's reputation.

Charles Byrne is the third generation of Byrnes to be bred into and grow with the business and now, ensuring continuity and their unique brand of passionate care and attention, his daughter Geraldine, a cellist and classical guitarist, has become the fourth. "It's absolutely marvellous that she has come into the business," says Charles. "She knows her music, can talk to people and has a very, very kind heart."

Geraldine, behind the counter playing a violin for a customer, doesn't hear but thinks he's wonderful too.

The four of us, Charles, Geraldine, the customer and me, take up almost all the floor area in the tiny shop. The walls have cabinets stuffed with violins, mandolins, bouzoukis, bodhráns. Charles

Byrne, on a low stool in the middle of it all, is the white-haired, benign, apron-covered lord of a world apart, uniquely secure and sensibly aware of the value to the wider world of the commodity it deals in.

The story of the Byrnes and music begins in 1870, when Charles's grandfather, David Byrne, a musician who played and studied music, opened the Luthier Workrooms for the repair and reconstruction of string instruments in Annesley Avenue.

When his son Charles (father of the present-day Charles) met and married Christina Monaghan he married into both her family and the Stephen Street building, which was owned by the Monaghans. Charles Byrne the First opened Charles Byrne Musik Instrumente there in 1920. "We're linked to the building on both sides, my grandfather's and grandmother's," Geraldine points out, "so it's very much a part of the tradition."

Framed bills, mementoes of the early days of the business, show that in 1901 Mr D. Byrne estimated that a "set of gut strings, 15 pegs and regulation of the machinery of a harp" cost The Science and Art Institutions of Dublin a princely £1.

Christina Byrne died giving birth to her son Charles so he lived with an aunt until he was eight years old. "Then I came to live here with my father," he says, "and from that day on, even when at school, I've worked with musical instruments. I've never regretted a second of it. My father and I used to talk together about musical instruments in the way others would talk about football. He said to me once, when he was 80 years old, that he was only fit to go back and learn more. My grandfather worked for nothing for his first year as an apprentice, 1/- in his second year, 1/6d for the third. By the time he was seven years at it he was earning 7/6d per year. Apprentices weren't allowed to frequent dances of the day, and there were lots more restrictions besides. When I first read his apprenticeship papers I thought he was training to be a monk."

The family, Charles says, "has always lived with instruments the way others live with sport. I was very young when my father showed me how to bend and recognise the ribs on a violin – his own instrument, not a customer's. In the early days I swept the floor and made glue. I lived here until I got married, then moved out." Overhead is these days taken up with repair workshops and filled with instruments.

Once, when Charles thought he might get away from work and instruments for a bit, he took up fishing and went to Moorkens in Abbey Street to buy a fishing rod. "I walked in and a lovely young lady came out and served me and that was that. We both loved music. Marie-Thérèse caught me and it was the best catch I ever made. It's been a fascinating life and we've been through a lot of things together."

Their first born, also Marie-Therese, lives and works as a teacher in Bristol. Their second daughter, Frances, is an accountant who "lives at the foot of the Wicklow hills" with her husband and three children. Geraldine, who did a BA in history and English and a postgraduate degree in media studies, came into the business after a fire in the building in 1992.

Customers meet and talk in the shop as if they'd known each other a lifetime. "They may never have met before," Charles says. "They're just sharing a musical experience. Jazz, whatever, it doesn't matter so long as it's good music." He thinks musicians work seriously hard and that it's only the very famous who get properly rewarded.

Not every string instrument brought to Byrne's is taken on for repair; it has to be of a certain standard. "Sometimes the work would be more costly than the instrument," Charles says. "If it's got sentimental memories we'll stretch a point and do the best we can. Second and third generation customers come in all the time." He remembers the conductor Prionsias Ó Duinn coming into the shop when he was 14 years old. "You could see music was in his soul. John Sheehan of the Dubliners and many, many other traditional musicians have been coming in here for a lifetime."

Geraldine shows and plays a €4,000 violin to a customer and Charles talks with deep appreciation of a couple of violins they managed to get hold of and sell recently. "The maker used the wood from organ pipes that were 100 years old and maple that had been seasoned for 25 years for the back and ribs. He only had enough materials to make 100 and we waited two years and then got two of them. They were beautiful." They sold for €6,000 each. Geraldine, momentarily free of customers, tells her story.

"We spent the summers here as children, my sisters and I. The fire in 1992 could have been a disaster but it was an ill wind blowing good. The great thing about these old buildings is that, though the fire was intense, the walls are so solid they held up. I took a year off to help out and during that time we evaluated things. We looked at what we were, what we could do to improve different areas, how we could rejuvenate others. It really gave us a unique opportunity; we wouldn't have done it without the upheaval of the fire. It changed hugely how we've moved on."

She believes keeping their service personal is very important. "No length of time is too long to give a customer. The heart of the business is connecting with people. We're on the Internet and have a web site now and do mail order. All of this is very high tech for us and we've worldwide customers, but we keep it personal. I've introduced a few new things to the shop too. We sell bodhráns and handmade mandolins and bouzoukis and novelty things. Musicians are mad and they love anything to do with music – cufflinks with bass clefs, mugs with instruments on them."

Talking to her, she has her father's passion. Charles Byrne Musik Instrumente is in good and safe hands.

Jonathan Mitchell, chairman and managing director, with Peter Dunne, director,
Mitchell & Son, Wine Merchants, 21 Kildare Street. *Photograph: Eric Luke*

Mitchell & Son

Wine Merchants, 21 Kildare Street, Dublin 2

Mitchell's, in the 1800s, was the Grafton Street place to go for tea, confectioneries and the odd sympathetic tipple. The last was a discreet extra, port served in teacups to the ladies-who-lunched of the time and who couldn't be seen imbibing publicly.

And it was in those comforting sups that the seeds of Dublin's most venerable wine merchants were nourished. Mitchell & Son moved in time from tea and cakes to whiskey and wine and, seven generations and a decisive resistance to take-overs and the multinational route later, are a nobility among the city's wine merchants.

From 21 Kildare Street, the elegant Georgian building the family bought in 1887, Mitchell's has for several of those generations been selling fine wines, spirits and its own Green Spot Whiskey. In 1918, it would have sold you a dozen bottles of St Emilion for 32 shillings, white Claret by the dozen for 36 shillings or 12 bottles of John Jameson & Sons whiskey for 108 shillings. They would have paid the carriage to the railway station too – and you wouldn't have been charged for the bottles.

R. Jonathan Mitchell is managing director and chairman of today's company. He's closely abetted by Peter Dunne, also a director, who joined the company in 1970. Robert Mitchell, son of Jonathan, manages the company's other wine shop, opened in Glasthule, Co. Dublin, in 1997. Mitchell's employs 15 people and will be 200 years old in 2005.

Jonathan Mitchell, with an easy affability, tells the Mitchell story over cups of dark black coffee. It's too early in the morning for anything else. Peter Dunne, an equally relaxed presence, adds anecdote and fact. There's nothing hurried about the mood in Mitchell's.

"The family business began as a confectionery and bakery in 1805 at 10 Grafton Street – where McDonald's is today," says Jonathan. "It was started by William Mitchell, my great-great-great-grandfather, who was a baker and came from the north of England." The company grew, supplying wedding cakes countrywide and opening tea rooms and private dining-rooms on different levels in the building.

Redoubtable women with sometimes remarkable names come and go through the Mitchell story. Sarah, who married George Patrick Mitchell, son of William, was one of them. She took over when her husband died, in 1847 at a far too young 32 years, and by 1850 had garnered the first of many royal warrants and become "Confectioner to Her Majesty".

During Sarah's reign things went from good to better. Mitchell's bought numbers 9 and 11 Grafton Street and, through what was Grafton Street's coffee-house hey-day – with the street knee-deep in the likes of Bewley's, Fuller's and Robt. Roberts – Mitchell's, with its variety of restaurants, was the place to go.

Jonathan remembers going there as a very small child, before it closed. "It was awe inspiring," he says, "with great stained-glass windows to the back and window displays of iced cakes and ice sculptures to the front."

He remembers the legend too, the story of how polite ladies poured port from teapots into teacups of an afternoon, unknowingly heralding what was to come.

The first Robert in the family, son of the redoubtable Sarah and of Patrick Mitchell, took over the company in time. In 1887, with the sale of wine making an ever-increasing contribution to the family business, he bought 21 Kildare Street from the then Provost of TCD, John Hely Hutchinson, and expanded into whiskey bonding and wines.

How Robert became a family name is a story in itself. "The first Robert was a great friend of Robert Emmet's," Jonathan explains. "It's said that on a visit to him in jail, he promised that the first-born sons in succeeding generations of Mitchells would be called Robert – and that's how it's been."

Back in the 1800s when Robert, son of Sarah and G. Patrick Mitchell, was expanding into wine and spirits, the family home was in Ailesbury House, now the Spanish Embassy. Jonathan has pictures of the family then, with Robert at the centre of formidable gatherings of Mitchells.

Jameson and Power were the big Dublin whiskey distillers when Mitchell's went into the business of whiskey bonding in 1887. "Findlaters would have been around then," Jonathan says, "and Gilbey's. We had special whiskey cellars in Fitzwilliam Lane where we bottled our Green Spot whiskey and matured it for 10 years."

Green Spot, since the 1920s, has been a continuing success. Up there with Black Bush, it's distilled, matured and bottled for Mitchell's and, in 2003, won the gold medal in Best of the Best Whiskey Tasting, run by the prestigious *Whisky Magazine*.

The first marriage of Robert Mitchell ended with the early death of his wife. His second marriage, many years later, was to Agnes Fairburn Jury, of the Jurys Hotel family. They had three daughters and a son.

"Robert Noel Mitchell, the son, was my grandfather and very much their last child," Jonathan says. "When his father died, Agnes was thrown into the running of both Grafton Street and Kildare Street. Robert Noel eventually took over and ran Grafton Street until the 1950s. A nephew, Harold Mitchell, ran things in Kildare Street – which meant the business hopped out of the direct line for a generation. Harold died young, in 1947, and his widow, the famous and formidable Beatrice Ruby Mitchell, became madam chairman of the company for a while until my father, Robert, was whistled in from the army, which he liked, to do his duty by the family."

The young Robert Mitchell travelled extensively and built up the company's wine portfolio. "He developed contacts, went out to growers we still deal with today," Jonathan explains; he took over from his father in the mid-1980s.

Peter Dunne says he joined Mitchell's "virtually from school. As Jonathan did, I learned things from the bottom up, picking grapes in France, bottling, going through the whole gamut. It's a tough but lovely business to be in."

He's full of interesting detail, explains some of the practical realities and latter-day great changes in the business. "We imported wine in casks until 1978," he says, "and had a Heath Robinson-like machine which bottled gin, rum, sherry, port — all of which came in casks. People returned their bottles, or if they didn't, were charged for them. We didn't bottle everything, of course. At the very expensive end of the market, as with Château Margaux, they bottled their own. By the late 1970s and early 1980s, the EU was changing the laws appertaining to wine bottles almost by the hour until it reached a point where, along with other importers, we had to bring in wine already bottled in its country of origin."

In 1978 Mitchell's converted the cellars into a wine bar and restaurant. The diversification ended in 1999 and Bruno's Restaurant now leases the space. In 1999, refurbishment doubled the sales-floor area in Kildare Street.

Wine consumption in Ireland has grown steadily since the early 1990s, the same decade in which new-world wine has come into serious prominence. Mitchell's, however, was importing containers from Australia and Chile in the early 1970s.

And Peter Dunne talks about the original emergence of these wines in 1560 as if it were yesterday.

"The line between new- and old-world wine was drawn when Mexico started to grow and make wine, after Jesuit missionaries started bringing it in for altar wine. Nowadays, countries like Slovenia, in particular, will be interesting to watch, and Hungary, which has of course been producing wine for a very long time."

Mitchell's believes in the personal touch and intends remaining a family business, dealing directly with the château and vineyard owners who are their suppliers.

And so to a Mitchell recipe from 1922 for sunny days ...

Bottle of champagne
Glass of curaçao or brandy
Two bottles of soda water
Slice of cucumber or pineapple
Let the whole remain an hour or two, then add lumps of clear ice.

The same year, Mitchell's recommended that when drawing champagne all wire, string and tinfoil should be removed before pulling the cork. Wine, they advised, would be spoiled by allowing it to run over mouldy string and rusty wire.

Tommy Brown (left) with Lorraine and Dermot Dunne at Dunnes depot near Baggot Street Bridge. *Photograph: Cyril Byrne*

Dunnes Fuel and Garden Centre

Percy Place, Dublin 4

The service is second to none in Dunnes Fuel and Garden Centre, Percy Place. Dermot and Lorraine Dunne, who will talk you through plant and shrub care in the summer and sort your log and coal needs in the winter, are genial, living proof that there's a part of the heart of old Dublin beating still in Dublin, 4.

Situated by Baggot Street Bridge, Dunnes is one of only two of the original canalside fuel depots left in the city. "There's only ourselves and Gordons at Portobello Bridge left now," says Dermot, with some regret. A historian, steeped and bred in the area and with a passion for military history, he's more aware than most of the loss to the community of older, more personal ways of doing business.

Lorraine, a fifth-generation local on her mother's side, feels just as strongly about the area.

But that comes later. First there's an endless stream of plant-buying customers to see to and, in between, the story of the yard. And of the Dunne family.

"This place was established in the late nineteenth century." Dermot, perched on the high stool in the sales reception hut, tells the tale with a historian's precision. "Coal and turf depots were set up beside the canal. Imported coal was taken from the docks on barges. Barrels of Guinness were transported from James' Gate by canal too. The barges would go down the country loaded with Guinness and coal and come back with turf."

With the scene thus set he really gets into his stride. "The business was started by an uncle of my grandmother. The space was an awful lot bigger then." He gestures to the Grand Canal, mooching past the other side of the yard. "I think it stretched all the way to Huband Bridge."

"My grandmother inherited from her uncle and married Tim Dunne, a member of the Dublin Metropolitan Police. That was about 1908. She was a Balfe from Kildare originally. Her name was Catherine, though she was called Kitty. She owned and basically ran the place by herself. They lived in a cottage on the grounds here."

He looks severely over his glasses. "You might remember the Clanwilliam ambush?"

I say, "Of course," and wait for him to tell me.

"In 1916 the Sherwood Foresters, marching from Dun Laoghaire, were engaged around here. There were lots of casualties with a great deal of the firing coming from the yard. Eventually, when the Rising collapsed, they arrested my grandfather and my grandmother's brother (who was also in the business) and interned them in Wakefield prison.

"My grandmother went to Kilmainham Gaol looking for them and, when she wasn't allowed in, persuaded a soldier to let her pass. As she walked in she saw James Connolly being shot, all bandaged and tied to his stretcher."

We take a minute to appreciate the scene: the young woman who'd talked her way in, witness to a scene not meant to be witnessed. Dermot goes on.

"Anyway, they turned up in Wakefield. A while after they came back it was discovered they'd TB. The uncle died and the whole bloody family got it. My grandmother had four children and two of them died of it."

Dermot's father, Paddy Dunne, luckily escaped. He left Haddington Road school at 14 and went to work with his mother in the yard in 1941.

The Second World War was on, turf was the fuel and the years busy ones, with people queuing with prams for their turf. Kitty Dunne had horses and barges then and the place was known as the Turfbank. Her son helped load the barges on the canal and make horse and cart deliveries.

In the mid-1950s Paddy Dunne married Maureen ("a wonderful seamstress from Ranelagh" is how Dermot describes the woman who became his mother). In 1958, the couple had the cottage in the yard knocked down and built the house, on the boundaries of the yard, where Maureen Dunne still lives today. Cheap oil and central heating saw a decline in business in the 1960s; the oil crisis and a demand for solid fuel saw it rise again in the 1970s.

When Dermot was 10 or 11 years old he "was chopping logs and serving customers. Same as my own son, David." He worked in the yard while he studied English and History at UCD, and he and Lorraine married in 1980. Smokeless fuel and gas-fired central heating brought the next crisis and, in the early 1990s, Dermot says, "business took a horrible dive. In the first year of smokeless fuel, it halved. That was a bit of a shock. A lot of people were put out of business. The people left in the business are old – I'm considered young and I'm in my forties. There's no young generation."

Paddy Dunne died in 1994. "Dropped dead right here in the yard," Dermot says. "Fell down and that was it," says Lorraine. "I came over to him and he was stretched," says Dermot. "He went the way he wanted to," says Lorraine.

Dermot took over the yard and Lorraine came to work full-time. She takes over the story. "We were in at the deep end and fuel just wasn't keeping us going. In 1996 we went into plants and flowers; it fits with the fuel because it's seasonally based and we've got the space. The fuel ends in March and we go right into plants and flowers. It's hard work but we're interested in horticulture and we like it. Our son David is something of a horticulturist and wants to train in the Botanic Gardens."

They've become expert over the years, learning from customers, courses and experience. They supply landscapers as well as retail customers and find their city-centre location an advantage. "People are glad," Lorraine says, "not to have to travel out of town for their plants. Tommy Brown came to work with us seven years ago and he's a great guy, our right-hand man. He knows everything and the customers love him. We're all here five days a week." Tommy, in the yard, is already bagging logs for the winter ahead.

"There's not a great future in the fuel business but we've room for expansion in the plant end of things," says Lorraine, a woman of no small passions. She greatly laments local developments. "I grew up in Baggot Lane and I don't think the area's improved over the years," she says; "it's full of offices and big business and fast-food joints. None of the kids go to school locally any more. Years ago neighbours looked out for neighbours but people in the apartment buildings don't even know one another. It's not safe at night anymore. But I suppose it's the same everywhere."

Dave Pembrey at Greene's Bookshop. *Photograph: Cyril Byrne*

Greene's Bookshop
16 Clare Street, Dublin 2

Fashionable as the Millennium Wing of the National Gallery may have made the TCD end of Clare Street, it will never have the cachet Greene's Bookshop gives the Merrion Square end.

This is to compare chalk with cheese, of course, because Greene's is low on the grandeur scale and the only queues it ever attracts are students and frazzled parents with school booklists in hand.

What Greene's has by the shelf-full is a past, an atmosphere and a story to tell. Not that Greene's does much to proclaim itself; the term low-key might have been invented with the shop, and its owners, in mind. It also has all the quiet peace and dogged eccentricity of a real bookshop.

For years the favoured browse of the late greats of literature, religion and politics, in Greene's you'll find today's practitioners coming and going too. New and secondhand books have been sold on two floors of 16 Clare Street since 1843, when it was set up by John Greene as a lending library.

Before that it was the place to go in Dublin for ladies' hosiery and before that, when it was built in the late 1700s, it was the four-storey-over-basement home and workplace of the original owners.

In 1892, a family called Quinn took over and in 1912 one Herbert Heymour Pembrey arrived, from Oxford via Combridge's bookshop in Grafton Street, to become the new owner.

H.H. Pembrey's family still own and run Greene's Bookshop. Today's owner-manager is Herbert's great-grandson, David. The proud father of a young son, he's gently hopeful the tradition of first-born sons going into the business will continue. The women in the family have not, he says, tended to go into bookselling. He and his mother are the directors of the present-day company. His brother and two sisters have chosen not to become involved.

When H.H. Pembrey died in the 1940s, his son Herbert Seymour, who had joined the company in 1928, took over. Herbert Seymour's son, Eric Joseph (David's father), came into the business in 1954. Herbert Seymour died in March 2000 and Eric Joseph Pembrey died in October 2000.

Eric Joseph believed that keeping up an old world image — and keeping the computer system well out of sight — was an integral part of the Greene marketing strategy. The family business ethos is based on the principle of working on a fair percentage, resisting the temptation to "make a fast buck".

The Greene's building is Grade 2 Listed and the distinctive glass canopy to the front was put there in 1917. The book-filled wooden tables, outside winter and summer, look as if they were put there at the same time but are actually a bit younger. It's all painted green — what else — and the letttering is the same as it was in 1843.

Greene's lending-library activities ceased in 1958 and these days (in response to demand) you can buy newspapers and sweets on the ground floor as well as new books and school books. There has been a sub-post office on this floor too since 1986.

The basement and the second and third storeys are used for storage and a wide and winding 100-years-plus stairs leads to the second-hand books on the first floor. This is where founder John Greene was laid out when he died in 1899. It's also where staff fried breakfasts over an open fire in the 1940s. Notable and familiar features include the great mirror at the turn on the stairs as well as reasonably intact ceiling roses and plasterwork. A trio of cast-iron fireplaces are barely visible behind the shelves of books, floorboards are hollowed by the years and three sash windows with shutters look out over Clare Street and the building which housed the offices where Samuel Beckett's father earned a living. (Beckett father and son bought their books in Greene's.)

A quick browse on this floor reveals gems as diverse as a 1921 eight-volume *Commentary on Canon Law*, an 1840 edition of Thomas Aquinas's *Summa Theologica Minuta*, an early 1900s edition of *The Poetical Works of Wordsworth* — with original engravings and steel portrait — and Jack Charlton's biography from 1996.

David Pembrey is happy with his piece of the world and works all year round, taking only short holidays.

He's happy to have Greene's go on as it is, unchanged. The newspapers and sweets happened because a nearby newsagent's shop closed and regulars kept asking him to fill the gap. You sense he did it to more to oblige than because of any perception that it might be a smart business move.

A bit like his by-the-way admission that the Millennium Wing has brought "some extra passing trade" and his aside about "the famous ones who came here, Kavanagh and Behan and all that lot, as well as the Yeatses, Liam O'Flaherty, Frank O'Connor and Mary Lavin". They and others came for years to Greene's, it being the sort of place both customers and staff are loyal to. David Pembrey has ten full-time employees as well as four part-timers — "men and women, a good mix".

Which brings him to Miss Rochford, "The Roch" as she was known in the shop. She came to work in Greene's when she was 16 and was still working there, six days a week, in the 1980s, when she was in her eighties, mostly on the first floor where "climbing ladders and shelving were no bother to her" according to David Pembrey. She dozed off and died one Saturday going home on the bus. "She knew everyone," says David.

He looks around, happy with the way things are. "I've never done anything else," he admits, "and I'm not about to change. This keeps me occupied. "Business," he assures me in his low-key way, "is fine. Ticking over."

James Healy at work in Healy & Hicks' workshop off Camden Street. *Photograph: Bryan O'Brien*

Healy & Hicks
Furniture Restorers, Pleasants Street, Dublin 8

A chair is a lot more than just a chair in Healy & Hicks, furniture restorers and fifth-generation craftsmen. It would be hard to find a corner of Dublin in which chairs are more appreciated, more cherished, more loved than in their workshop in Pleasants Street, Dublin 8. They are what Healy & Hicks care most passionately about, the piece of furniture in which the art in their craft is most beautifully seen.

Father and son Jim and Des Healy produce chairs, one after the other, from corners everywhere in the Byzantine-like, low-ceilinged workshops, to demonstrate the glorious use to which they put wood, fabric, horsehair, buttons, webbing and coiled springs. There's every kind of seating about the place, from a Victorian boudoir chair to an earlier nineteenth-century gents' chair and its companion ladies' chair to Edwardian chairs, dining, carved, upright, sloping, ornate and plain chairs.

"The chair encapsulates everything we do," says Des Healy, the fifth-generation representative. "Taking a chair asunder and restoring it can involve a carving element, stripping and French polishing, reupholstering in the traditional way with horsehair or real coiled springs." Ignoring the creamy, damask seduction of the boudoir chair (valued at €2,500), I sit on a stool to hear more. No one ever sits on the finished product. Not in the workshops, anyway.

The company, these days, comprises the Healy father-and-son team along with Tony Hicks, himself from a family as renowned in the world of cabinet making and furniture restoration as are the Healys. "We're basically a three-man operation now," Des says. "It's Dad, Tony and myself." They were bigger once, and times were different, but small is definitely beautiful these days. Small is also hard working, time consuming, precision driven. Small is proud, too, of jobs well done and uncompromising about the craft involved.

Des begins their story. Jim, coming and going, fills in detail. Tony Hicks pays a benign, silent visit and goes back to working on a chair.

"I'm the fifth generation," Des confirms, "and my Dad, obviously, is the fourth and the one before me. Before him there was his father, my grandfather, James Alphonsus Healy, a fine cabinet maker and known to us as Alec. Alec's father was Reginald Healy, an upholsterer like his father before him, who was also called Reginald Healy." So far so clear.

The business got off the ground when Reginald Healy the First came to Dublin from Cork via a furniture factory in Edenderry and went to work for Lalor Briscoe on the Quays, doing a lot of internal upholstery work on traps and carriages. His son Reginald also became an upholsterer and opened a place on the North Strand. When this was bombed during the war, Reginald the Second went freelance, becoming a journeyman upholsterer and working in people's houses.

Things moved on apace when his son, James Alphonsus (Alec) Healy, a cabinet maker who worked with T&R Scott of Strand Street on office and church furniture and later as a foreman with J.V. Bowden & Co, specialists in quality chairs, went out on his own and set up Artistic Craft Wood Products in Pembroke Lane. He later took on a business partner and became Hill & Healy, with premises in Little Ship Street. When those premises were destroyed by fire the company moved to Rathmines.

The company had always had several family members working for it but around this time the wider world began to beckon and Alec's talented sons moved out and on. Colm, Gabriel and Donal Healy set up European Cabinet Makers in San Francisco. Colm Healy (uncle and godfather to Des Healy) is these days a renowned and much-appreciated Master Cabinet Maker in Atlanta, Georgia. Gabriel Healy still works happily in San Francisco and Donal, described by his nephew as "the academic one", is not, for the moment, working with furniture.

Jim Healy, Alec's eldest son and Des's father, went into business on his own after the Little Ship Street premises burned down. "He opened a place at 46B Arnott Street," Des explains, "just around the corner from where we lived on Vernon Street. We still use it for storage or as a place to work on big pieces of furniture. There was a shortage of work in those days and Dad had to diversify, doing van deliveries and getting what work he could."

Jim takes up the tale. "In the seventies we were going around on bikes; I used even do a bit of knocking on doors. You could get a telescopic table for between £10 and £15 then. They cost about £7,000 now. People didn't know what they were throwing out. In the early 1970s we did piano removals, did stripping and French polishing, did whatever we could. The business grew. About 20 years ago we'd a big factory up the lane from here where we concentrated on producing individual pieces. We'd a big staff up until the late eighties, did a lot of work restoring furniture which had been damaged over winter due to water tanks bursting.

"Then the insurance companies stepped in and decreed the tanks should be plastic and the work dropped off dramatically."

He's got no regrets. The company moved back to basics. "It was a headache, employing a lot of people," he admits. "We still get calls from people wanting to be apprentices but we don't take anyone on unless they've a real passion for the work."

Des, though bred to the business ("Dad wouldn't let me out to play until I'd practised my dovetails and cuts"), took time out to do economics and marketing in TCD and spent eight years studying classical piano in the College of Music. "My mother's passion is music and it's mine too," he explains, "apart from furniture, of course. Even when I was in college I worked here."

Healy & Hicks have done a lot of work for Tony O'Reilly, both in his Fitzwilliam Square home and in Castlemartin. They're regularly commissioned for handcrafted work and have done restoration on furniture for corporations and bodies such as the AIB and Bank of Ireland.

We wander through the maze of work finished and half done. Jim Healy is in the process of making a lady's writing bureau in Brazilian mahogany. Only part of the way there and it's already shaping up to be something of a masterpiece.

Elsewhere there's work in progress on a small Edwardian sewing box and on a set of chairs for the Eye and Ear Hospital, which are being stripped down, having coil sprung seats fitted and being reupholstered and French polished. Another chair is to have a new mahogany leg fitted, repairing the damage done by a "cowboy" who drove a large nail through the original.

Jim stops beside a chair in solid rosewood and walnut. "You don't get many of these now," he says and goes on to lament a lack of appreciation in today's generation for traditional workmanship. "They buy everything in Habitat or Foko and then ring me up, show me furniture my father made and want me to modernise it." Words fail and he becomes, relatively, silent.

Healy & Hicks intend keeping things small. Jim Healy is coming up to 70 and, even if he wanted to, his son is not about to allow him retire. "He's got too much knowledge to let him stop working," he says, laughing. "He got me into it so he'd better stay."

Gerald Davis in the Davis Gallery. *Photograph: Alan Betson*

Davis Gallery
11 Capel Street, Dublin 1

As Capel Street, cutting its swathe to the river's edge, is to the heart of Dublin 1 then Gerald Davis – painter, gallery owner, critic, patron of the arts, sometime businessman and oft-time personifier of Leopold Bloom – is to the heart of Capel Street. Man and boy, he's been an essential part of the street for more than 50 years, since, as the only child of Sydney and Doris Davis, he first began to help behind the counter of the family business at 11 Capel Street.

And 2004 is exactly 50 years since, as a 16-year-old with an Inter. Cert. from St Andrew's College, he became a full-time part of the business. Much has changed and much has stayed the same and through it all Gerald Davis has been a passionate, opinionated champion of Capel Street – and by extension the rest of the city.

He tells the Davis/Capel Street story with the zeal he brings to everything. "My grandfather came from Lithuania and got his naturalisation papers in 1904," he says. "He would have arrived, like all of that wave of Jews, in 1883–4. He brought his wife over later, which wasn't uncommon. My father and the rest of the family were born in St Kevin's Road, Dublin 8, which was an all-Jewish street at one time. My mother, Doris Miller, was born in Longwood Avenue, which was almost all Jewish too."

Sydney Davis left school at 14 and went to work. "The details are scant," his son admits, "but like everyone else at that time he started selling stuff on a weekly basis – clothes, household goods, blankets. He travelled. He discovered Portmarnock. He used go to Kildare. My first memories of my dad were of him going off in the car to sell around the country for the week."

Sydney Davis eventually bought a small shop in Liffey Street where, as the Second World War ended, he sold "small wares; shellac, hobnails for boots, razor blades. After a few years he bought in here, number 11 Capel Street, which had sitting tenants.

"He was by then wholesaling toys and fancy goods, and he rented rooms to a Mr Barrett from Birmingham, who used take orders for rubber stamps. They became partners when my dad, on his travels around the country, began getting rubber-stamp orders for Mr Barrett. But Mr Barrett went back to Birmingham and, in 1950, Barrett Davis & Co. became The Rubber Stamp Shop and, gradually, the biggest seller and manufacturer in the country of rubber stamps."

By the 1960s, and with the range of the business extended, the name had changed to Davis Stationery. "My Dad bought another place up the street, at number 25 Capel Street, and rented a place in Strand Street from where he imported and distributed toys. This left the running of the Capel Street business to myself and a Mr Murphy, who'd worked with my Dad and essentially ran things. I was supposed to be the boss but, I mean ..."

What Gerald Davis means is that he was a half-hearted businessman at best, an established painter by this time and not averse to telling his father how he felt. "I said to him, 'I'm not enjoying this business,' and he said to me, 'So, who enjoys business?' which is a typical Jewish answer. I'd been painting and exhibiting for a long time by then but he thought this a bad idea. My mother, who would have been interested, died before my first exhibition."

He's grateful to the business though: "At one stage we had 23 employees – retail, wholesale and manufacturing. It educated and fed my family."

In 1970, when the sitting tenants moved out of the first floor at 11 Capel Street, Gerald Davis opened an art gallery there. "I thought it would be a nice thing to do," he says. Chief Justice Cearbhaill Ó Dálaigh did the opening honours; the show was of drawings by Edward Delaney. Twenty-five years later, in 1995, then president Mary Robinson opened a jubilee exhibition showing work by 25 artists.

"I learned about the practicalities of business from my father," Gerald Davis admits, "which is why I've been able to make a go of the gallery." Davis Stationery Ltd carried on until 1981 and the death of Sydney Davis.

"I let it go when he died," his son explains, "and through the 1980s rented it to different tenants. Towards the end of the 1980s Frank Mooney, a guy up the street who'd worked for my father, took it over and continued trading as The Rubber Stamp Shop. After a while he bought 14 Capel Street and moved the shop there. When that happened I made a total commitment to the art-world side of things and moved the gallery to the ground floor. It's nice that there's continuity and that The Rubber Stamp Shop is just up the street." He remembers and loves it well. "I can remember when there was two-way traffic and horses and carts in Capel Street. I've seen it seriously neglected over the years, take an awful lot of bashing and neglect by the corporation and council, historically."

He warms to his theme. "I think the kiosks by the river are disgraceful, an affront to anybody. A visual affront to the city. Totally contrived. Nobody wants them."

He's unforgiving, but optimistic too because "in the last year there's been a huge amount of refurbishment and rebuilding on the part of private people in the street. There are some marvellous people on the city council and some good employees but there's a distinct lack of vision. Our city fathers are to blame for what's happening. There isn't the culture of a pit pony in the lot of them."

Passion far from spent he talks about his pride in the gallery. "The 2004 Charlie Cullen exhibition, which was the best Joyce exhibition in Dublin, was very successful. He first showed with me in 1971. There weren't many galleries in the city then. Many artists who're now big names in the country had their early shows here – Charlie Harper, John Kelly, Edward Delaney, John Devlin, Martin Gale – they've all gone on to become very well known and regarded.

"I think we did great things in this gallery and I think it's been vastly underestimated. I was the first gallery to show quality craft work and sculpture. My policy over the years has been to show the work I believed in. Now I show only paintings. My taste would definitely eschew the so-called conceptual; I'd radically oppose it. Also, I've always run the gallery with the policy of showing work people can buy, sensibly priced for people who want to build a collection of their own. As a painter myself I'm aware of all aspects."

He's adamant that, in the 30-odd years he's been running the gallery, his standards haven't changed. "I've shown avant-garde stuff here but it's been good quality and that's my main criteria." He says he's always been loath to show his own work in the gallery. "My own career is very successful and now, after 40 years, my work is sought-after and appreciated. The future? I've never known what's going to happen next year, what I'm going to do."

Bill Coyle at his famous hatter's shop. *Photograph: Frank Miller*

Coyles & Co.
Outfitters, 8 Aungier Street, Dublin 2

Until he retired in the spring of 2004, Bill Coyle reckoned he was the only hatter left in the country. He was 76 when he closed-up shop – but before he did he reminisced about the good old days and played an old sweet song.

After explaining that he was the only remaining hatter in Ireland, how he was apprenticed to Pims in the 1940s and how his hat shop had been on Aungier Street since 1925, Bill Coyle produced a Stradivarius and played for the two of us, with haunting sweetness, in his empty shop. Bill Coyle is not simply one of a kind; he made the mould.

His father, born in 1898, set up Coyles at 8 Aungier Street in 1925. Bill joined him when he finished his apprenticeship in Pims of South Great George's Street. He worked in the shop for the best part of 60 years, opening every morning at 8 a.m., closing at 5.30 p.m. – except for Wednesday half-day and early closing at 5 p.m. on Saturday. For 30 of those years, he rose at 5 a.m., driving from Artane to get to the shop by 5.50 a.m. Between 6 a.m. and 7 a.m. he would push up the shutters and generally get the shop ready for the day.

From 7 a.m. to 8 a.m. he performed an hour's worship, "reading the Bible and playing music to the Lord on my Stradivarius". Homeless people, leaving nearby shelters and making their way daily into town, own the street at that hour. "They break my heart," said Bill Coyle. "It's a terrible thing to see them. The street's changed.

"There's only myself and Kavanagh's sweet shop two doors up left of what used to be." He had plenty to say about the standards of selling in clothes shops these days. "In my day you'd be sacked for not doing all you could to help the customer," he said. "People don't know the business any more. When I worked in Pims in 1944 as a sales apprentice, the charge-hand was the first to get the sale, then the senior staff and last of all the apprentice. I got 12/6d a week and 1/5d taken from that for a stamp, so I got 11/1d into my hand. The big thing was commission at the end of the month. For every £1 you sold you got 3d commission. That was real money." He gleefully told the story of how he managed to make a sale of 100 yards of black cloth to a nun in 1945.

He began in haberdashery in Pims, moved on to leather goods and from there to piece goods (material by the yard). "I ended up in ready-to-wear, which was a very good department, and then came on here. My father worked in Troys in South Great George's Street, another hat shop and outfitters. He was there in 1916. Three days before he opened his own place here, he'd no shirts to sell.

"When the manager of Somax, the shirt factory opposite Troys, asked what was up, my father told him the problem. But Mr Troy said to Somax, 'If you supply Coyle you can forget me.' So the Somax manager said to my father, 'Pick what you want and you needn't pay for three months.' My father did that and never looked back." He ran, momentarily, out of steam and gave a small sigh. "Somax is gone now and all of the Troys dead. Sad. Every one of them gone."

His shop was high and narrow, with dark wood presses and drawers, a couple of long mirrors and every kind of hat lining a wall of shining wood shelves. There were red hat boxes from Christy's of London, stetsons, panamas, wool felt hats, summer hats and Donegal tweed hats. Yearly, he did a big trade in Joycean boaters. He showed me a wonderful brown wide-brimmed Cheltenham hat – another good seller at certain times of the year. A lot of his hat sales were repeats. Customers are wont to lose their headgear on buses, in pubs, all over. Within days they'd be back in Coyles for a replacement.

Being an outfitter's, Bill Coyle also sold school uniforms, pullovers, slipovers, cardigans, ties, socks and shirts. He did good business, a fact he puts down to knowing the business and looking after his customers. "I'm the only qualified hatman left in the country," he said. "Practically anyone who wears a hat comes here. They come up from the country, from everywhere. I sell the hat to them . . ." he gave me a sharp look. "You've a double crown, do you know that? You should be bright enough. Einstein had three crowns. The circumference of his head was 28 inches." He came back to today's way of selling, lamenting the lack of professionalism among latter-day shop assistants.

"Convenience shopping is all. I sell. It's all in the selling but it's all serve yourself in the city these days. It used to be you sold for a commission and you wanted the money so you sold. You learned how to move around people. It's so important." He told me about his five daughters, all married, 10 grandchildren and two great-grandchildren.

"The great-grandchildren make me feel old," he said, not meaning a word of it, relishing his sprightliness. His daughters all helped in the shop over the years, before they married.

Bill played a game of golf every Wednesday in Howth, off a 14 handicap. He was proudest of all of the fact that he's a "qualified musician with the Association of London Colleges of Music.

I'm a singer too, and play the guitar. I worked with Jack Cruise and Chris Curran and all of them for years in the Olympia, in the evenings. I used do the musicals there, and all over the city too, running the shop by day."

He grew up in Artane and went to "Joeys" in Marino, where he was doing his Inter. Cert. when Charlie Haughey was there doing his Leaving Cert. When he first came to Aungier Street, "the trams used to run down the street. There was a certain niceness about it then, not all this gallivanting and rushing you get today." He shook his head. "Five people killed in Dublin last weekend ..." Words failed him.

"I never have trouble here. God is good. Never been touched, thank God." He remembered his aunts working down the road in Jacobs factory and how both families, his mother's and his father's, used to gather on Sundays between 7.30 p.m. and 10.30 p.m. on Wyndle Road in Drumcondra to sing around the piano.

"Any time now I hear one of those old songs it breaks my heart. It brings tears to my eyes. I can see them all, still." He thought then that he might retire at the end of the year. Might. He owned the entire building and thought he might sell it too. Might. His father retired at 72 and died a year later, of cancer. His working day was a long one, "but I just love it here. I think it's marvellous. I wouldn't have done anything else. The music was the big thing in my life, and I did a lot of singing. I've had a lot of customers from the Dáil, of course, and big businessmen. I do a fine hat trade. Garret FitzGerald bought hats here and Dick Spring.

"But I wouldn't know the half of them. As far as I'm concerned they're customers, that's all."

Jimmy Delaney (centre) with his sons Brian (left) and Paul outside the
T. Delaney & Son bike shop at Harold's Cross Bridge. *Photograph: David Sleator*

T. Delaney & Son

Bicycle shop, 7 Harold's Cross Road, Dublin 6

Jimmy Delaney's grandfather got on his bike from Kildare in 1917.

Thomas Delaney came from Kildare in 1917 to set up a bicycle shop at Harold's Cross Bridge. At the back of the shop, in a location then bordering the countryside, he and his wife reared three boys and a girl while building up the business which has supported generations of Delaneys since.

Today's bicycle shop, which still carries the name T. Delaney & Son, has a betting office to one side, an estate agent on the other and traffic coming from four directions in front.

Inside, where the heady smells of rubber, oil and grease betray a serious bicycle shop, the entire ground floor, and Thomas Delaney's one-time home, is taken up with the business. The shop is an Aladdin's cave of hanging wheels and tyres, helmets, oil in cans and bicycle gear of all kinds.

It's not very big; the early Delaneys were reared in restricted conditions. "I don't know how they managed in such a small space," Thomas's grandson Jimmy Delaney admits, "but they did, somehow. People did, then." Jimmy Delaney, with sons Paul and Brian, looks after the business today. (His third son, Fergus, teaches engineering in Cork VEC.) He's been in the shop since 1949, when he was 17, which makes him 72 years old. Maybe it's the bikes and bicycling, maybe it's the scuba diving and wind surfing and teaching in Kevin's Street College of Technology he does as a pastime, but Jimmy Delaney has the agility and appearance of a 50-year-old.

"Apart from scuba diving, bikes are all I know about," he says. He's held on to what he knows, too, and tells the story of the shop's survival with a typical, modest calm.

"When I got married, 30-odd years ago, we went to live in Rathfarnham. Then this here block was sold to one of those developers who upped the rents. The next-door barber, whose son was ready to go into the business, had to go but myself and the butcher on the other side decided the only way was to buy our premises from him. So my wife and I sold the house in Rathfarnham, and paid him more for this building than he'd paid for the whole block, and moved in to live overhead. It was the only way out of reviews and exorbitant rents."

Jimmy Delaney now lives overhead on his own, in "oceans of space" since his three sons married and moved out. His wife, Monica, died in 2001.

The business, in some ways, has come full cycle. T. Delaney & Son, in those early years of the twentieth century, sold motorcycles as well as bikes. "The motorcycles had gas lamps." Jimmy Delaney makes a drawing to explain. "They had a small cylinder with carbide in the bottom and the top half filled with water. A tap was turned; the water dripped down causing gas to go off and was ignited. When I started here there were still belt drives in operation. They're back in fashion again on mopeds and a few motorcycles, though the material in the belt is much advanced."

Things have moved too from a middle period, in the 1940s, 1950s and 1960s, where bicycles were the preferred mode of city travel, back to a bigger business in mopeds and motorcycles.

When Thomas Delaney died, his son Denis (Jimmy's father) took over. Jimmy came into the business at the age of 17 because he didn't like school.

Denis died 20 years ago and, until his own sons were old enough, Jimmy Delaney had to employ people to work for him. Remembering this, he shakes his head and says, "There's nothing like working with your own family." He recalls the cycling changes too. "In the 1940s, 1950s and 1960s, we hardly sold anything with an engine. There was more room on the road for bikes then and parents didn't mind their children cycling on the road, not like now, when you can't blame them for being afraid. Children used go to school on a bike; now they're driven everywhere."

He reflects again. "It's surprising how circumstances affect business. Mopeds began to come in the 1960s and really picked up in the 1970s. We started with European ones and then the Japanese moved in and took over." Mopeds are today's big sellers. The craze for the moped has grown, Jimmy Delaney believes, "out of laziness, people wanting a motor to get them along. But you can't hold on to a bike either and fewer and fewer people are buying them because there's no place to park without them being stolen. It's getting that way with mopeds and motorcycles too."

He's enthusiastic about mopeds himself. "They're very light and fully automatic. If you can ride a bike you can ride a moped. You just sit on it and off you go. The insurance is quite cheap and if you've a car licence that'll do. Moped customers come in two types," he says. "Teenagers who want one to charge around on and adults tired of sitting for hours in traffic in cars. A moped costs €5 a week to run and means a saving of €20 week on petrol, not to mention time. There are special jackets available now, too, so you can stay quite dry." He cycles a bike himself, says it takes him three minutes to get to town from Harold's Cross Bridge.

The basic bike has changed very little over the years, according to Jimmy Delaney. "Except for the gear systems," he concedes. "You get bikes now with 25 gears. All you really need for daily use are the basic three speeds.

"When I started here, the only bike you could sell to an Irish person was a Raleigh. Now, in Nottingham, Raleigh is closing down." Racing bikes are a specialised business but he says mountain bikes are still very popular, though not often used for the purpose for which they were made. "There's a new sort of bike now, a hybrid bought by the older bike rider, which has the mountain-bike fittings on a racing-bike frame."

When he cycles himself, or when Paul and Brian take to the saddle, they use bicycles from stock, rather than owning individual models. "We've got a 50-year-old insurance policy which covers domestic and trade use. You wouldn't get a policy like it today."

Herman Koster, managing director of Knights of the Green, at his hair centre at St Stephen's Green Shopping Centre.
Photograph: Cyril Byrne

Herman's Klipjoint
81 Grafton Street, Dublin 2

In the beginning there was Herman of Holland, a talented young hairdresser in demand in the salons of 1960s Grafton Street and environs.

Then, in the flash and razzmatazz that was the start of the 1970s, there was Herman's Klipjoint, over the China Showrooms on Grafton Street, the country's very first unisex hairdressing shop, where no appointment was necessary and where good hairdressing didn't cost the earth.

Herman's Klipjoint opened in Grafton Street in 1971. It was a shop, he says, not a salon. His ad with the slogan "Feel like having it off?" was refused by newspapers. "We were the birth of unisex," he says. "People said it wouldn't work, that it wasn't possible to have a man and woman sitting side-by-side having their hair cut. But it did work, from the very start, too. We had queues down as far as Switzers [now Brown Thomas]. I played Thin Lizzy's 'Whiskey in the Jar' from 10 in the morning till 10 at night.

"Our logo was designed by Jim Fitzpatrick and we advertised great sounds and great prices. We had chocolate-brown walls and orange chairs, which was unheard of. We did the hair for all the Noel Pearson productions, from *Joseph and His Amazing Technicolour Dreamcoat* to *Cabaret*. Phil Lynott came in and we gave him a farewell party before he went to London for *Top of the Pops*. He defined the early 1970s too. I followed a dream, as my daughter tells me now!"

Between 1971 and now, there's been a life well-lived, a passion for hairdressing, reinvention, moving on and, always, the principle that the customer comes first, second and third. And behind it all there's been Herman Koster, born in Rotterdam, Holland, as the Second World War came to an end, a troubadour with scissors in hand who arrived in Dublin in 1959.

"The only Dutch people here then were graphic artists," Herman remembers, "and there was no good coffee to be had at all. I would walk a mile-and-a-half looking for a decent cup ..."

He's affable beyond belief and entertaining to boot. His memory's prodigious, full of anecdote and colour and insight. When he opened Herman's Klipjoint, it was in response to a need he saw for a hairdresser's which would deliver style and value, cut through the mystique and salon pretensions of the time. When he consolidated in the 1980s, it was to concentrate on colour, cut and training a new crop of hairdressers. By the 1990s, when everywhere was unisex, he'd gone back to barbering, to what he calls "the long forgotten tonsorial art of shaving".

In between he'd worked on beehives and piled-up curls, wash'n'wear haircuts and the shaggy look, Afro styles and spikes and colouring of all sorts. Through it all he's operated his own MBE. "Management by Encouragement," he explains, "it's the only way."

Herman's is still on Grafton Street, a more conventional hair salon now than it used to be. Most of his time these days is spent in his St Stephen's Green Centre barber shop, Knights of the Green.

He was a teenage adventurer with a hairdressing qualification which took him everywhere. The Dublin he arrived in aged 20 in 1959 was, he says, "a very small city, everything within walking distance. Stillorgan was still a place of fields and meadows." He fell into the early folk culture of the time, his Vandyke beard a familiar sight in places like Neary's and the Coffee Inn.

"I lived in a succession of small flats where the walls were so damp there were mushrooms growing in them," he roars with laughter, "and there was no magic in that, I can tell you! So instead of going home after work I went to the pubs and mixed with the student life."

He remembers 1960s Dublin looking to London for style guidance. "Mary from Cavan became Monique of Bond Street when she became a stylist, that sort of thing. I was called a Continental and had to sign up every six months in the aliens' office." He worked first of all in Leons, at the top of Grafton Street, and later with Jacqmal of Mayfair in Dawson Street. Then he moved on, scissors in hand, across Europe, adventuring, cutting hair on the beaches of Greece, coming and going through the 1960s. He wrote, too, newspaper columns of advice on hair care. Ahead of the posse even then, he wrote in praise of home treatments, advocating hair "foods" like marrowbone oil, olive oil, eggs, lemon and beer.

In between, he'd met Brenda, his wife to be and mother of their three children. "A wonderful woman," he says. "I met her in that ballroom of romance, the CIE Ballroom in Marlborough Street! She's always been a support to me in my business and a wonderful mother."

By the beginning of the 1970s he had a clear view of "the enormous potential in Ireland to create something different, to reinvent the point of hairdressing salons, do away with the mystique and falseness and create an honest-to-God decent service where personal attention was important and available to all, not just those with loads of money."

In the 12 months of 1971 Herman Koster opened three outlets. The first, in Dundrum

Shopping Centre, was called Herman's Hair Care, the second was Grafton Street and the third in Galway Shopping Centre.

"Everyone thought I was utterly and totally nuts," he says, "and it's only now I realise that I was. I'd get up at 5.30 a.m., be on the road at 6 a.m. and open the Galway shop by 9 a.m. I did that once a week until it was established, as well as running my other two places."

He opened, too, in Pat Quinn's Sports Hotel in Kilternan, in Kimmage Shopping Centre and in Dun Laoghaire. "One day you realise you're deluding yourself," he says, "and that you can't be everywhere. If I'd had a laptop and mobile and fax I'd have had 24 shops. But what I did in the 1980s was spend time consolidating." After Hermans became All-Ireland Irish Hairdressing Champions in 1981, he concentrated on training — "what I used to call growing your own roses — and on the things that really mattered, like colour and cutting". The decade, he says, was one in which more was learned about the structure and texture of hair than had been learned in 100 years. Old, strong chemicals disappeared and a new education began. But it was also a time when attracting juniors was difficult.

Herman is adamant that hairdressing is a career, not a job, and feels strongly that hairdressing is still not properly legislated for. "I campaigned for 30 years for registration and proper training schemes. Things are changing at last. There are strong people running the Irish Hairdressers' Federation and there's proper guidance on health and safety. Guidance for trainees is really coming on too."

His outlets these days are in St Stephen's Green Shopping Centre, Grafton Street and Ballinteer and Dundrum Shopping Centres. But now, the wheel coming full circle, he's getting ready to open in the new Dundrum Town Centre. "It's to do with going back and reinventing yourself," he says. "Nothing stays the same but the principles remain. Fashions change, as they say, but style remains. We will go on! We've had many people imitating our ideas but we've survived. I've tried to teach my children that they should find a job they like so they don't have to work every day of their lives. Doing something you like isn't work at all."

By that criteria Herman Koster hasn't worked a day in his life — and has loved every minute of it.

At Barnardo's on Grafton Street: Ms Caroline Barnardo with her grandchild Harry
Barnardo Byrne and her daughter Elizabeth Barnardo Byrne (left). *Photograph: Cyril Byrne*

J.M. Barnardo

Furriers, 108 Grafton Street, Dublin 2

"An ancestor of mine married Wolfe Tone …" As an opening line for a family history, Elizabeth Barnardo's is enviable. And true. With the help of her mother, Caroline, she matter-of-factly works out the bride's place in the family. Mrs Tone was a great-grand-aunt, they agree, adding that her wedding dress is on permanent loan to the National Museum at Collins Barracks.

The fashion note, in a twist that has more to do with fate than design, has followed the family through the centuries. Barnardo Furriers, at the foot of Grafton Street, has to be one of the more window-shopped frontages in town. Through good times and bad, for most of the last 130 years, it's reliably displayed a touch of luxury, glamour and exotica.

What's not so obvious from outside is the hard work and tenacity which has kept the business in the family for almost 200 years and made the Barnardos, according to Elizabeth, the oldest family of manufacturing furriers in Europe.

A fifth-generation Barnardo, Elizabeth runs today's business with her mother, Caroline. A multi-tasker if ever there was one, she tells the story between dealing with customers, reassuring her small daughter and keeping an ear to demands on the phone.

"The first Barnardo, John Michaelis, arrived on the Clare coast in a fishing boat in 1810. As far as we've been able to make out, the family was originally from Venice but moved to Germany. While in Clare he met and fell in love with a Miss Elizabeth O'Brien. He went back to Germany but returned in 1812, married Elizabeth, came to Dublin and started a fur business in 4 Dame Street. It's said that he was a taxidermist by trade."

Mrs Barnardo died giving birth to their sixth child, a girl called Elizabeth who died when she was a month old. As was common at the time, John Michaelis married his wife's sister.

He and his second wife, Abigail, went on to have 13 children. Of the 19 children fathered by John Michaelis Barnardo, one would become renowned.

Born in 1845 and the thirteenth child in the family, Thomas John grew up to become the Dr Barnardo who founded the Barnardo children's homes. His younger brother Henry Lionel (born

1847) took over the business when John Michaelis died in 1874. Things were going well enough by this time for the company to have been appointed Court Furriers every year from 1832.

Towards the end of 1874 Henry Lionel moved family and business to 108 Grafton Street. When that building burned down in 1882 he seized the hour, had a great sale and created a purpose-built fashion shop at the corner of Duke and Grafton streets. The sale, of "the best goods uninjured by the fire", offered fur-lined circular cloaks in every kind of fur from 14/6d up, fur carriage rugs from £2.6.0d to 3gns and seal bag muffs mounted in nickel silver frames from 10/6d.

Henry Lionel Barnardo, for reasons more than typical of his time, made life difficult for his son and successor, Henry Cecil, when he fell in love with Ellen Josephine McDonald, then working in the shop.

Disapproving of the match, he sent his son to Canada to work as a lumberjack. Henry Cecil's ardour remained uncooled and in 1912, six months after his father's death, he returned, took over the business and continued keeping company with Ellen Josephine. Ten years later, in 1922, they married in St Andrew's Church in Andrew Street.

"She'd worked in the shop since she was 14," Elizabeth explains, "and was the serious business person in the relationship, running things while he went off to antique auctions and conducted the Dublin Philharmonic Orchestra. He was known for his extravagant generosity to 'touchers', or beggars. Josephine was generous too, but of a more practical nature."

When they lost all their money in the crash of 1929 they survived by selling the second shop, loading laundry baskets with the fur stock and wheeling the lot back down to 108 Grafton Street to continue trading. Henry Cecil and Ellen Josephine had been aged 43 and 44 respectively when they married.

They had one child, a boy they named Thomas Henry, who grew up to marry Caroline, father Elizabeth and create the internationally known, fashionably aware furriers Barnardo's has become.

Henry Cecil himself died in 1944, cycling home to the house he and Ellen Josephine had bought in Blackrock in 1932. He was found dead on a bench on Avoca Avenue.

"That left Harry, as my father was known," Elizabeth explains. "As time went on he took a very international attitude to the business. Aer Lingus was up and going then and he started supplying stores in the US and abroad, putting on fur fashion shows in all sorts of places – Bermuda, Switzerland, France, America. He always used Irish models: Winnie Butler, Lady Antonia Wardell, Hilary Freyne, Rosemary Smyth and Adrienne Ring. He did the MC bit himself, reciting snatches of Percy French."

In 1971, in St Andrew's Church, Harry and Caroline married. Caroline had been working up the street in Bewley's but they met through a shared passion for badminton. Caroline, remembering, laughs.

"He was one of the most eligible bachelors of the time and was 20 years older than me. He just bided his time, waiting for me to grow up!" Harry Barnardo, sadly, died of cancer seven years later, in 1978. Elizabeth, the only child of Caroline and Harry, was born in 1972.

The year they married, Harry Barnardo bought Rohu furriers in Castlemarket for Caroline to run. She'd already spent their engagement year in London, studying fur and business at the London College of Fashion. When her husband died she took over his role in 108 Grafton Street. Rohu is still owned by the family.

Elizabeth, whose family home is in Rathfarnham, laughs when she says she "grew up under the counter here, just like my own two children are doing today". Over the shop there's a cheerful playroom and young Harry and Elizabeth come with her and are cared for there during working hours – when they're not perambulating on Grafton Street.

The family story has been diligently researched and lovingly handwritten by Olive Harris. She came to work in the shop aged 14, became secretary to three generations of Barnardos and, much loved by customers, started selling again towards the end of her time with the family.

Barnardo's today exports sable, mink, fox, musquash, lambskin, leathers and suedes across the world, has workrooms on the premises and cold-storage facilities for customers wanting to protect their furs during the summer.

"Since Dad died the business has been in the hands of two women, myself and my mother," Elizabeth says. "We're a great team; she keeps my feet on the ground when I get some of my wilder design ideas. I worked here every Saturday from 12 years of age and in 1990 went to the London College of Fashion where, as well as design, I learned how to run a business.

"Today's customers are far more aware of trends, more travelled and able to buy anywhere in the world. We have to be the best to get business. I'm very proud of our name. When I go to auctions in Seattle and Copenhagen to buy skins, as I do four times a year, it doesn't matter how much I spend because the Barnardo name in trade and business holds good."

The anti-fur movement didn't affect them much, she says. "Our agricultural background in Ireland gives people an understanding of animal life. We're members of the World Wildlife Federation and use farmed animals and so don't endanger species."

We go upstairs, to a room of shining wood and mirrors, and I get a real feel of today's furs. Elizabeth and Caroline, gleefully and with confidence in their product, dress me in exotic, featherweight furs: a floor-length Sapphire mink which reverses to denim, a knitted mink jacket, an opera coat in bronze taffeta and multi-coloured dyed fox collar.

These are all designed by Elizabeth, who says the key is "wearability and ease" and that inspiration "comes from everywhere. We do sizes 8 to 26 and have a vast collection every season. The raw techniques and materials available today are wonderful – my grandfather didn't even have zips to work with!"

Sarah and Kitty Joyce in the Cleo showroom, Kildare Street. *Photograph: Matt Kavanagh*

Cleo

Handknits and Weavers, 18 Kildare Street, Dublin 2

Cleo has been a moving, fondly regarded landmark in the area between Trinity College and St Stephen's Green for the best part of 70 years. It has been the place to go for uniquely designed clothing made from natural fibres. The wools and linens used are Irish, and the designs are mainly drawn from Ireland's past.

Kitty Joyce was born to Cleo. Her mother, Kathleen Ryan, was its founder and only begetter and Kitty's destiny, as an only child, was an almost foregone conclusion. She spent some time nursing but the lure was strong and today, with the company just slightly older than herself, Kitty Joyce can look happily back on a lifetime of passion and commitment to "wearable artworks" and satisfied customers.

She and Sarah, the youngest of her six children, run the business with the indispensable help of Maureen Lewis, "a super person".

Cleo sells the work of craftspeople from all over the country: sweaters with designs based on the entrance and backstones at Newgrange, handmade hats of all descriptions, felt jackets and sculptures, replicas of men's evening cloaks from the nineteenth century and silver jewellery. Wearable art indeed, and hugely individual.

The great, good and beautiful have dressed themselves in Cleo for decades but Kitty is not giving names away. Prevailed upon, she reveals that Dior was a customer in the 1950s and that Perry Ellis also came calling. The world well knows that stars of the stage, screen and catwalk have gone and go there but Kitty's not for turning — the customers' privacy is sacrosanct.

Kitty is a natural storyteller, beginning at the beginning and joyfully digressing through the streets and history of twentieth-century Dublin.

The beginning was in 1912, when her mother, Kathleen, came to Dublin from Tipperary. She was apprenticed in Switzers, then moved to Cathcart's in Ranelagh and then opened her own business in Molesworth Street.

"She had two milliners working for her," Kitty says. "At that time Dublin was the second city of the empire so there would have been good trading with colonels and their ladies and a lot of posting of hats in special paper so they didn't become affected by mildew when crossing the equator."

When Kathleen married Bryan Ryan, a Spirit Grocer with premises in Mountjoy Street and Abercorn Street, she stopped working. "That was the pattern at the time," Kitty says. "In the 1930s the business began to go down: in America they were jumping off skyscrapers. My father moved us from Mountjoy Street to Abercorn Street to concentrate things there. But things got worse, so in 1936 my mother started Cleo at 10 South Anne Street. That's where it was until 1950, a tiny shop with a little basement.

Calling it Cleo had to do with economics — the name was painted over the door, so she kept it. She sold separates — skirts, tops, little jackets. She had a very good maker called Mrs Lyons and did for individuals and what were known as awkward sizes.

When Bryan died in 1944, the Abercorn Street premises had to be sold and Kathleen rented the top floor of Findlaters in Rathmines for herself and her daughter to live in.

"It was a huge area," Kitty says. "She took in about 12 lodgers, all of them characters. She was a fabulous woman. Every morning she would clean out their rooms, empty the grates and set the fires for when they came home in evenings. Then she would head for Cleo."

When change came in Cleo it was to do with a lodger, "a man whose soul needed to work in the unspoiled countryside in the summer". Kathleen Ryan asked this lodger to keep an eye out for any especially good knitters or spinners — and so came to know Maggie Dirane of Kilronan on Inis Mór. "Maggie and her daughter Dymphna were wonderful and did a lot of original Aran patterns," Kitty says. "She also invented the *crios* hat we sell to this day."

In 1950 Cleo moved to a basement in Molesworth Street. "It turned out to be a fabulous position," Kitty says, "near to the Hibernian Hotel. My mother had built up a pool of knitters, some extremely good ones in Donegal as well, and was still selling separates. As the war came to an end it was as if America discovered Ireland and there was an explosion of tourism. My mother could hardly cope with the surge in business between May and September — she was getting on and becoming tired."

Kitty helped in the summer and, in between, studied nursing and midwifery.

"But I gave it up and decided to go into the business because my mother was falling asunder and she'd done a great deal for me. Within six weeks I was having a love affair with it. I'm still having a love affair with it. Those were wonderful years in Ireland; the country was fresh then. Then CTT and Bord Bia and the rest came along and organised everything and took the simplicity out of it and didn't contribute much to small people. We had wonderful times in Molesworth Street — customers are still coming from those years. They were terribly exciting times — people would queue on the wooden steps to the basement and shout for things they'd seen and wanted to buy. The Aran wasn't done to death then and anoraks and ski clothing weren't worn so much, so woollens were used as outer garments."

In 1961 Kitty met Tom Joyce at a conference in the RDS; they fell in love and married.

Kathleen Ryan died, too young, in 1964. Through the sixties, seventies and even into the eighties Cleo used the likes of The Weaver's Shed in Kilmainham for their fabrics and master tailors such as Austin Lendaro to make suits and coats.

"There was much more space for individuality of design and make then," Kitty says. "Now there's the worship of the technological mode. There's more work for everyone, of course, and you can't quarrel with jobs!"

In the early seventies Cleo moved, for a short two years, to Dawson Street. "Those were hard times in Ireland but we survived," Kitty says. "We moved here [Kildare Street] in the mid-seventies. This building had been in retail use by Maureen O'Hara's mother and aunt — they would have sold couture to every lord and lady in the country. We bought blind; the place was too big for our needs, and we weren't sure we'd ever sell a thing here. But it gradually came together. I stopped grieving for Molesworth Street and like it here now!"

A second Cleo, opened in Kenmare in 1985, is these days owned and run by Kitty and Tom Joyce's middle daughter, Helen. "She's wonderful at retailing and loves Kerry," Kitty says.

Sarah joined the company after she'd taken a BA in Maynooth. "We work fine together, the two of us and Maureen," Kitty says. "I've been taken up with this business all of my life and, though Cleo is here to stay, there are no dynasties involved. The family members know they don't have to continue when I'm no longer on this earth."

Albert Kelly outside the Classic Cinema in Harold's Cross. *Photograph: Cyril Byrne*

Classic Cinema
314 Harold's Cross Road, Dublin 6W

Sadly closed in the summer of 2003, the Classic Cinema was so loved and passionately patronised that its place here is a given.

Albert Kelly was the Classic Cinema. Without him it would never have become a cultural icon – the last show was screened only because his doctor told him he had to stop "doing a seven-days-a-week job".

If he hadn't bought what was then the Kenilworth Cinema in 1974, it's a safe bet that the building, and late-Friday-night home of the *Rocky Horror Picture Show* for almost a quarter of a century, would have been gobbled up by development. If he hadn't believed in film as entertainment, in the judgement of his patrons and in a hands-on work ethic, he might have been forced to close his doors anyway.

We met at noon in the Classic before it closed. He was on crutches. "I'd a car accident after we spoke." His jaw hurt too, but he was smiling. "I didn't want to disappoint you."

Fragile and very, very buoyant, he laughed about his age and said, "Tell them I'm 100." He had the enthusiasm and energy of a lively 30-year-old. "You have to love this business to be good at it," he said, telling me to sit but standing himself; the doctors had told him to keep on his feet. "We're lucky. We haven't had a loss in 24 years. This is a great business but, second to oil, it's the most corrupt in the world. As long as you know that you can handle it." Gently humorous, as entertaining as anything he could show on the Classic's two screens, he told his story.

"When I was young, about 10 years old, I ran a cinema at the end of our garden in Larkfield Avenue. I showed slides and charged 1d in. After the war I bought a 16 millimetre soccer-coaching film and went around the country showing it. Then I became a projectionist, first in the Grand Central in O'Connell Street, then in the Sundrive."

He didn't know it, but he was on the way to owning the Classic, built as a cinema in 1953 and called the Kenilworth. The owners, Sundrive Cinemas Ltd, already owned the Classic in Terenure as well as the Sundrive, on Sundrive Rd.

In the early 1970s they sold the Sundrive and gave their projectionist charge of the then Kenilworth Cinema. When the managing director of the company died suddenly, in his office in the Classic, Albert Kelly was, he said, "pushed into looking after the two houses, the Classic in Terenure and the Kenilworth in Harold's Cross".

Because it was difficult for independent cinemas to obtain mainstream films, he turned the Classic "into an arthouse, running French and Russian films and the like. I bought the Kirov Ballet *Sleeping Beauty* and we ran it for a month every year for three years.

"Everyone came. Micheál MacLíammóir and Hilton Edwards were great customers. They loved ballet, of course. People used come from Belfast. In 1974 the company offered me a chance to buy one of the two houses. This [the Classic in Harold's Cross] was the newer one. I'm here since then."

He credited Michael Dwyer, the *Irish Times* film critic, with bringing the *Rocky Horror Picture Show* into his life. "I was in Terenure when he said to me: 'It's a great picture, play it!' and I said, 'We don't play horror,' and he said, 'It's not horror,' and so I got it and it took off, late night in Terenure. When Terenure was sold I brought it here, changed the name to the Classic.

"We had so much fun with it. It was a great audience-participation film. I remember a night when a hearse drew up with a guy in evening dress in the coffin and 11 other guys in evening dress in two mourning cars. They carried the coffin to the stage area and the corpse got out and bowed to the audience, who went wild. At the box office they wrote a cheque for admission for the whole lot of them." *Rocky* (as he calls it) went on to become a financial success. "The geography of the house suited it. The screen was three feet off the floor, good for audience participation." He stopped looking at it himself 10 years before the end but was in the house most Fridays anyway. "There were guys and girls coming every week for years; their sons and daughters were coming at the end. *Rocky* was singular. There will never be its like again."

The greatest change to the Classic came when it was twinned in 1980. "We hated doing it," Kelly admitted. "We had 1,100 seats before, in one cinema. Then we had two cinemas with 200 seats in one and 300 in the other. I gave part of the building back to Sundrive Ltd, who had gone into property." He retains a great affection for the company.

He lamented, more in anger than sadness, the way the film industry has changed.

"The soul and glamour have gone. The old cinemas were decorative as well as functional. Today, every square inch has to pay for itself. The old Savoy had 2,400 seats, the Royal 3,400, the Adelphi 2,000. Today's complexes can have eight screens but they've the same number of seats." He gives me a torch and I take a look around an empty Classic: high vaulted ceilings, silent rows of seats, low-down screen. The torch is weak and I don't stay long. The ghosts of too many films fill the empty dark.

He had views, many critical, on the Irish film industry. "I could talk for hours about the errors it's made. Art is only okay if it's entertaining too. The most successful Irish films I've ever shown were *Waking Ned* and *About Adam*. The most successful other films were *Gone with the Wind* and the original *ET*. *Out of Africa* ran for six months, a record, a lovely picture."

He made "some wonderful friends among patrons. You have to know your patrons. I always try to stand at the door when they're leaving and they tell me whether they liked the picture or not." He had no regrets. None at all. He'd do it over again if he had a choice.

Joe McNamara, director, Corrigan and Sons. *Photograph: Matt Kavanagh*

Corrigan and Sons
Funeral Directors, 5 Lower Camden Street, Dublin 2

Joe McNamara, who has attended more than his fair share of funerals, believes firmly in their healing power. "They're a part of life, not an annexe," he affirms. "That's the Irish way and the longer I'm in the business, the more certain I am that we've got the balance right. Up to now anyway."

That last is more than a throw-away remark. Joe McNamara, embalmer and funeral director, sees change in the culture of death and burial in this country. He's philosophically accepting of it, if not altogether happy. "People weren't aware how much they relied on the church in death. I feel an anger in people when I'm out and about, a feeling in them that the church has let them down.

"There's an ongoing healing power in connecting back to the community and parish of the dead person which I feel is breaking down. People are turning more and more to grief counselling to cope."

Funerals are Joe McNamara's business. As director of Corrigan and Sons, Funeral Directors, of 5 Lower Camden Street, he's part of an unbroken line of family involvement in a company set up by Patrick Corrigan in the latter part of the nineteenth century. Dapper, discreet and diplomatic, he's the essence of the Corrigan and Sons ethos, respecting death, the dead and the feelings of the bereaved.

Dignity is the key. Joe McNamara carries a bowler to funerals and wears it "by times. It's useful when people are looking for a focus because it helps to identify me. I don't wear it for any other reason."

Ostentation, extremes of any kind, are not part of the Corrigan/McNamara way of burial. The company uses Mercedes-Benz cars only and an E-Class hearse and the premises has an on-site chapel of rest, an embalming theatre, a garage with private parking and a reception. Coffins used are, the company's director assures, "classic and traditional. The unusual we don't have."

Joe McNamara was born into the undertaking business and is the fourth generation to run the company: he is the son of Gerard McNamara, who became part of the Corrigan dynasty when he married the granddaughter of the original founder.

Marriage, since the very beginning, has been the way of continuity and consolidation in the Corrigan firm. The company's founder, who had a carriage business, started the trend when he married Dora Head, daughter of a Cook Street coffin-maker. The combined companies made for an undertaking business which was consolidated when Dora and Patrick moved, in 1884, to the Camden Street site still occupied today.

Corrigan's, from the beginning, brought panache and a dignified style to the business of burial. The original premises had hay, oats and coffin lofts. The stables could hold up to 30 horses and work started at 6 a.m., when they were taken out, cleaned and fed. The role of the horse was crucial: the animal drawing the hearse wore white plumes if the deceased was unmarried, black if the person was married.

The slow move from horse-drawn vehicles to motorised ones began about the time the second generation of Corrigans, Patrick and Peter, joined their father in 1900. A time followed when Corrigan's offered lots of choice: you could go for motor hearses and limousines or horse-drawn hearses and carriages.

Patrick Corrigan the Second's son-in-law, Gerard McNamara, joined the company in 1954 and 28 years later, in 1982, his son Joe, returning from work experience in the UK as embalmer and funeral director, became a full-time employee.

So – what makes a good funeral director? "Temperament is the key." Joe is unequivocal. "That, as well as the training and ability to understand grief and the stages it goes through – loss, denial, acceptance. You have to be able to deal with this, to understand and guide people along for their own good. Because I grew up with the business, I'd an interest from an early age. You become embroiled without realising it – that's the way things go."

Corrigan and Sons is the undertaker for the city's three medical schools (UCD, TCD and the Royal College of Surgeons) and take care of the burials or cremations of those who have donated their bodies to medical research.

Then there's the embalming side of the business. Joe McNamara, with scant prodding, moves from a discussion of the art as practised by the Egyptians some 5,000 years ago to the fact that these days "embalming is becoming more and more acceptable" and his belief that it, too, "helps the healing process. And embalming means there's less likely to be deterioration of the body of the person who has died before the funeral. People are more anxious than ever before about what death looks like, so, as an embalmer, you need to be sensitive to how a person looked in life. A photo is useful; so is a person's own make-up. In the end, though, it comes down simply to whether or not the family have confidence in you as an embalmer. If they've had any bad experiences, they don't want to know. There's a code of ethics around embalming which involves confidentiality and respect for the dead."

Funerals should reflect the dead person, Joe McNamara believes. "Many people, especially men, are laid out in their own clothes. Families might want particular items to go into pockets, or pictures from grandchildren or such to go into the coffin. We always co-operate."

He also believes the dead person is "a part of the community. I would approach the funeral as an inclusive situation, a bringing together of people in healing and reconciliation." He elaborates on his feeling that things are changing in this respect, his conviction that "there's going to be more involvement with grief counselling. People are definitely easing away from church involvement – and not just from the Catholic church. People are going through hoops trying to construct a service which includes healing.

"I'm not sure people have appreciated the healing power of a funeral up until now, the fact that it takes place in community with other churchgoers, the ongoing healing power of connecting back to the parish of the dead person. We, as funeral directors, are embroiled in this ongoing situation and are finding ourselves with the new function, in some cases, of reintroducing people to the parish community when the bereaved meet in church. I believe it's important to have the dead person in the church overnight but my guess is that this too is going to end and the funeral will become a day-long event. These things may, of course, resolve themselves. I hope they do."

Joe McNamara has three children. He would never presume to decide their futures, nor expect them to go into the undertaking business. But, given that he's there for the long haul himself, the future of Corrigan and Sons seems assured.

Linda and Liam Finnegan in the museum of the Waldorf Hairdressing and Shaving Saloon on Westmoreland Street.
Photograph: Cyril Byrne

Waldorf Hairdressing and Shaving Saloon

13 Westmoreland Street, Dublin 2

Liam Finnegan appreciates the rich value of sounds: the tap of steel heels across a terrazzo floor, the slow clunk of a towel-steamer closing, the snap of a cut-throat razor folding, the clip, clip, clip of scissors cutting hair.

Old sounds. Everyday sounds in Westmoreland Street's Waldorf Hairdressing and Shaving Saloon. "A salon is for women," Liam points out, gently, "a saloon for men. It's a nice distinction." There's a lot that's distinguished about the Waldorf.

Linda Finnegan, his daughter and co-owner, is both distinguished and an essential part of things. She is also, in large measure, responsible for the existence of today's saloon. When the old saloon, which started life across the road in 1929, came up for sale in 1995, Linda was the visionary who marshalled her father, and the support of her brother and husband, in pursuit of a legend which was in danger of dying.

Her persistence paid off and when she and her father bought the company for £10,000 they found they'd more than a business on their hands. The six older barbers who'd owned and run the place as a co-operative had passed on an institution, a veritable and living museum, a showcase to the excellence and versatility of the art and craft of barbering and its many ancillary services and delights.

The going's been tough since 1995 but the dream has prevailed and Liam and Linda Finnegan are today in charge of a recreated business and newly created cultural phenomenon in the basement of 13 Westmoreland Street.

In a long terrazzo-floored underground room, only metres from O'Connell Bridge, you can have a traditional Waldorf razor cut (with cut-throat razor), hot oil treatments, singeing (in which wax tapers singe and seal hair ends to prevent breakage), Indian head massage, beard, eyebrow, nose and ear maintenance (quick and painless, the last three), facial mud packs, nail clipping Pakistani-style (again, painless and quick – I'm personal testimony), buzz cuts, shoe shines and much more.

This is a barber's in which the old and the new Ireland blend nicely.

Then there's the museum. The Back Room, the Finnegans call it, where shelves, cupboards and worktops are stuffed with a donated, bought and sought-out collection of barber artefacts and therapeutic remedies. There's a Travelling High Frequency Generator from the 1920s, delivering shock treatment for hair loss and warts. From 1826 there's a box sharpener holding ivory-handled razors. A barber's coat in heavy cotton dates from the 1920s. There are weighing scales once used to make up old recipes and cures, a cunning magnifying device for examining the scalp, a seven-day razor set. There's also a large cauldron in which whirring blades mix the ingredients for today's Waldorf Hair Tonic, used to soothe and stimulate the scalp. The recipe comes from old-time barbers and customers and nothing, but nothing, will persuade the Finnegans to reveal the ingredients.

To give an idea of what was *de rigueur* by way of treatments in the early 1900s, Liam produces *The Preemo Book of Simple Recipes*. Nitrate and nickel sulphate were used to dye hair, brilliantine was made with mutton suet and lard. None of these, he assures, go into today's tonic. "In the old days, on Wednesdays," Linda says, "all they did here was prepare and bottle formulas and tonics and shampoos for sale. It was big business and we absolutely intend going back into production here, in this room. Very soon. We love doing it."

Slowly, and at last, we get back to the beginning. The original Waldorf barber's was set up in 1929 by Mr Thomas J. O'Byrne in the basement of 37 Westmoreland Street, the building now occupied by the Westin Hotel. Mr O'Byrne had worked as a barber on a liner out of Cobh and subsequently in the Waldorf Barbers in New York where, Liam says, "there were 66 chairs and they worked 24 hours a day, seven days a week". The dream of a Dublin Waldorf was born there too.

By 1946, Mr O'Byrne was doing sufficiently well to open a second Westmoreland Street establishment. Today's Waldorf began life as the Waldorf-Adare, underneath the then Kildare Men's Outfitters.

By 1969, long-haired male hairstyles were doing for the barbering business, and Mr O'Byrne closed number 37 to concentrate on number 13. When he retired soon after, and paid his staff redundancy, they organised themselves into a co-operative under Mr Alexander Parker and kept the business going.

To avail of a government grant, they were required to modernise and consultants decreed that the terrazzo flooring, curved Art Deco-style ceiling, stainless-steel handrails and more should all be done away with.

While the members of the barbers' co-operative worked on and grew older, Liam Finnegan trained and worked in his father's barbers in Inchicore. When a customer told him the Waldorf was for sale, Liam wasn't interested but Linda, working alongside him and a trained, traditional barber, crossed town to have a look. She thought the place "fantastic".

When Liam Finnegan came to view the shop in 1995, his daughter wanted him to buy it, even though it reminded him of nothing so much as a "Spanish café", with squares of lino covering the terrazzo, the ceiling encased in wooden beams, basins contained in booths. He fell for it all the same, but was "more interested in making a weekly wage. I'd a family to support, everyone was against it, there was too much at risk." Linda, who'd just been crowned an International Champion Barber, was undaunted. She brought her husband, Patrick Carr, on board and encouraged her brother Brian to come home from London to join up.

The fact that the Waldorf barber's could only be bought as a going concern frightened other would-be buyers, but not Liam. "I knew the men and I trusted them," he says. "Mr Alexander Parker was a union man and you could trust him with your life." Which was what he did, or at least his livelihood.

For the first two, very tough, years Paddy Carr and Brian Finnegan worked with Linda in Westmoreland Street while Liam remained running things in Inchicore. "Then a friend suggested I move here, that the customers would follow," Liam says. "So I did and they did. But those were rough, rough times. We worked from 7.30 a.m. until 7.30 p.m. But I enjoyed it. It was exciting. The funny thing is, I feel as if I've been here forever."

Slowly, the Finnegans brought the place back to what it had been. They began with the floor. One of the earlier barbers, who'd had a limp, had worn a hole in the lino around his chair and revealed the terrazzo. The ceiling was opened up, chrome fittings and hot-towel steamers replaced and wooden shelving and cupboards brought back.

Then they decided to revive the old treatments and ways of doing things – and to add to them. Riaz and Fiaz, barber brothers from Pakistan, work there now, as well as Karen, from Belmullet, who was trained in Linda's expert hands.

"Riaz and Fiaz had their own way of doing head massage and friction and we'd ours, so we combined the two," Linda explains. "Now we've our own special treatment to offer customers."

The work of restoration, renovation, refurbishing and recreating goes on, the Finnegans constantly looking for artefacts, memories, photographs and recipes for tonics and hair treatments.

"We'd love to hear from anyone who remembers," Linda says, "or who has any old things we could add to the place."

Colclough Doran at The Old Stand pub in Exchequer Street. *Photograph: Dara MacDónaill*

The Old Stand

Public House, 37 Exchequer Street, Dublin 2

Michel Doran makes no claims about the antiquity of The Old Stand. He's much too civilised a publican for that. The Old Stand, in any event, is well able to account for itself. Its venerable historical credentials are impeccable. And recorded.

"Our public-house licence is one of only 20 in Dublin which can be traced to the mid-1600s, when Charles II renewed licences across the city," says Doran, who owns the pub with his brothers.

"Others from that time include The Brazen Head and The Bleeding Horse and no one knows, really, which of us is the oldest."

He grins, as unassuming as The Old Stand itself, and goes for a play on that famous lager ad. "In the way that Carlsberg claims to be probably the best beer, we're probably the oldest pub."

The Old Stand, situated where Exchequer Street turns into Andrew Street on one of Dublin's more individual corners, is unmissable. Even its name, which comes from the old rugby stand in Lansdowne Road, has the distinction of being instantly recognisable. Its style – of both service and decor – is traditional and reassuring. Today's building is Georgian and some 200 years old. In the 1990s the pub was "tidied up", as Michel Doran puts it, but without radical change. Where floorboards were viable they were retained; an ornate Welsh dresser behind the counter displays Willow and Wedgewood; the seating is lush and comfortable. There are no bouncers on the door as you go in. "We don't need them," Michel Doran says. "I can't remember when we had trouble in here. It's not that sort of place." They don't serve drunken customers either.

It's never been "that sort of place", not in its lifetime with the Doran family anyway. Their involvement in the licensed trade goes back to a great-grandfather who moved from a shebeen in Wexford in 1889 to set up Doran's licensed premises in Marlborough Street.

Michel Doran's father, Michael Doran, in time took over in Marlborough Street. Something of a dynamo in the trade, and one-time president of the Licensed Vintners' Association, Michael Doran opened what his son describes as the "first modern lounge in Dublin, a place where women were welcome and able to go alone for a drink".

Dublin wags, ever-inventive and in reference to the closeness of the city's Catholic cathedral, used to call it the "Pros Cathedral".

In 1942 Michael Doran added to the family portfolio when he bought Davy Byrnes (of *Ulysses* fame) from Davy Byrne himself, "a bachelor from Wicklow", according to Michel Doran.

The Old Stand became part of the Doran family business in 1969–1970. Michael Doran Senior died in 1995 and, between them, his three sons now run both pubs. Davy Byrnes ("only about 150 years old", Michel points out) is in the charge of Redmond Doran, while Michel looks after The Old Stand with his brother Colclough.

The Old Stand had a lively business life before the advent of the Dorans. Not much is recorded about the very early licence holders but papers exist on James McLean, who opened a provisions store in addition to his pub on the premises in 1817. It remained a pub/grocery through various owners until John Cox took over in 1885 and reverted to pub-only use. The premises became known as The Monico and that's what it was called when Michael Collins used to drop in from his office in Andrew Street and hold meetings there with the illegal IRB. The owner before the Dorans, one Michael Daly, gave the premises the name it has today.

The rooms above The Old Stand have had various occupants over the years – the name Gillespie still attaches to one of the old bells at street level from the time journalist and writer Elgy Gillespie lived there in the 1970s.

The major change in the pub's business has to do with food. "It makes up more than 40 per cent of our turnover," says Michel Doran. "If we closed the kitchen tomorrow we'd lose 60 per cent of our business, given that customers come to both eat and drink." The Old Stand serves a non-stop, full food menu seven days a week – anything from stuffed braised beef to open fresh salmon sandwiches.

Its city centre location attracts a particular sort of local customer. When Bertie Ahern was lord mayor, The Old Stand became his local. "These days we've three different kinds of regular," Michel Doran explains. "At lunchtime we've an 80 per cent return business, mainly people working around the place. At tea-time we get those relaxing after work and at night it's people out for the night, at the theatre or whatever. We've a big and traditional rugby-following clientele too."

A rugby-ball sign outside attests to this and when either Wanderers or Lansdowne rugby clubs win a cup it's customary for them to bring it in to be filled with champagne. Louis Dignam, legendary barman with more than 40 years service in The Old Stand, used to host the Sam Maguire celebrations in the pub.

Drinking tastes have changed as well as habits. "Young people want Bacardi Breezers and

Smirnoff Ice. They like their drinks in the bottle and by the neck, preferably long. There's a growth in the sale of white spirits but not in whiskey. What we don't sell any more is Guinness by the bottle. We'll get the odd old fellow from the country looking for one and have to tell him we don't have it; no one in Dublin drinks it any more."

The business of drawing a pint of Guinness has changed too, all to do with temperature and the perfect head. Time was when the black stuff was kept at cellar temperature. Later it was carried in pipes through ice banks. Now it's stored in pub cold rooms subsidised by Guinness. "The result is a perfect head and no waste," says Michel Doran. Before joining the family business, he studied law and became a barrister, but he's glad he gave it up. "I'm happy here and I've no regrets."

Cyril Greene in Greene Marine, Harold's Cross. *Photograph: Dara MacDónaill*

Greene Marine Ltd

Boats, Engines Repairs and Sales,
38 Clareville Road, Harold's Cross, Dublin 6

Ethel Greene, who has been married to her husband Cyril for nearly 50 years, says of her husband that "no man in Ireland knows more about engines than Cyril Greene. When he's dead the world of his knowledge will go with him under seven feet of clay."

Few, if any, of the countless boat owners who've called on Cyril's services over the last 60-odd years would disagree with her.

Greene Marine Ltd is a modest-looking operation with an immodest, legendary reputation. Cyril Green describes his business as simply "the repairing and selling of outboard engines and the occasional boat" and has been working on engines of one kind or another in the converted garage attached to his home on Clareville Road, Harold's Cross, since 1943. Out the back there's a German MZ250 motorbike, wherein lies the rest of the Green Marine tale.

Cyril Greene's father, T.E. Greene, built the first motorbike in this country. The Wellington Special hit the roads in 1912 and T.E. went on to become a legend in his own time. He'd already won the French Grand Prix in 1902 and throughout the 1920s raced in the Isle of Man and other hot spots, becoming a friend of Stanley Woods, the racing icon who won the TT half a dozen times. His passion became a business when he set up the Shamrock Cycle Co. in a basement in Blackrock. His business became as legendary as himself when he moved it to Clareville Road and converted the garage to take on the care of motorbikes for Des Manson and Ginger O'Beirne and the Irish Speedway Team.

Cyril spent his childhood in that garage, "messing around in there all the time with my father. When I was 16 I moved in and started working proper with him. At that time, it was the early 1940s, insurance for a motorbike was about £5 a year and tax was 5/- a year." He makes the move into boat engines sound a logical, simple move.

"Buckley's Accessories were agents for outboard engines and when I went in for parts I got talking to a mechanic. In time he passed his overflow to me and when Buckley's closed that's what started me. The first engines I sold were three-cylinder 60s. That was 1968. I graduated from that to what you see now."

What I saw was a modest and crammed reception/office fronting a workroom stuffed with engines and parts. It wasn't yet 10 a.m. but customers, arriving in a steady and demanding stream, made the telling and hearing of Cyril's business story difficult. Ethel, who keeps the books and looks after the tea-breaks, suggested the house as an alternative. Over strong tea, and surrounded by T.E. Greene's trophies and the Greene family in photographs, Cyril and Ethel shared the telling of the story of Greene Marine, the business.

The present workplace replaced the one T.E. Greene operated out of. "I took it down in about 1985 and built the two-storey structure you see today," Cyril says. "We did a lot of boat sales at one time but we ran out of storage space when our son Stuart moved from Mounttown to Blessington. He was in this business but he turned completely and went into alternative medicine, in which he'd always been interested." Stuart Greene is one of four offspring. His brother Norman was a banker for 20 years until he left to make model boats, cars and planes. A daughter, Adrienne, works mornings alongside her father and another daughter, Pamela, is a teacher and organist studying for a mathematics doctorate.

We're not even safe in the kitchen. Adrienne comes through on an intercom to tell her father that "The Chinese man with his problem is back and the man from the Aran Islands has arrived." Cyril advises and Ethel says, "Cyril's known the length and breadth of Ireland. I'd never go to Dun Laoghaire because it would be 'Cyril, would you come over and hear my engine?' on every side. When I go out, it's to the Dublin mountains where there are no bloody boats about."

Cyril says the boat business has changed. "When I started in boating it was a more leisurely experience, with older people involved. Boating people are younger now and it's not so leisurely, more about speed. The majority of leisure boating is done on the Shannon, where a lot of business people retire on big boats. We service them. Also, there are more and more people coming into the business nowadays."

Ethel says they've always had a "nice kind of business with a nice kind of person. It's very seasonal. Between March and October you could work day and night. The rest of the year you'd be doing work on laid-up boats and the like." They also work for the army, on a contract for the Rangers' boats, supplied the engine to the new *Asgard*, the first Garda boat for the Garda Diving Unit, and the first boats for the Customs service. "Diving clubs come to us too," says Cyril, "and you've to keep standards high if the business is going to stay." The question everyone asks them, and so do I, is how they work on boats in virtually the middle of the city? The answer has to do with Cyril's knowledge of engines. "He'll never die in the house," Ethel says. "He'll die in that garage and I'll lay him out in the garage." Cyril grins.

He remembers how things were in the 1980s, when he was an agent for Johnson Outboard Engines. "They used to give us 'sales incentives'. We got a trip on the Orient Express and to Hong Kong and to America and to Yugoslavia and to Gibraltar where the apes are. That was what was given out in those days. Companies were great then and lovely to deal with."

He's got "no great interest" in speed boats, would prefer a leisurely weekend on the Moy or Slaney or some of the "good rivers doing a bit of salmon fishing". He's also "big into motor-car and motor-bike racing. I've Ethel cultivated so she's an ardent follower too. We go to the San Marino race in Italy and Silverstone in England plus, if we can, the German and Belgian Grands Prix. We have to pick races that happen at slack times of the year for us."

What about retirement? "I'm waiting," says Cyril, "for someone to come and give me a hand out for the place. The way to retire is to get someone else to do what you used to do. There are no signs or plans at the moment. No one's made me an offer." Ethel says that if Cyril could "reduce his work load to three days per week it would be okay. I can't see him doing it, though." Cyril says he'll "be around as long as my health hangs out. I gave up smoking 32 years ago and I feel grand."

Ethel says she's as fit and supple as ever she was and hasn't an ache in her body. She puts it down to hard work, her only exercise, and shows me her impeccable, large-ledger book-keeping method. She can't abide computers and will have nothing to do with them.

Cyril says a "not too big cabin cruiser is the best boat for anyone to have — it's not too difficult to manoeuvre or to run. I'm not interested in speed on water, though maybe on a jet ski — it's exhilarating. When I'm boating, once I step into the boat, I never give a thought to business. I relax absolutely and completely."

Ethel and Cyril definitely have the suss on marriage and sharing. "We love each other, don't we?" Ethel says to her husband and Cyril grins, agreeable and gentle. They're a class act, the Greenes of Greene Marine.

Róisín Pett in West of Grafton Street. *Photograph: Bryan O'Brien*

West of Grafton Street

Stepping into West of Grafton Street – Goldsmiths, Jewellers, Silversmiths – is an experience. The door opens when you discreetly knock and closes after you as you step onto a royal blue carpet and into a world of grace and taste which some people like to imagine was what an older Dublin was all about.

Shutters are closed against the life of the street outside; inside, separate mahogany and curved-glass counters display delicate, tasteful, handmade jewellery.

Robert Halpin steps forward. "I've been standing here since 1966," he says, "when we moved from 102 Grafton Street, where River Island is now. The year before, Desmond West, the sole owner at the time, was killed at 41 years of age coming back from the races in Killaloe when his Rolls Royce crashed into a telegraph pole.

"Death duties meant the building had to be sold and the company was liquidated. His sister Geraldine West inherited and asked me a year later to come back from London, where I was a jeweller, to run things. The goodwill for the company was there and she was adamant it should be kept going."

It's peaceful sitting there, on one of the high, elegant eighteenth-century chairs, designed to allow the customer to see easily into the glass cases. The shop floor covers a deceptive 600 square feet and is not awash with customers.

"We're not a volume trade," Halpin explains. "If we deal with six people a day, that's as much as we expect. But then we only deal in the making and selling of fine jewellery."

That's the way things have been, more or less, since 1720, when the original West & Son opened on Capel Street. "We're the oldest jewellers in Europe." Halpin takes a silver trowel from a glass case. "This was presented by the artists employed by the company for the laying of the foundation stone when we moved to College Green in 1845. The next move was to 102 Grafton Street, then to this location."

He looks, reluctantly, through the glass of the door at the scurrying crowds. "The street's changed, and for the worse. There's such a traffic in people and the condition of it on a Monday morning! It doesn't befit the premier street of the capital city of Ireland. Then, too, most of the best shops are gone. My cleaning lady said to me one day that Grafton Street died the day they stopped using knives and forks in its restaurants. She was right."

The company has six employees and the shop opens at 10 a.m. daily after an hour's "setting up". A day's work includes repairing, revaluing and cleaning jewellery. "It's time consuming but well worth it," Halpin says. "The quality of our work brings the client back."

The company also designs and makes jewellery to customers' specifications. "Our workshops are here on the premises," he explains, "as is the case with other, older jewellers. For security reasons we're the only tenants in the building. We carry Lloyds Insurance and they're very, very strict."

Keeping the door locked is not a security measure, however. "We don't want hordes of people hanging about and using us as a meeting place. We couldn't deal and talk with customers if that were the case."

Geraldine West — who lives in England, where she breeds Great Danes — owns today's company along with Joseph Moran of IWP. Robert Halpin talks to her every second day on the phone.

West made the original chain of office for Dublin's lord mayor in 22-carat gold and, in recent years, made the replica more often used these days. The company made its own silver in the 1700s and 1800s and at one point the antique silver it sold included its own.

"We were the King's Jewellers," Halpin explains. "We'd a coat of arms over the door. That sort of thing doesn't impress me though. There are a rake of people who have the same thing.

"Business has changed greatly over the years. We had wonderful characters who used to come in here. Lady Wicklow was one of them. She used to prod me, playfully, with her cane, her enormous chauffeur by her side. That was before the street was pedestrianised and you could park and have your hair done, then lunch at the Hibernian or Russell and stroll over to see what we had here, in Wests.

"A lot of the racing people were customers. Those were more gracious days and people had more leisure. Today our clientele is made up largely of successful business people, which reflects the economy of the country.

"But I've clients I've had for more than 30 years and, more importantly, their children — whom I remember looking up at me through those glass counters."

Robert Halpin is a jewellery designer and says, "90 per cent of the jewellery we deal in is handmade. The cost of handmaking a ring, which takes eight hours, is lost in the value of the diamond. Ninety-nine per cent of jewellery is machine-made in factories in places like Italy and England, where they just churn it out and drop a diamond into the centre.

"But if a customer of ours has an idea for a ring, we'll sit down and talk. There's no limit to what we can make by hand. We buy loose diamonds, already cut. There's no point us cutting diamonds when we can get the best in the world already cut from Israel."

To demonstrate what they do he removes from the window an exquisite oval-shaped diamond in a platinum setting, on an 18-carat chain of white gold. You could buy it for €40,630. It's very difficult, according to Halpin, to "make a good diamond ring for under €1,270. Jewellery prices here can start at €635 and go up to unlimited amounts. Below that, it's not my market.

"If I haven't got whatever you want I can make it for you. A piece of jewellery worth over €500,000 is a showpiece and you'll have it for life. If you want something of really fine quality there are two things involved: craftsmanship and design, diamond and metal. It's all to do with hand and eye. There are still many good jewellers around; it's not at all a dying craft."

He dismisses the idea of there being any mystique, "anything artistic", about design. "It's not difficult. You could do it on the back of an envelope coming in on the bus." (Which he does, frequently, on the 46A he's been getting at 7.30 a.m. each morning since the mid-sixties to get him to Bewley's by 8 a.m. to breakfast and chat with friends).

"There are certain things we don't sell and certain standards below which we will not go in this firm," says Robert Halpin. "That's how we are."

Fred and Frank Smith at their garage on Sandford Road. *Photograph: Matt Kavanagh*

Sandford Service Garage
79 Sandford Road, Ranelagh, Dublin 6

The Sandford Service Garage has been there for Dublin city's automobiles in the aftermath of two wars, tended the Fords (60 per cent of all cars then) and the Austin and Morris cars of the 1950s, the Ford Anglias, Volkswagen beetles and Minis of the 1960s — and in passing earned itself a memorable place in literature.

In the beginning, in 1918, there was Mr William McCabe, builder and property owner, who rented the Sandford Road site for use as a garage. A few years later, in 1925, a very young William Smith, aged 13 and living in Albert Place off Charlemont Street, arrived to work as an apprentice mechanic.

The garage never looked back: William Smith's sons, Frank and Fred Smith, run today's highly regarded business.

The work and times of the Sandford Road garage may chart the city's dance with the automobile, but it was a fire on the premises, in or around 1925, which made it the dramatic high point of a story by writer Maeve Brennan. In one of her *Stories of Dublin*, written in the 1950s in New York, this is how she remembers the fire: "It was a really satisfactory fire, with leaping flames, thick, pouring smoke, and a steady roar of destruction, broken by crashes as parts of the roof collapsed. My mother wondered if they had managed to save the cars, and this made us all look at the burning building with new interest and with enormous awe as we imagined the big shining cars being eaten up by the galloping fire."

Maeve Brennan was about 9 or 10 years old when the Sandford Service Garage went on fire. Frank Smith adds a few of his father's memories.

"He recalled the flames reaching to the sky," Frank says, "and told me how the pit later used for working under cars was originally built for the storage of petrol in old two-gallon cans. I would imagine those cans were the cause of the fire being so strong. In those early days, people came with empty two-gallon cans and exchanged them for full ones which were stored underground for safety. In this instance it looks as if they went up . . ."

Set well back from the road, in a quietly industrious niche surrounded by the sort of red-brick Ranelagh house Maeve Brennan once lived in, the garage is much as it always was. The kerbside petrol pumps by the entrance are still there – and will remain when Dublin City Council, in the interests of safety, fills the holding tanks underneath with cement.

On a timeless wintry evening in his small office, Frank Smith tells the story of the garage and the Smith family. "My father worked here until 1931, then moved on to a job with Huet Motors in Mount Street. They worked on bigger cars there so it was more experience for him. Then the war came; there were no cars on the road and mechanics were all let go. My father worked around Ireland for those years, doing compressors in airfields and railway stations, anywhere he could. I was born in 1942 and I remember him not being at home when I was very, very young."

The Smiths had travel, as well as cars, in the blood. Frank's grandfather served as a cavalry groom with the British Army in countries such as India and returned home to a job with Gunn's. His son, William, married Rose (*née* Rorke), who came from Milltown, and they had nine children. Frank was born on Ranelagh Avenue. "I haven't moved much over the years," he admits, without regret. When the war ended, William Smith went back to work in Huet Motors, where he heard that the Sandford Garage had failed to reopen. "He decided to rent the place himself; after a few months, he left Huet Motors and moved here."

A brave step for a man with a wife and a growing family (the first of William and Rose Smith's nine children was born in 1935, the last in 1955). By 1946, the Sandford Service Garage was an up-and-running business.

"At that time a lot of cars had been off the road and laid up for a long time, needing work done," Frank explains. "My father would get them going again and back on the road. Because he'd been working with Huet Motors, they sent him Bentleys and Rolls Royces, the old-fashioned box kind. Even up to 1951 there were cars arriving by train from west Cork and Kerry with tags on them to be stripped down. I remember them too well," he says, with a rueful look at his hands.

"The chassis had to be lifted off and the engine taken out and sent to England to be worked on. The chassis would be here for up to eight months." He nods towards the darkened area of the garage. "I would work on them, scraping them down for repainting and respringing.

"I was working here when I was 10 years of age, during the summer. Can't say I loved it; it was just part of my life. We were living in Drimnagh by then and used go home at lunchtime – the traffic wasn't so bad then, the journey only a 15-minute drive along the canal."

Frank began working full-time in Sandford Road in 1956. "I never wanted to do anything else. Fred's eight years younger and used come in to help before he started full-time in 1964. We took over the kerbside pumps in 1956.

"In 1956 cars were serviced at 1,000 miles and at 3,000 miles; 60 per cent of cars were Fords, 99 per cent of them were black and most female car owners were widows. Austins and then the Morris 8 were popular too." Mechanics Steve and Johnnie, along with Frank and his father and apprentice Ernie Dickson, made up the garage staff in the 1950s.

Then came the 1960s and the Ford Anglia 105E, with an improved engine and greater power. "They were the first car to be hyped big, with yellow and pink models paraded around Dublin," Frank recalls.

"It was a dramatic change from the black. The Mini had come in 1959, then the Austin 1100 and Morris 1100. The Volkswagen Beetle arrived – a complete change of engineering for us and, because Germany had a bad reputation after the war, no one else would work on them at the beginning. We could take the engine out of a Beetle in 20 minutes! There are still Beetle maniacs out there but we don't get them any more."

Oil crises came and went too. "In 1965 we were selling Arrow petrol from the kerbside pumps for 6d cheaper than elsewhere because we weren't tied to a garage. There were queues up and down the road. Changes came in the business with the introduction of electronic ignitions and fuel injection systems where before there had been plugs and contacts.

"Now we're into fuel management systems and there's a lot more equipment needed for testing. We now use synthetic and semi-synthetic longer life oil too and service cars once a year or every 10,000 miles. Or even after 20,000 miles in some cases."

Notable customers and cars which have been through Sandford Service include a young Michael Smurfit with his E-Type white Jaguar in the 1960s and Senator Michael Yeats with his Morris Minor in the same decade.

Dr Ciaran O'Driscoll, ex-Master of Holles Street, had a Peugeot 403 cared for there – "a lovely car at the time".

William Smith died when he was 86 in 1997, Rose two years later. "My father continued as boss/consultant until he died. We were a three-way partnership, my mother and father as a unit along with me and Fred." Cars continue in the family blood – Frank's son, Derek, is a member of AA Patrol.

Frank says he usually drives "a banger – a Toyota Corolla at the moment. Fred drives a BMW. We'll continue to work here – I love my work. If I retired I'd only be looking at cars and wondering what sort of transmission systems or fuel injection systems they had." He would too.

Millets Camping, Mary Street. *Photograph: Brenda Fitzsimons*

Millets Camping

61–62 Mary Street, Dublin 1

Camping has changed. Radically. Those who took on the great outdoors in the 1950s and 1960s did so under heavy-duty waterproof canvas. They cooked on a Primus stove and saw what they were doing by the light of a tilly lamp. Today's enthusiasts have a much easier time of it. Tents are made of lightweight nylon or polyester, food is heated on triple-burner gas cookers and multi-function emergency lanterns have remote controls.

Millets of Mary Street has seen the changes come, and sometimes go, and is in the business for the long haul. Today's camping and outdoor-equipment store, a by-word in the city's hill-walking, hiking, climbing and camping communities, is living testament to the rewards to be had for hard work and persistence. It's owned and run by the Kearns family. Their ability to go with the times and a recent refurbishment have turned numbers 61–62 Mary Street into a business with 5,000 square feet of retail space on two floors and storage and administration space on two further floors.

Denise Kearns, in charge of things these days, says she works closely with "Mum and Dad", visiting them every evening "for a grilling" on the day's events. Her mother, Colette, retired from active service on the shop floor only a few years ago, and in recent years too a brother, Darryl, left Mary Street to set up his own newsagent's business. A sister and two other brothers are doing other things with their lives.

It all began with Denise's father, Timothy Kearns. Born and brought up in the nearby fruit market area, he left a city going through hard times for work in Canada. Things weren't a lot better when he came home in 1956 but, older then and more resourceful, he went into business for himself, selling second-hand clothes in Little Mary Street. The company name came about when he bought the sign and two truck-loads of name-printed paper bags from a shop closing in Henry Street. The shop was called Millets.

"He sort of fell into this business," Denise says. "Things grew in Little Mary Street until he was selling army surplus, workwear and rainwear.

"The market went on changing and he changed with it to where he had a business specialising in camping and outdoor supplies. We moved from Little Mary Street to this bigger building in 1996. The market's changed big time these last years and so we decided to renovate the whole place."

The new space means they've been able to open up the first floor, which used to have tents pitched on it, to create a fully equipped shop-within-a-shop, selling everything from compasses to socks by Welsh company Gelert.

"We've been dealing with Gelert's for years," Denise explains, "and the new arrangement leaves us more time to concentrate on other top outdoor brands, people like Lowe Alpine, Berguasus, Helly Hansen and Mountain Equipment. We've extended the back of the shop and ground floor."

All a long way, in time and culture, from Timothy Kearns's early business dealings and the stories he has to tell. Like the one about the time he bought a container of seconds wellingtons in Leeds. They arrived in Dublin full of pin holes so, to separate the usable from the leaky, he had to fill each and every boot with water. Only one customer, a cousin who'd been sold his boots at cost price, complained about the subsequent bargain wellies.

Then there was the time Timothy Kearns brought in a consignment of suits from England and had them hanging outside the shop during Easter week. April showers turned to torrents of rain and the hanging garments shrank so much he had to sell them off as Communion suits. In another wellington story, he opened a container-load of brightly coloured wellies to find them neither paired nor sized. He paired them off in matching colours and sold the lot to Hector Grey.

Millets was there, and on the ball fashion-wise, when army surplus coats and jackets were *de rigueur* in the late 1960s, 1970s and even early 1980s. Denise is convinced army surplus gear will have its day again, maybe in 10 years' time.

Millets was also the place to go to get the old external-framed rucksacks which Denise remembers "only came in yellow, royal blue or red and were imported by us from Czechoslovakia". Millets sold the old-style army poncho oils too.

The Kearns have always been a hands-on business family. Growing up, household conversations were about the shop and, every Saturday, all or some of the Kearns children would help their mother in Mary Street.

"She worked six days a week until a few years ago," Denise says. "She thought she'd miss the place but she's actually enjoying her free time. I used come in a lot on Saturdays myself. We went camping as a family, all packed into the car, and in different parts of the country. Camping has always been popular. It was the one holiday people could manage when they didn't have much money.

"People would rent caravans and put tents outside for the kids. We used to get lots of

customers too from among those going to the Fleadh Ceoil and music festivals. What's really popular now are charity walks. People doing them come in to be fitted out from head to toe. We equip people going on mountain expeditions as far as initial base camps too."

Leisure wear is a fashion statement these days. Army surplus and old-style anoraks are historical curiosities with the demand now being for brand names, for jackets which are waterproof, breathable and capable of being worn every day. Tents have domes, different compartments and fibreglass poles. Buckets are foldable and dogs are restrained on dog tethers.

Millets employs 12 people. Denise Kearns, who has two small children, has no idea how many hours a week she herself works. "There's always something to do and I work as long as it takes," she admits. "It's great though – no two days are ever the same. Of course I take work home; it's not like a normal job. Yes, I'll stay with the business. Its future is assured, what with everyone more health conscious and activities like hill walking more popular than ever."

Her own obvious fitness comes from "running around this building all day, keeping things up and going".

It's easy to believe her.

George and Lee Rogerson, with their son Darren, owners of Ocean Marine in Monkstown Farm. *Photograph: Moya Nolan*

Ocean Marine

Fresh and Frozen Fish Suppliers,
22 Monkstown Farm, Dun Laoghaire

The story of Ocean Marine, the Monkstown Farm suppliers of frozen and fresh fish, is a lot more than the tale of how a hard-working family built a fish-selling business.

The sea surges and rolls, giving and relentlessly taking through generations of the Rogerson family and Ocean Marine saga. This is a business with impeccable credentials of the seafaring kind, going back to the 1800s, a family of fishermen, sailors and fish sellers which has known tragedy, sadness and recovery and is very familiar with resilience.

George Rogerson, ably abetted by his wife, Lee, tells how it was in laconic style. His story and Lee's, by virtue of lives lived together since their teenage marriage, is the stuff of both social history and a good yarn.

"We're trading here since the early eighties," he says. "Before it was Ocean Marine it was George's Fish Shop. But I'm in the business since I was nine or 10 years of age, when I sold fish on the quayside in Dun Laoghaire."

His father came from a fishing family in Fleetwood, "between Blackpool and Liverpool. They had steam trawlers and my mother met my father when he came into Dun Laoghaire for supplies. She was a Shortall, selling fish on the pier with the rest of her family, who were well-known in Dun Laoghaire for looking after boats and selling fish. Her name was Ellen. My father was James. They're both dead now.

"My mother went to live in Fleetwood but my father's people were staunch Protestants and she was a Catholic and they didn't get on, so they came back to live in Dun Laoghaire. They'd three kids by then and got a council house. My father carried on fishing, with one of his brothers, out of Dun Laoghaire."

George Rogerson is a great man for the dramatic detail. He tells of a court case, and how his father and uncle made history.

"They were caught fishing this side of the Kish Bank; the demarcation line goes down as far as Arklow now. They were the spawning grounds for prime fish and the English boats used come in at night. My father's and uncle's nets were confiscated. Herman Good represented them and they won their case." He shakes his head, remembering. "The life I had. Never went to school. Satchel under the hedge more often than not. We'd be fishing off the Arklow bank and our parents would be searching everywhere for us."

He grew up on York Road, one of 13 children. His brother Harry drowned when he was seven years old, on 7 October 1943. As George explains it, "he went down between two boats and banged his head coming up. He wasn't found until the following day."

Two uncles, along with a companion, drowned almost a decade before, on 5 December 1934. The story, in all its wintry tragedy, made headlines. The three men, Richard and Henry Shortall (aka Reggie and Hairy Man) and John (Freckles) Hughes, had been engaged in the dangerous pursuit of "hobbling". This involved four men rowing out in a skiff to intercept incoming cargo boats so as to earn the 7/6d fee for piloting them in to port.

"The boats coming in would be strangers to the waters," George explains, "and nine times out of 10 wouldn't stop to allow the pilots on. The men in the skiffs would be towed along, trying to get a man aboard. On that day the uncles and the two men with them got the job and earned the 7/6d. One of the men, Garret Hughes, stayed in Ringsend to collect and the other three decided to row the skiff back to Dun Laoghaire. It turned over. They all drowned. There's a monument to them on the new pier in Dun Laoghaire."

When George was 16 he went to work on the building of the Kish Lighthouse. This is a story in itself: how the lighthouse was made in telescopic fashion, the amount of work it brought to Dun Laoghaire, the men killed and injured over the years of its making, how George came to be the last person to leave when it was finally finished, left to man things because he was the youngest and single. Another story.

"A storm came up," he explains, "a force 8–10 southeasterly. I went up through the tower, opened the door to the platform. It came off its hinges, went out across the sea like a lump of newspaper, even though it was solid teak and four inches thick. The life-boats went in the wind too, torn away along with the 10 RB crane and three big compressors. I was there for three days; you'd hear the Kish rocking on the bottom at night. That was 1965."

Lee comes on board then, reminding him that was also the year they got married. "I met her in the Town Hall and she'd a yellow dress on." George nods. He was 19 and she 17 when they married in Monkstown Church. George went to work for Irish Lights, stayed 15 years, all the time wanting to go back to either buying or selling fish.

It was Lee who began building customers, getting orders. "We'd no money but went looking for a premises," she says. "Maggie Maloney, who used have a fish shop in Glasthule and who'd been widowed and was alone, gave us a hand. We found this place. It was an old, broken cottage at the time and we borrowed £4,500 to lease it for 13 years."

The story of them obtaining the loan, of how George, in the bank in his working clothes, was refused and how Lee, appearing in a fur coat, clinched the deal, is one for all times. Lee reported the bank's manager (who'd been the one to refuse), did business thereafter with the assistant manager and says that "to this day, I take every customer as they come, as they are".

The cottage was repaired, the wilderness yard ditto and they worked, together with Maggie Maloney, to build the business. "She was very good to us," Lee says. "She showed me how to fillet. We were broken into every other week in those days and George was back where he'd started, on the quays every morning buying fish. But we had things up and going within six months. We had three of the children by then too."

George went all over the country buying fish, leaving at 5 a.m. on Mondays for Kilmore Quay, Helvick, on to Dunmore East. Cod, ray and plaice were popular and he worked five days a week on deliveries as well as in the shop.

"The hours were long," he admits, "until nine and ten at night or filleting until two in the morning with Maggie. Ten years of that. It was hard work." Lee agrees, adding that "nothing in life comes easy".

The business today deals mostly in the supply of frozen and fresh fish to hotels and restaurants. "The Royal Marine was our first hotel," Lee says, "and then came the Gresham and the Royal in Bray. Then the pubs – McCormacks, The Merrion Inn, about 30 in all now. Three of the people we supply were in the 2003 BIM Seafood Circle."

They closed the shop in 2000 to concentrate on the wholesale side of things but Darren, their second son and the one of their four offspring to go into the business, reopened it in 2000 after a lot of renovation and enlargement to the rear. Tastes have changed.

These days, according to Darren, the demand is for frozen tuna, sword-fish, halibut steak, prawns. They're turning over more than €1 million a year and are at last involved in the negotiations to buy the building. Things are rowing along nicely for Ocean Marine.

James Gorry at work in his studio at Molesworth Street. *Photograph: Eric Luke*

Gorry Gallery

20 Molesworth Street, Dublin 2

James Gorry puts me sitting in his father's chair. "I run the business for him," he says. "He died in 1967 but I still consider I'm running things for him." He indicates a portrait of a moustachioed gent on the wall behind me. "That's my grandfather you're sitting under, painted by my father in 1923. He's the man who started the business more than 107 years ago. James Joseph Gorry was his name and he was born in James Street Basin in 1870.

"He began as a cabinet maker then went to work in Combridges, at the corner of Grafton Street, before opening his own shop, dealing in antiquarian books and restoring and dealing in pictures, on Ormond Quay. My father, James A. Gorry, was born in 1900. That makes me James the Third."

He tells the story of the Gorry Gallery seamlessly, without prompting, a man who loves what he does and freely admits to living for it too. The Gorry Gallery, 20 Molesworth Street, is discreet and enduringly dedicated to fine art. James Gorry, the most unpretentious of men, a picture restorer and sometime painter himself, specialises in eighteenth- and nineteenth-century Irish paintings, shows "a small number of living artists" and occasionally hosts a retrospective show. He works night and day, including weekends, with his wife Thérèse as his right hand. He is the Gorry Gallery and this is his story.

"My father went to the Metropolitan School of Art, Kildare Street, and studied to be a painter. He went on to become quite a decent painter and an RHA exhibitor. But he gave up painting and went to London and stayed there for 19 years. He trained there as a picture restorer with Ralph and Sid Warner, who were world-famous specialists in the restoration of seventeenth-century Dutch, Flemish and Italian still life and flower paintings. My father, who was a real specialist in restoration, was all the time buying up pictures in London and sending them home to my grandfather."

He digresses here, mentioning *en passant* that his father and grandfather were fine cross-country runners, his father becoming an English champion, covered in medals from all over the Thames Valley. He resumes the gallery story with the tale of how fate, in the shape of the Second World War, intervened and brought his father back to Dublin.

85

"He'd nowhere to live but he was a friend of Sean O'Sullivan RHA since their days in the Metropolitan School of Art and Sean was vacating his studio in Molesworth Street. So my father took over the lease and opened the Gorry Gallery here, at 20 Molesworth Street, in 1939, in what was Sean O'Sullivan's old studio. He and my grandfather worked on together until my grandfather died in 1943.

"My father was devastated by his death and nearly gave up the business. But he decided to continue and to hold exhibitions."

The second James Gorry had brought a wife home with him from London. Constance Lucy George was, her son says, "a Londoner of Welsh extraction". They lived in a flat on Grafton Street, and their son James was born there in 1948. "My father was 48 when I was born, so he was a much older man than me. I remember growing up on Grafton Street, how my father loved the life of the city at the time, how his haunts were places like Jammets and the Theatre Royal. He knew all the writers and artists of the time, from Patrick O'Connor to Sean Keating, Maurice McGonigal and Patrick Kavanagh.

"I left school at 15 and went to night classes in the National College of Art, as it was then known, and worked here in the gallery during the day. That was 1963 and it was the best thing I could have done because my father died in 1967 and I was able to continue on.

"It was quite a struggle but I dedicated myself, my work and the place to my father, whom I idolised. It brings tears to my eyes still to think of him … He was a wonderful man and I was very fond of him. He knew everyone, landed, titled, they all came in here."

He points to the chair I'm still sitting on. "That chair hasn't been moved since the day he died, and the cushion's never been washed."

James Gorry III has expanded the gallery, creating another gallery space downstairs where once there was a store room. The gallery holds twice-yearly exhibitions of eighteenth-, nineteenth- and twentieth-century Irish paintings gleaned from all over the world.

"We spend seven or eight months getting it ready, collecting pictures, buying, getting them sent from places like Canada and the US. We employ academics to write articles for the catalogue. People queue for the openings in sleeping-bags."

He stops, takes a serious breath and talks about his approach to the business. "I don't like the word 'Art'. Painting is a craft. It's a trick, a *trompe-l'oeil*. You're putting paint on a surface to give a 3-D effect. Some are better at it than others. If you paint pictures you're a painter, if you sculpt you're a sculptor.

"All the word 'Art' does is elevate it above the general public, make the work inaccessible.

Admittedly, I come at it from a restoration point of view so I study pictures in a technical way. I come from a painting/restoration background and am more a hands-on person. I'm like a detective, looking at the wood in old frames and all of that – earlier pictures require a different approach."

He's a member of the Irish Professional Conservators' and Restorers' Association, of the Irish Antique Dealers' Association and an associate member of the British Picture Restorers' Association.

The Gorry Gallery also holds one, sometimes two, exhibitions by living artists during the year and a studio or retrospective sale of the work of a deceased artist – in 2002 it showed the work of Nathaniel Hone RHA (1831–1917).

"I regard this place as a club," the gallery's owner says. "We're an open house; people come in for a chat and I give free advice on pictures. I'll help where I can, look up books and so on. It's a service and it's a deliberate thing that we're hidden away, with no shop front to advertise ourselves. We're very well known among a certain number of people but the general public mightn't know us so well. People have to ring the bell to come in."

He doesn't paint any more but restores all the pictures for the gallery, sourcing and restoring frames too. He's particularly interested in early gilt frames. Downstairs we take a look at pictures being cleaned, restored and getting their frames organised for an exhibition next month.

There are treasures of all sorts leaning against the walls – *The Gas Meter* by Harry Kernoff with a £10.10.0 price tag on the back, a gloriously cheerful Walter Osborne, abundantly gilded and decorated frames from all periods.

He's proud of the frame he found for a restored 1810 picture of the early Poolbeg lighthouse. "It's of the same period and for me it's pleasurable to be able to match the two. This work is not just about making money. The right frame on the right picture is a joy. I work seven days a week and at weekends behind closed doors. It's a hobby that I make money out of! I have to make money, obviously – I have to keep my books and pay VAT and pay rent. But I do it because I love it. I try to run it as a serious business, not just a commercial enterprise. I cultivate the club atmosphere and we give people time when they come in. We don't push people to buy and we're careful not to put people off."

Sam (retired) and Adrian (managing director) Caplin of Homestyle DIY, Mary Street. *Photograph: Alan Betson*

Homestyle DIY Ltd

1 Mary Street, Dublin 1

"By God, but this shop's been here a long time," said a man buying door handles in Homestyle DIY Ltd. His tone held satisfaction and a bit of wonder, a common response in the small but perfect cornucopia that is the Mary Street shop.

Door handles apart, the walls and surfaces everywhere groan with the weight of locks, glues, ornamental iron work, door pulls, leg plates, bolts – the sort of DIY necessities you might search far and wide for before inevitably finding them here, the place you should have gone to in the first instance.

"We're something of an institution," admits Adrian Caplin, third generation MD and owner of the company. "We've also got the biggest selection of door handles and knobs in Ireland." This seems modest; you'd believe him if he said they'd the biggest selection in Europe. The Caplins have been in the business long enough to know what they're doing, know what their customers want – and definitely long enough to become an institution.

In an upstairs office, where a map of the veneer timbers of the world (crafted in veneer timbers) takes up a wall, Adrian's father, Sam, in his eighties and retired, tells the early part of the story of the family and the business.

The first Caplins, like many other Jewish people escaping the pogroms of the time, left Russia after the Great War. Jacob Caplin, with his wife, four sons and a daughter, arrived in London in (probably) 1918–19. For reasons lost to history, one of his sons, Israel, didn't settle and moved on instead to Dublin. That was in (about) 1920 and was a decision which gave rise to the business and the generations of Dublin Caplins since then.

Sam, with a bewildering and typically Dublin amount of anecdote and detail, tells how it happened. "He worked for someone else initially before opening his own factory in 67–69 Jervis Street in about 1922, one of those tall old buildings that used to be there. He was very young. He'd served an apprenticeship in London and his apprenticeship piece was a beautiful little bureau. He called the company Caplin & Sons Ltd, Artistic Furniture Manufacturers. He decided he wanted to make and sell only the best of furniture, that he would make a name for the company throughout the world. He employed the best furniture makers of the time and they stayed with him, for 40 years some of them, and called him Charlie, never Israel. Caplins, in time, supplied exquisite handmade furniture to most of the Irish establishment."

The company's business card of the time fills in some detail. Caplins, it says, made "all classes of modern and reproduction furniture", as well as "satin and figured walnut bedroom suites, plain and inlaid mahogany bedroom suites, beds, bureaus, cabinets and bookcases".

Sam remembers the Jervis Street factory "consisting of a ground floor filled with the machinery for cutting and a second veneering floor, where the likes of curled mahogany veneer was put over mahogany doors". Adrian briefly interjects to lament the passing of the "lovely figuring work" and the advent of "MDF and laminated finishes".

Charlie/Israel Caplin took Ireland's turbulent times in his stride and in 1921 brought his parents, three brothers (who joined him in the business) and sister over from London to Dublin. "They all lived together," Sam says, "until my Dad met my mother, a lovely, lovely girl from Latvia, very modest and reserved, no arm holding or anything like that until they were married in 1922. I was born in 1923." He had a sister too, Pauline, and two brothers, Gerald and Harold.

In 1935, when Sam Caplin was 12, he went to Wesley College, then on St Stephen's Green. He didn't last long. When he was 14, "Charlie gave me a choice and I decided to go to London and learn the veneer trade."

Sam Caplin's time in London is both a tale onto itself and a tale of the times. For a while he pushed a handcart in the East End, later met a young Frenchman who promised to take him to his father's veneer-cutting mill in France and in between fell victim, more than once, to violence at the hands of Oswald Mosley's anti-Semitic followers.

The times and another war decided his future. "When the Second World War broke out my ma and da came to London and dragged me home to Dublin. The Frenchman was shot down very early in the war so I didn't get to France; he was a lovely man. Charlie was knocking out a nice living in Jervis Street but I wanted to go out on my own so I borrowed £50 from him and started up in a tiny place in Swift's Row. I paid him back every penny because I've never cared to be under a compliment to anyone."

The business slowly expanded and he moved to Parnell Street, to become Modern Veneer Importers Ltd, dealing in everything for the cabinet-maker. "I was about 17 and Richie Timmons, who came with me from Charlie's factory, was 16 and we were the managing director and manager in Parnell Street," he relishes the telling. "Richie went on to become the All-Ireland Ballroom Dancing Champion three times."

Securing an order in those days could (and did) entail Sam cycling as far as Navan on his pushbike. By dint of such energy the wholesale and retail business was expanded to premises in Granby Lane and later, in the 1960s, made the move to Mary Street. By the 1970s there was a company wholesale warehouse in Wolfe Tone Street too.

The Parnell Street premises had meanwhile been taken over by Dublin Corporation. More importantly for future Caplins was the fact of Sam meeting, falling in love with and marrying Moreen in 1953. "We live in the same house today as we did then," he reveals with pride, "and they've been 50 very good years."

And so to Adrian Caplin's story and today's business. The youngest of Sam and Moreen Caplin's four children, Adrian was born in 1962 and became the one who would choose to go into the business. "I came straight from school in 1978," he says. "Dick Timmons was still here, as well as Brendan Partridge. I learned the business from them and from my dad, going on buying trips to places like London and Germany and Italy. I went out repping on the road for a few years and loved it – I love dealing with people and prefer the retail side of things. We sold the wholesale when Dad wanted to retire and you could say things had come full circle when I took over the shop in 1995."

In 1985 he married Sharlotte (who assists in the business) and they have three children. With justification and without fear of argument he says that "people are delighted to find we're still here. Specialists and customers don't get the attention in bigger places they get from Aidan Kavanagh, who's the manager here, or from Derek Wright and Liam Rutter, who work with him in the shop."

He acknowledges the thousands of items packed into the small space, says the entire building is in use for storage and as company offices. He's confident about the future too. "This is a great, up and coming area," he points out. "It's becoming more residential all the time and the people who live in the new apartments come to us for their needs. We do quality stuff. Chrome and satin-chrome handles are the thing of the moment, but brass handles are good sellers and will always be in fashion."

There's another side to this quiet businessman. Adrian Caplin can sing. He sings in the synagogue, sometimes taking the service. Coaxed by his father, and for a minute of spine-tingling pleasure, he sings for us in the small office. The world of music will probably never know what it has lost to the DIY business.

Brady's Pharmacy on the corner of Camden Street and Harrington Street. *Photograph: Frank Miller*

Brady's Pharmacy
12 Upper Camden Street, Dublin 2

Dr Colm Brady has an acute memory for detail, especially of the historical kind. He grew up over the family pharmacy at 12 Upper Camden Street, still practises next door in Harrington Street and recalls the years since his father took over the pharmacy in 1924 with an enthusiasm that makes the story write itself.

"It has been a chemist since 1894," he begins, like the best storytellers, at the beginning, "and was owned then by Dr Ryan MPSI. It was a prominent chemist shop, even in those times. Dr Ryan was the pharmacist to Jacob's and made up medicines extemperaneously, on the spot from stock bottles. As they did in those days. As my father did too."

He reflects on this, fondly, shows me a 100-year-old bottle used for holding ginger. It's still half-full. Bottles were a certain colour if they held poison, green or blue if they held liniments or rubs. Aspro was available in tablet form and so were Beechams Pills, three of them for 1d.

"Dr Ryan died in 1924. My father had been managing the shop and he bought it, then built it up. I remember well how it was in the 1930s and 1940s: there were no antibiotics, pharmacies remained open until midnight and my father would deliver medicines personally to patients after that. In those days there weren't very many doctors so patients went to the pharmacist first."

He casts a fond eye on the busy street outside. "This district was very congested, teeming with people now gone. The old style Camden Street is gone, too, and Charlotte Street/Harcourt Street station was a busy place – the people around here went from it to Bray.

"The developments of office blocks in the area means we're dealing with a different kind of customer now. The older customers were families and constantly in and out of the shop for advice on medical matters. Simple matters, easily managed. My father would refer them to the local doctor if he was worried."

Colm Brady's father was Philip Brady, pharmacist and, later, Lord Mayor. He met Kitty Deery, who would become his wife and the mother of his seven children, when she was working as a medical rep and selling to pharmacies.

"My father became interested in politics because of the deprivation he saw," Colm goes on. "He represented the area along with Sean Lemass, became Lord Mayor in 1960 and died in 1995, his 102nd year. He'd been a pharmacist for over 78 years by that time. As a family, we were initially reared over the shop but eventually moved to Rathgar."

He describes how the shop once was: "A Georgian building with steps up to the door. My father wrote 'Steps to better health' across them but in the 1960s levelled them to allow access to disabled people. In the early days the dispensing department was to the left and on the right was what was called the store. There were two large windows, one onto the Camden Street corner and the other on Harrington Street, and displayed in them were large containers and carboys, to show people you were a pharmacy.

"We had the first neon sign in the area, made by Taylor's of Portobello in 1939. We used have to turn it off during the war black-outs."

On Camden Street there was a small side "wine window. People came for Buckfast or Wincarris or Cardinal de Salis tonic wines," Colm Brady explains, "and it wasn't the honey in Buckfast they were looking for! There was terrible poverty around this area in the 1930s so pharmacies would try to make some money selling sugar and chocolate. Later we took on sundries, like cosmetics, to bolster income. Then, too, the production of medicines was very time-consuming.

"Brady's cough mixture was made up according to a formula of my father's and cost 2/6d for eight ounces. It had huge sales. People came from far and wide. Many people had their own formulas for tonics and such, often based on sulphur. People came for eucalyptus, wintergreen – the pharmacy in the 1930s was a sort of alternative-medicine centre, with a great many herbs in use.

"You walked into one in those days and there was a lovely herbal scent from the storage of medicines. Leaves and roots and bark – they all had a smell. It was a much more intimate business then. That's one thing I miss: knowing everyone. Your knowledge of people ran to thousands."

His brother Fergus, also a doctor, pops in and together they remember Ben Daly and Jimmy Hayes and how they spent their working lives in Brady's Pharmacy. "They were bricks of the place," Fergus says. "I remember a Mr McCarthy, too, and Ms Dymphna Williams, Pearse Farrelly – all the names of people from years gone by."

Their mother worked all her life in the pharmacy; two of their brothers, Philip and Des, carried on the tradition and became pharmacists; Gerard is an optician (and TD), Frank a surgeon and their sister, Una, is now involved in care for the elderly. "The medical aspect came through in us all," Colm says, and goes back to remembering.

"There were quite a few doctors living around, working in Surgeons and UCD and attached to

Portobello. Prescriptions would come in with just a number on them and my father would know the formula and make them up. You wouldn't get away with it now — everything has to be tabulated. In the 1940s and 1950s messenger boys or the family had to do medical deliveries on bicycles with wicker baskets which had 'chemist' written on them in red and white. My father would send me on a bike to Tallaght and to a family in Three Rock Mountain in the late 1940s. It was easy, only a cycle run to the country. Micheál MacLíammóir and Hilton Edwards used come in here in the 1940s. Micheál always liked to smell the perfumes: his preference was for Houbigant and Chelque Fleurs. We stocked a special stage make-up just for him.

"We supplied medicines, too, to Portobello House, which used to be a nursing home, and I remember delivering there to Jack Yeats at the end of his life."

Things changed, medically speaking, in the 1940s and 1950s. "New medicines came in, treatment for TB and for ordinary infections, antibiotics and steroids. The pharmacy began selling medicines which came ready branded and the way of dispensing changed."

Sunday mornings in the early 1950s were lively times in Brady's Pharmacy. "It used be packed to the doors with people coming from mass. They would buy small things, a soother or something, but really they just met here. You rarely see anyone on a Sunday now. We lost lovely people when they moved everyone out! And there was a beautiful, soft Dublin accent that was typical of this area."

He casts an eye over life outside the window again. "This used be Kelly's Corner, after the sweetshop across the road. All the streets were cobbled until they took them up with the tram tracks; four tracks converged here and you wouldn't believe the number of wires crossing this corner! Now they've put down Luas tracks right beside us.

"There were always large numbers of immigrant people living around here. The early-twentieth-century Jewish people have been replaced by Muslim and Hindu groups but medical needs don't acknowledge religion! We're all the same. We still have a loyal customer base of regular customers but nowadays it's very much more a passing trade, especially office workers at lunch time. It's a different style of thing altogether but the function remains the same. A skilled pharmacist is a wonderful person to help people."

Colm Brady reflects on another change. "From being a predominantly male profession, pharmacy is now predominantly female," he says. "Possibly because the hours suit women who want to be in a caring profession."

McDowells, The Happy Ring House,
O'Connell Street. *Photograph: Frank Miller*

McDowells,
The Happy Ring House
Jewellers, O'Connell Street, Dublin I

To talk about McDowells, The Happy Ring House, managing director Peter McDowell sits in his first-floor office, a quiet room overlooking the famous timepiece. The passing minutes tick reassuringly, confirmation that some things really don't change. The McDowell clock is one of only three mechanically operated clocks in the capital.

"I've purposely kept it manual," says Peter McDowell. "I'm quite interested in mechanical movements. I don't wear a quartz watch either."

The Happy Ring house is a bit like that: plenty of quiet tradition and a sort of solid confidence about it. It's been a landmark in O'Connell Street for over 100 years, witness to history parading through the capital's main thoroughfare since 1902. The McDowell jewellery business itself has been around even longer, since 1870, when Peter McDowell's great-grandfather opened a shop in Mary Street.

Today's MD (Peter McDowell runs the business with his cousin John) has no idea how or why the family first came to the jewellery business. "The family origins are in Scotland," he offers by way of a clue. We don't pursue it. The reason it's called The Happy Ring House is easier, self-explanatory really. Engagement and wedding rings are as much the mainstay of the business now as they were when Peter McDowell's great-grandfather first came up with the name.

Peter McDowell and his cousin John are the third generation of the family in the business. Peter thinks they must be the oldest family-owned operation on O'Connell Street. "What's important from a business point of view is the private-ownership aspect. Given the nature of this business there's a lot of trust involved. People like to know who they're dealing with when they hand in personal jewellery for repair, or whatever."

His father was a vet, but Peter was happy to go into the business with cousin John when their uncle and previous owner Jack McDowell died without a successor. Peter McDowell studied business in TCD and joined the family business 33 years ago.

Stories about The Happy Ring House are legendary, and true. There's the 1916 tale about how, with the GPO coming down, Peter McDowell's grandfather and the porter refused to leave the building, hoping to prevent looting. "But things got so bad they had to make a run for it," Peter says, "somewhere between here and Cathedral Street. The porter was shot dead and my grandfather was hit in the leg. This building was more or less demolished and looted anyway. It was rebuilt using girders from the ruined GPO. We sent a bill to His Majesty and got compensation after some negotiating."

One of the greatest boosts to the business came because of a horse called Caughoo. Owned by previous owner Jack McDowell, and trained by Peter McDowell's father, Herbert, Caughoo won the fog-obscured 1947 Grand National. With no television cameras to prove otherwise, rumour had it that Caughoo had gone round the course only once. "He was paraded up and down O'Connell Street," Peter says. "It was a huge boost to business, the best thing which could have happened."

During the Second World War, with no gold available for jewellery purposes, McDowells gathered what scrap gold they had, refined it and used it to make wedding and the then-fashionable signet rings.

In the 1930s, 1940s and 1950s, great numbers of Happy Ring House customers came from the country. "It was the thing to come to town, meet your girlfriend by the pillar and buy the ring in McDowells," Peter explains. "People still come to us from the country but towns everywhere have jewellers now. We've our own workshops on the premises as well as our own jeweller and watchmaker.

"We've always had a very good, loyal staff, something which is fundamental to the success of a business this size. We like to think we understand our staff and any problems they might have, and work with them. We've a lot of long-term employees, people who have 30, 40 or 50 years with the company. One lady was here 55 years, coming in when she was 12 years old. Our long-time jeweller Noel Geraty retired recently after 67 years. In all that time he was only absent two weeks, and then with appendicitis. His father was here before him and brought Noel in when he was 14. They worked side by side, repairing chains, sizing rings. He's been replaced by Des Rooney.

"Our present watchmaker, Raymond Martin, has been here 34 years. His father brought him into the company too. We've a staff of 18 full- and part-time workers and use the entire building, from top to bottom, for the business."

As the clock quietly ticks we look at catalogues and pictures of earlier times in The Happy

Ring House. In the late 1940s you could buy an 18-carat gold ring with platinum setting and nine-stone diamond cluster for £10. Watches came with a 10-year guarantee. Gold drop earrings were 12/6d a pair. A photograph dating from the early 1920s shows the McDowell name set in stone above curved glass windows. "It was a lovely window," Peter McDowell laments, "but the wood rotted and the insurance people said the curved glass wasn't bandit proof so the lot had to be replaced."

One thing hasn't changed. Rings, marriage and engagement, are still the mainstay of the McDowell business. "We've a constant stock of between 900 and 1,000 rings," Peter McDowell says, laying flat, elegant boxes on the desk. "We can make whatever the customer wants." He opens the first to show diamonds, shining white and expensive looking. "We import all our diamonds loose, from London. We've the most complete and comprehensive stock in the country." The other boxes hold rubies, sapphires and emeralds.

Fashions have changed. Brooches and tiaras are long gone. Customers these days are more likely to look for 18- and 9-carat chains in various weights and lengths, or for bracelets and earrings. Sales of the once ubiquitous three-piece silver tea-set on tray have "died the complete death", according to Peter McDowell, "though silver jewellery is quite fashionable. It's cheaper and people can get bigger pieces for their money. Clusters of stones are out for engagement rings; single- and three-stone settings are popular. Women are still keen on a ring. We're selling more and more but the approach to buying is different: women are often married and with children before they come for an engagement ring."

He's passionate about O'Connell Street's place in the scheme of the city and feels that the current revamping is 20 years overdue, "far reaching and welcome". He likes what he does. "It's a nice business to be in, particularly since it's well-established. We've had bad times, naturally, particularly in the early 1980s when we'd to deal with 33.3 per cent VAT charges. It nearly put a lot of us in the luxury trade out of business. But here we still are." He has two sons who may, in time, when they're old enough to decide, go into the business. What's virtually certain is that McDowells will not be going out of the family.

Betty Ann Norton (sitting) with Carol O'Neill, administrator and drama teacher, at the Betty Ann Norton Theatre School, Harcourt Street. *Photograph: Eric Luke*

Betty Ann Norton Theatre School

11 Harcourt Street, Dublin 2

Betty Ann Norton is a passionate woman. She fills the high, bright rooms of her theatre school at 11 Harcourt Street with energy, spreads passion generously and infectiously around as she talks about the school's 45-year history, its students and tutors, her own growing-up in Dublin, her brother Jim. In no time at all you're feeling passionate and generous about life yourself.

Anything's possible, life's a doddle and a joy, people are wonderful and Dublin will survive the Luas works if Betty Ann has anything to do with it.

But more of the last anon.

First, with the sun spilling through the windows, she talks about passion as her not-so-secret ingredient for a happy life. "The secret of life is to know what you want," she says. "I've always known that I wanted to teach voice and acting."

Her own voice is crystal and clear, a tribute to an early training at the Ena Mary Burke School at 20 Kildare Street. She was seven when she went there with her brother, the actor Jim Norton. "Burkey had taught Maureen O'Hara and Milo O'Shea," Betty Ann says, "and later Joe Dowling and Brenda Fricker. She did plays, shows, *feiseanna* across Ireland."

Her father, Professor Burke, had taught elocution in Maynooth in the 1870s. "I feel I'm in a direct line from all of that!"

She puts aside, briefly, the drama and entertainment of her early life to make a few salient points about life and today's Harcourt Street school. Adamant that the school is "not a one woman show", she explains that she's co-director of the school with husband Michael J. Cunneen, that Carol O'Neill is its invaluable administrator as well as a part-time speech-and-drama tutor, that the school has a dozen tutors altogether (most of them past pupils) and has Sir Michael Gambon as its patron.

"Teaching and performing happens on all four floors, sometimes in the hall as well," Betty Ann says, "six days a week, sometimes seven. Students come from everywhere, some even from the country on Saturdays. Not all of them want to be actors or public speakers. Many come because they find speaking publicly or socially difficult and want skills and confidence. In recent years we've opened other centres too."

She does a bit of everything herself. "Voice, acting, teacher-training, English literature, improvisation and writing original work for students. We have students doing the theory of speech, film acting and directing, mime, stage acting and diploma training."

Evidence of the school's varied activities is in bookcases stacked with everything from Shakespeare to the Bible, with volumes on Greek drama, costume, make-up, set design, and in shelves of novels, plays and poetry. Among photographs on the walls there's a younger, passionately smiling Betty Ann and, hanging in a frame above her, a dreamy, blue-eyed Jim Norton.

"There were only the two of us," she says now, "just Jim and I. We lived off the SCR when we were children. My mother was a housewife; in those days ladies didn't work after marriage. She was a violinist and had an amazing interest in theatre. Our father was a shy man but she was a dramatic lady, an actress *manqué* I suppose.

"My father, Eugene Norton, was manager of the Bacon Shops in Grafton Street. He was a meticulous man for whom preparation was all. I remember him getting into his Morris Minor on Stephen's Green and Brendan Behan, passing by in an open shirt, yelling, 'Hey, Norton, you'll never be as good a man as your son.' Behan had met Jim, who was by then working in the Radio Éireann Rep."

A fine storyteller (as was her paternal grandmother, a Monaghan woman) with a prodigious memory, Betty Ann is well into her stride by now.

She went as a child to the St Louis Convent in Rathmines, "a small school in those days, in a Georgian building. We used sit around an open fire on settees to be taught."

By the time she was 19 she was studying for a Licentiate teaching (speech and drama) diploma in London's Guildhall. She got 91 per cent in her final exams. "While I was at it I went on to get a diploma from the Royal Academy."

Back in Ireland she travelled the country, in a yellow Ford Anglia bought for her by her father, teaching speech and drama. She remembers classes in Enniscorthy, Wexford, Bunclody, and teaching fishmonger Peter Caviston in Glasthule, Co. Dublin. "He was a star pupil. He could have been an actor if he'd chosen to be," she says.

She opened her own school in 1959, at 57 Harcourt Street, a building now gone. "It was quite revolutionary, a woman running her own business. I taught adults as well as children and it never occurred to me that I couldn't do it. I just concentrated on how it could be done. I do the same now. It worked out wonderfully. I was still living at home and my brother was making his way in the Rep."

She met her husband on the Aran Islands when, riding a bike, she literally knocked him down.

That was in the summer of 1965 and they married in 1967. "He was in display and design but also had a huge theatre background in amateur drama and set design. He came into the business with me and we bought the house in Dun Laoghaire in which we still live. It was and is a beautiful house."

In 1969 the growing school moved to 27 Harcourt Street. "We had all of the basement – five rooms with two big studios and a lovely patio out the back. I put two camellias into tubs in the front and they grew and grew and when we left my gardener took them to Dun Laoghaire and they're just splendid, red and crimson and a memento of number 27. We moved here, to Clonbrock House, which used be the home of the Dillon family, in 1991."

Her face doesn't darken, exactly, as she begins to talk about Harcourt Street and the Luas works. It's more a case of fierce resolve taking over. "I was the drama queen of Harcourt Street until Luas came and tried to knock me off my perch," she says, "but they didn't succeed. They were irresponsible and insensitive while they worked here. When they started there was lots of goodwill for them in Harcourt Street but I don't think anyone had a good word to say by the time they finished. Our rates alone are almost €10,000 this year. Trying to put on showcase shows for parents and videos in the front rooms was impossible with the level of noise."

Carol O'Neill joins us and is equally adamant. "We went out into the street to talk to them," she says. "They told us they had to do their work but I told them they were preventing us doing ours." Betty Ann says too that they had to replace their computers, damaged by the dust from the works.

She is anxious to name and give credit to the work of her tutors. "Vincent Lambe runs our film course. He's a fine director himself and won first prize for his film *Broken Things* in the Cape Cod Film Festival. Our other tutors include Rebecca Bartlett and David Horan of the Abbey."

Harcourt Street remains the working and booking hub of things but expansion means the school now has centres in St Louis High School, Rathmines, York Road Presbyterian Church Hall, Dun Laoghaire, the Dominican College on Griffith Avenue, in David Lloyd, Riverview (members only), and very lately in the Brackenstown Resource Centre, Swords.

Betty Ann Norton is genuinely shocked when asked about her future, about the idea of retirement. "Why on earth would I want to give up something I enjoy so much?" she asks. The question is not rhetorical – this year the school is for the first time offering students the opportunity to do a Guildhall teaching diploma in conjunction with an acting diploma.

Betty Ann Norton believes real talent "always outs". Dervla Kirwan, Barry Lynch, Hugh O'Conor, Emma Donoghue, Eleanor Shanley, Moya Doherty – the list of those who've been through the school is long. "We've a much wider programme now," says Betty Ann, "everything's improved. Standards are higher everywhere."

John Myley, owner of Curran's Shoe Repairs at Baggotrath. *Photograph: Moya Nolan*

Curran's Shoe Repairs
Baggotrath, Dublin 2

Curran's Shoe Repairs, Dublin 2, will never be anything other than Curran's Shoe Repairs. It's of no matter that Mr Michael Curran, who started the business in 1937 and was its life-force for 50 years, is retired since 1987. Mr Curran's work ethic, pride in the craft and customers are all solidly in place. Not to mention his spirit and the powerful memories which don't so much haunt as inhabit the place.

Things might have been different had John Myley not happened upon Curran's Shoe Repairs at an early, and definitely impressionable, age.

John and Mr Curran first met over the family dinner table in the Myley household in the early 1950s. John was eight when he began spending time in the shop with his father and Mr Curran, 11 when he began helping out during the summer holidays and 16 years old when the seemingly inevitable happened and he became an apprentice shoemaker. (A cobbler, he explains, "was someone who fixed shoes on a three-legged last balanced on cobblestones; a shoemaker is a craftsman and a different thing altogether".)

Today's business is in John Myley's capable and caring hands. And will be. "No. No. No. I'm not going to sell up." He's adamant: "I'm here for the next 20 years. I love what I do, love seeing a shoe come in in bits, putting it together and giving it back whole to the customer."

The shop looks much as it ever did: a single-storey, garage-like building in a Baggot Street landscape of towering office blocks, Georgian houses and the Merrion Hotel; there are just six inches between Curran's and the hotel's walls. The floor is wooden and uneven, the back walls made of white painted brick, the whole place uncertain looking.

Appearances are misleading: the shop will definitely, John says, "see me through those next 20 years". An Adler sewing machine dating from 1927 dominates the waiting area; the bench behind is a museum of ancient, worn-down knives and hammers.

John Myley is adamant too that he owes everything – training, knowledge and the continuing existence of the shop – to the craftsmen who worked there before him. Their combined working lives come to more than 180 years and there will never, he thinks, be their like again.

Mr Curran is Mr Curran, always. It's how John Wyley refers to him and no one ever called him anything else.

When Mr Curran bought the Baggotrath premises in 1937, there were shops all around. The coffee shop on the corner was then a creamery, and for a while, Mr Curran walked out with a young woman who worked there. But the romance didn't flourish in the way the business did.

"He used arrive at 7.30 a.m. and not leave until 11 at night," John Myley says. "He did the counter and all the inconvenient work – handbags, patching shoes, sorting things out.

"He was religious and used make us all genuflect and bless ourselves when the Angelus rang at midday. He went to mass every single day and to a Men's Holy Hour on Sunday.

"He never married and lived alone in Fitzwilliam Lane in an old, stone coachman's mews. It had four bedrooms; he lived in one and blocked off the rest. He was very friendly to the customers, a perfectionist who knew what he wanted in the finished product and could be hot-headed."

His employees were the legendary Joe Simington (who used to repair de Valera's shoes), Patrick Thornton, "the best ever shoemaker in Ireland" according to John, and Dominic O'Neill, who knew more than most about stitching and finishing.

"Everyone got their shoes done here," John explains, "all the doctors in Fitzwilliam Square and the nuns from the convents around. They had to be collected and delivered back.

"Often the doctors would keep you waiting a couple of hours, until they'd examined the shoes, before paying.

"Mr Curran couldn't afford a stitching machine, so that work was done in Harcourt Street, where two brothers had a stitching machine in a basement. Pat Thornton's job was to deliver and bring back the shoes from them. He was always complaining about his bike wheels getting caught in the tram tracks along Stephen's Green."

Pat Thornton ("a great man for stories") would cycle in every morning from Dundrum to be in the shop for 7.30 a.m. In later years, he took to using a Norton motorbike.

The shop opened at 8.30 a.m. and closed at 6 p.m.; still does. "In those days," John says, "there was a summons for trading after 6 p.m. When the shutters came down, Mr Curran went on working until 11 at night."

During those years too there were about four shoemakers in the area. Patrick Thornton, over the half century he worked there, saw 13 shoemakers start up and close down. The explanation is simple, according to John Myley. "You have to give quality workmanship or you'll be found out. We pay attention to detail, doing repairs for lots of solicitors and barristers who have to go to court well shod."

John's own story follows the tradition of dedication to the craft of shoemaking. His father,

Hugh Myley, an employee of the British United Shoe Company, got to know Mr Curran both through selling him shoe machinery and meetings at the Men's Holy Hour. After John's first three-month summer stint in the shop, Mr Curran gave him a hammer, Pat Thornton a "little nipper" and Joe Simington a driving file. He still has them.

He still refers to their skill and knowledge too. "If things go wrong in here I go back to the way the lads would have done it," he says.

When Mr Curran, prior to retiring, decided to sell up in 1984, and there were doubts about whether or not the business would continue, Hugh Myley came to a gentleman's agreement with Pat Thornton, Joe Simington and Dominic O'Neill and bought the place.

John Myley did his apprenticeship "under the wing" of Dominic O'Neill, a learning time of about 18 months during which he "stripped shoes, taking off the old leather and repairing anything which had to be repaired on the shoe". He absolutely believes the adage which claims you can tell a man by his shoes. "An Armani suit is nothing without a good pair of shoes," he says.

When Pat Thornton retired six years ago he was on his own. Still is. "I was very sad when he left," John admits. "He'd become a father figure to me. I still do things the thorough, old-fashioned way and still have lots of customers from the Dáil, some TDs who've been coming for over 30 years.

"I've a customer I've never seen, a man in Greystone, Co. Tipperary, who sends shoes every three months to be looked at and checked. One pair at a time, black and good."

He wears Italian shoes himself, slip-ons usually. And Caterpillar boots for work, "for safety reasons. The last pair of laced shoes I had I made myself. When Pat and Dominic were here we'd often sit down of an afternoon and cut and pattern and make shoes from scratch."

The Celtic Tiger bit them a little, for a while. "People were buying more new shoes all the time but in the last year they're coming in for repairs again." Tailor Louis Copeland sends customers to Curran's and has his worn shoes repaired there.

He does repairs for customers of the Shelbourne and Merrion hotels. Customer attitudes have changed. "In the early 1980s people were very bossy. They wanted Mr Curran's attention all the time. These days customers are more appreciative."

Like Mr Curran before him he often works until 11 at night "to get the work out to customers". He says that in the "near future" he'll be looking for "an experienced man who enjoys the job". But for now, it's work as usual, five days a week.

John Doyle's butcher's shop on Pearse Street. *Photograph: Dara MacDónaill*

Doyle Bros
Family Butchers, Pearse Street, Dublin 2

A butcher's shop is an intimate place. You get to know what people have for their breakfast, dinner and tea, as well as with whom and in what order they eat those meals.

If you're John Doyle and running a family butcher's in Pearse Street, you get to know an awful lot more about your customers than their eating habits.

"We've been here for over 60 years and have customers from 3 weeks to 89 years old," he says. "Our oldest customer recently turned 92. The people around here are everything, the most important thing in the business. I'd know 80 per cent of customers and would know the grannies and great-grannies of most of them. It's more than a butcher's, it's a bit of fun. You'd always know what's going on, the good and the bad. Who's been born, who's dead, who's pregnant and shouldn't be. It's a liberal community around here and I'd be liberal too."

He's had plenty of time to get to know his customers. Been at it since 1962, in fact, when he came as an apprentice to what was then his father's shop.

Doyle Bros was started by John Doyle's father and uncle, Jim and Pat Doyle, in 1943, when they arrived in Dublin from a small mountain farm in Donard, Co. Wicklow. "There were 11 of them in the family," John Doyle explains, "eight boys and three girls. The farm couldn't support that many of them so what else were they to do?"

Butchering was what seven of the Doyle boys chose to do. In 1945–46 Jim and Pat Doyle bought a second shop, in Terenure. The business split, when it came, was amicable. Pat Doyle moved to Terenure and Jim Doyle stayed in the Pearse Street shop and reared a family of four boys and three girls in nearby Sandymount. John Doyle is the oldest of the brood – and the only one to become a butcher.

"I was wasting my time at school in Marian College," he says, "but I liked the business so at 15 I started an apprenticeship here. My father at that stage had started a livestock auctioneering business in Blessington along with four of his brothers. A man called Jimmy Carroll trained me. He was a very, very good butcher.

"In 1965 I was sent by my father to look after a farm he'd bought in Tallaght, which was all land then, no houses. It was all part of the learning process, part of becoming a butcher. I spent two years at that, looking after cattle, sheep and pigs. I loved it. Still do. We've a farm in Newbridge now, where I live, and we're one of the few butchers left in Dublin slaughtering our own meat.

"One of our big selling points is that the beef and lamb we sell is from our own farm or a neighbouring one and is completely traceable. We also see the animals alive and dead so we know about their general well-being and all of that."

Because his father believed a butcher should know every aspect of the trade John Doyle also spent a couple of years as a cattle auctioneer in Maynooth and Blessington. "My father worked the ass off you," he says, "but I've no problem with that." He "works his ass off" voluntarily these days, opening the shop at 8.30 a.m. and closing at 5.30 p.m. as well as working on the farm in Newbridge.

The walls of the shop are hung with local community and family event pictures. Britain's Prince Charles is there, surrounded by customers when he visited the community, and local dancer Lee Oglesby figures prominently too. "People bring in their pictures," John explains, "or if we hear of something interesting we ask for photos. It means a lot to have them up there."

John Doyle took over the shop in 1968. Today's shop, bright, white and good-sized, has grown over the years from the much smaller original premises. "In 1943 it was two shops," John explains, "a butcher's and a dairy owned by a Mr Uzell who died leaving no one to take it over. The shops were knocked into one in 1957 and the whole place revamped.

"There was some updating over the years, but in 1998 I took the bull by the horns and did the complete update you see today: new fridges and air conditioning out the back, new floors and new plastic walling."

Something which doesn't change a lot in Doyle Bros is the staff, who are inclined to stay. Brendan Smith, butcher and "jack of all trades" has been with the business since the early fifties and his son Brendan joined up in 1986. Maureen McCabe, PA to John Doyle, came on board in 1985 and says cheerfully she's "a piece of the blooming furniture" and wouldn't work anywhere else.

Though Doyle Bros supplies hotels, restaurants and institutions with meat from their beef herd and sheep flock, the shop trade is the side which has become busier since the early nineties.

"It's because of the general uplift in the area," John Doyle says, "and with the building of apartments and new houses. We've huge numbers of Chinese, Russian, French, Italian, Canadian, Australian and New Zealand customers coming in, lots of them students. We have great craic with them too. The Chinese buy pork of all kinds but the rest buy everything, including fillet steak. There don't seem to be any poor students any more."

He reckons his prices are among the keenest in town but feels that eating habits have changed absolutely. "It used to be all stewing beef and mince and rib steak. Nowadays it's sirloin steak and stir fries, which we sell ready made. Girls are very hassled these days, juggling jobs and homes and children, and Irishmen are still disastrous when it comes to helping in the house. So it has to be easy and quick to make. I often have to tell them how to cook a roast."

His own (adult) children have "absolutely no interest in the business. It's the same with most butchers; the younger generation don't want to know. It's a six-day-a-week job and hard compared to other work. But I love it and would go mad in an office.

"I reckon I'll be still coming in here at 85, in a wheelchair. What else would I do? That's plenty of years away and I'll worry about the continuity of the business when that time comes."

The CAST bronze foundry team at South Brown Street, with a bronze cow by sculptor Jackie McKenna. From left are Ray Delaney, Colm Brennan, Paddy Graham, Barry Linnane, Willie Page, Leo Higgins, David Dunne, Walter McGuire and Emer Byrne. *Photograph: Cyril Byrne*

CAST

CAST, the bronze foundry in South Brown Street, Dublin 8, has a pre-history that gives it a status and importance in the culture of the country which belies its relative youth – it has only been in business since 1986.

There's no one more conscious of the foundry's role in things than sculptor Colm Brennan, co-founder of CAST with Leo Higgins. Brennan, a life-force as large as the bronze work in his foundry, is a man who passionately believes that sculpture is part of what life's all about.

"It's medieval," says Brennan with relish and accuracy as fires burn in crucible furnaces, bronze ingots arrive and time-worn tools such as chasing chisels, spatulas and die grinders are wielded all around.

"Technology wise, the single biggest change is that we're now using a process called 'ceramic shell'; along with Kinsale gas and electricity, it's about our only concession to the twenty-first century. We still use a process called lost wax casting. A Renaissance sculptor could walk in here, understand the process and start working."

Musing away, he takes things back a few centuries earlier. "The foundry tradition grew out of the itinerant bronzesmiths of the High Christian period," he says, "but even in the early bronze age it's reckoned many artefacts may have been made by itinerant bronzesmiths."

CAST is based in the Liberties, in what in 1850 was a tannery, and provides a total sculpture service to artists and commissioning bodies.

The fine art works cast by the company are seen across the land and abroad and include the GPO's *Cuchulainn*, Leo Higgins' gilded bronze torch set in stone in Killarney Street, Dublin I, which commemorates those who have died from drug abuse, medallions for the Air Corps and the monumental John Behan sculpture for the UN grounds in New York.

The company started when Brennan and Higgins came together and agreed the need for a new foundry in Dublin. Sculptors both of them, there's a synchronicity about their lives and partnership which boded well for CAST from the beginning.

Leo Higgins grew up in Finglas and at 15 was apprenticed as a bronze moulder to Daniel Miller's foundry works in Church Street. "I've been working at it since the late sixties now and conditions were Dickensian when I began. Apprentices came in a half hour before the tradesmen to light the fires and get things ready. They stayed later too.

"The work involved industrial moulding for distillers, ecclesiastical casting, railways for CIÉ. Towards the end of my time I developed a liking for the ecclesiastical end of things. It meant I could meet people face-to-face, artists like Oisín Kelly and Imogen Stuart. My horizons widened and I became completely interested in the art side of things."

It was 1967–8 and he talks of the great changes in Ireland at the time, how metal-working skills were "coming into their own, there was more money around, churches were being revamped, architecture was changing and different skills coming to be appreciated. It was an exciting time to be involved in metal work."

It was a natural move for him to join artist John Behan in the newly formed Dublin Art Foundry in 1970. "I worked there for 14 years. John Behan had left by then and set up successfully on his own in Galway. In 1986 I decided to have a go myself, went into partnership with Colm to set up CAST and here we are today, alive and kicking. We'll go on, too. I'll have to be carried out of here. No other way I'd leave."

Colm Brennan fills in his side of the story – as well as the gaps which round the circle. A Mayoman, born in Belmullet in 1943, his grandfather was "a rudimentary stonemason and I was happiest as a kid in the local forge. I very often didn't get home from school until after the forge closed – it was a kindergarten of fiery form.

"I met Leo in the early seventies, when I needed a piece of sculpture cast. I'd been working in stone and wood before that and was excited at seeing the foundry and all that could be done there.

"Years later we saw the need for a new foundry and CAST was born. The name's an anagram for Crucible Art Services and Technology – coming up with that was painful and kept me awake at night. We're so well-known now the anagram's forgotten and doesn't matter anyway."

Everything else does, however, in particular "a pour". We watch in the cold air as molten bronze leaves the furnace in a crucible and is poured, orangey gold, into ceramic shell moulds. It's medieval, as Brennan has said, and it's exciting.

On a quick walkabout he remarks that foundries have been compared to a cross between a bakery and building site.

CAST began life in the yard of the Daniel Miller foundry works in Church Street – where Leo Higgins had served his apprenticeship. "A lovely link," Colm Brennan says.

"We were there for about six years; we cast the Anna Livia figure for O'Connell Street there. Then we moved here, to our own purpose-built place. There were three of us then – David Dunne was with us in the beginning and still is. The company now employs 12 people, ranging from metal finishers to mould makers, wax workers and patinators."

CAST was well established by the time it moved to South Brown Street, to an area Colm Brennan says "was originally an industrial estate, home to silk and wool weavers as well as a tannery in this particular premises. Right now, across the road, they're excavating an early mill."

The burgeoning company was helped by what he says was "a general acceptance of sculpture that was a result of travel, a sense that it was a natural adjunct of streetscapes and landscapes."

Great work was also being done by the Sculptors' Society of Ireland and the Artists' Association. Nowadays, almost any public building scheme will have a percentage spending for the arts.

"A piece of sculpture can be a pleasant punctuation along a road, can re-establish a landmark and give a human measure to things. That's partly what public sculpture is about. I'd hate to see a piece of sculpture in sterile isolation. I believe the tactile aspect gives it a life in the community and reminds us of our humanity."

In this context he talks about Leo Higgins' sculpture in Killarney Street and how "it functions as sculpture has functioned for years – a focus for the community, almost a place of pilgrimage. A very important place for families."

He talks, too, about how the company has grown in tandem with "a stability and growth in the artistic community in Ireland. The big change over the years has been that visual artists who go abroad come back. It used be that they'd become disillusioned here and stay away. Things have broadened out in every sense – in the last few days we've had enquiries from Belfast and Paris."

Leo Higgins' work can be seen in the RHA and Solomon Galleries. Colm Brennan's work can be seen in public places such as the reception area in RTÉ's television building and, with *Rotations Space 2*, in Belfield. He also shows in Kelly's of Rosslare.

Terry Shaw of Shaw Tree Services. *Photograph: Brenda Fitzsimons*

Shaw Tree Services

I St Fintan's Terrace, Palmerstown, Dublin 20

Terence Shaw knows a thing or two about trees. He should. Trees are part of his seed, breed and generation, part of what the Shaws have been about since his father first started "working at timber" in 1925.

These days, Shaw Tree Services will do just about anything there's to be done with trees. They'll prune or fell them, remove stumps, clear sites and perform any and all surgery needed.

A man more than able to see the wood for the trees, Terence Shaw tells the Shaw tree story with style and clarity and, always, an acute care and understanding for the life and times of his father and grandfather.

The working lives of his grandfather, James Hill Shaw, a Parnellite from Tubber, Co. Westmeath, and his father, Clement William Shaw, who grew up in Co. Limerick, had all the drama and sadness of the twentieth-century decline and fall of the great woodlands and estates.

Terence (Terry) Shaw's work with trees in the twenty-first century ranges from urban care to suburban pruning and, always, the needs of the woodlands and countrysides.

"My late father started in the business as a boy," Terry, tuned to the natural way of things, begins. "He was brought up in Clarina, an estate in Co. Limerick owned by Lord Clarina. My grandfather was the steward on the estate, which was called Elm Park. He'd moved there from Co. Westmeath when my father was about six. He had four other children – Leslie, Constance, Beatrice and Cyril. A boy called Gerald died in infancy.

"Lord Clarina died when my father was about eight years old. He'd had a passion for trees, wouldn't even allow hay be brought through the woods in case it damaged branches, so the estate was still heavily wooded. A new owner came in and my grandfather, James Hill, moved to Rose Cottage at Clarina Cross, where he bought a small bit of land. The castle burned down in the early 1920s. The estate was broken up and all the trees cut down.

"At eight years of age my father was helping local timbermen cut down trees and sell them to the saw mills. With his brother, Cyril, he would hold one end of a cross-cut saw, a timberman the other. They got 1/- a day. Up until 10 or 20 years ago there were still lots of small-time timbermen."

Clement William Shaw worked so well with a timberman called Pa (Patrick) O'Shaughnessy that when his father, James Hill Shaw, died, Clement left the farm in the Clarina area and went into partnership with Pa. "They travelled on bikes," Terry says, "their domain predominantly Limerick, Clare, the tip of north Cork and a bit of Tipperary. They tied the cross-cut saw to the bar of the bike, the axes and sledge hammers on top of the handlebars and the wedge in the fork under the seat."

When the partnership with Pa O'Shaughnessy ended in the early 1940s, Clement William Shaw went into business on his own. "He had a Second World War jeep at one stage," his son says, "and used horses to extract and haul out timber. He was a big man, six foot three, with a lot of muscle power."

A venture with a saw mill didn't last, the lure of the woods proving too strong. Terry Shaw still has the tractor and winch his father bought in Sheils of Ennis in 1956 for £365 and £156 respectively. The old blade from a saw bench acts as a sign across the gate to his yard.

Clement William Shaw married Daphne in 1957 and Terence Clement, their only child, was born in June 1958. Clement William was 46 years old.

"At that stage," Terry goes on, "a lot of the estates were cut out and he was finding it hard to make ends meet so he and my mother moved to Dublin. He put a deposit on the house I live in today and through Jack Nugent, who had a mill at the end of Cork Street, got a contract to cut wood in Bray. County Dublin, in the late 1950s and early 1960s, was quite heavily wooded, with lots of gentlemen's residences, big houses on 20 acres or so with pockets of woodland. There was ongoing work for my father. He also began to supply fire logs around Palmerstown. My cousin Roger Ferrall, a son of my father's sister Beatrice, worked with him in those days."

As a boy, and before the serious suburban growth of the late 1960s, Terry spent his time in the woodlands with his father. "There were some lovely places then and I developed a passion for the woodlands which I still have. My father taught me the trade, the skills of felling trees and extracting timber."

His heart in the woodlands, he left school when he was 16 and went to work with his father. He was just 18 when Clement William Shaw died.

As a young man running a business Terry found it hard to get people to take him seriously. Jack Nugent was dead but his company, still going strong, gave Terry work hauling timber from Enniskerry to Cork Street. He was paid £2.50 per ton.

Business had improved by the early 1980s. "I'd developed my own art, a way of felling trees without damaging them," Terry explains. "I liked the life and lived in a caravan. In the late 1960s the elms began to die from Dutch elm disease and I got involved in dangerous tree felling."

He went into business with a merchant who sold high quality timber to the Continental furniture trade. In 1987, after the hurricane in the south of England, Terry joined him in Kent and they formed a partnership; "I was doing what I liked to do, extracting timber."

But the partnership dissolved, his mother's health began to fail and Terry came home. After Daphne Shaw's death, Terry went back to the woodlands, working for nine months on the de Vesci estate in Abbeyleix and for several years after that moving from one estate to another. By the mid-1990s mature hardwood was on the decline, the competition tougher and margins smaller. As the Celtic Tiger kicked in, Terry had people working for him, the dangerous tree and pruning work gathered momentum and that end of the service expanded.

"We had to re-educate ourselves to a certain extent in tree surgery and arboriculture," he says, "since there are standards to be adhered to. We were good at what we did and rounded the corner. The business began to pay the bills."

Shaw Tree Services employs four people – "all young men, though I've had women in the past and very good they are too. We're very good at woodland rehabilitation: that's our forte. One of the things I did with my father was look for faults in trees and, over the years, I've learned to spot faults, see trees uprooting, branches falling. I find now I rarely miss a problem in trees because I can bring this root knowledge to bare!

"We offer a complete tree service, from very large to very small jobs, and find ourselves in every sort of situation."

He says it's too early to say if his very young daughters Heather or Holly will follow him into the business. Heather, "on a good day", can identify trees. His own view of life and work is that "you've got two choices. You can enjoy your day or not. I'm still with trees and I enjoy my day."

Antiques cabinet at Mason Technology, which dates from 1780, showing spectacles and a volume on the islands of Ireland written by Thomas Mason, grandfather of the current chairman. *Photograph: Frank Miller*

Mason Technology
228 South Circular Road, Dublin 8

Standish Mason reckons Mason Technology is the oldest family-owned business in the state. They've been around, weathering storms as well as the peaks of success, since 1780, and the family roots went down a lot earlier.

"I'd be interested to find out if there's anyone older …" Stan Mason muses with all the quiet confidence of one sure of the family's place and in the certain knowledge that there's not a lot of competition. Chairman of Mason Technology, he's a ninth-generation Mason, and the seventh-generation Mason to run the company.

At the cutting-edge of science and technology, today's company deals in Olympus microscopes, weighing equipment, laboratory equipment and analytical instrumentation. The Mason family and business tale is classic, weaving a hard-working, sometimes turbulent, way through Irish life since 1712. That was the year Robert Mason, a leather worker from Seacombe, near Liverpool, arrived in Dublin. He'd been enticed by a government plan encouraging trades and businesses to expand in the provinces — what Stan Mason calls "the IDA of the day".

Robert Mason, as part of the deal, became a Freeman of the city — a distinction passed from father to son through the ages until, the way of things changing, the entitlement died with Stan Mason's grandfather.

Of an obvious go-ahead nature, Robert Mason set himself up as a tanner, with premises in Watling Street, and became head of the Guild of Skinners and Glovers. It was his son, Thomas, who sold the family property in Liverpool when he took over the business, broke the link with England and established the Masons as a distinctly Irish family. Thomas's eldest son and third-generation Mason, Seacome, would be the one to found today's business.

Seacome Mason was born in 1745 and apprenticed to a Monsieur Alment, a French optician and political refugee with a place in Capel Street. When M Alment returned home, Seacome Mason, optician, set up his own business at 8 Arran Quay. An ad in the Dublin Chronicle of 10 May 1787 has him giving "sincere thanks to his Friends and the Public for their kind Encouragement since his Commencement in Business".

His list of sale items included "telescopes, glasses, microscopes, concave and opera glasses, celestial and terrestrial globes of all sizes, electrical machines with apparatus … goggles for protecting the eyes from dust or wind, ditto for children with the squint …"

Things went well for Seacome Mason; he was in business until his death in 1804.

Stan Mason, who put together the family story in 1980 in celebration of 200 years in business, falls to musing again. "This company shouldn't be here," he says, without conviction. "Family businesses don't usually survive more than three generations – the first establishes, the second builds and the third loses it! That's the way it happened with us, too. The third generation of Masons were not good at business."

Seacome Mason had nine children. His sons, Thomas and Jonathon, moved the business to 11 Essex Bridge (now Parliament Street) in 1813. Thomas made history when he gave the family name to Mason's Hygrometer – the old name for the Wet & Dry Bulb Thermometer invented by Apjohn, one-time professor of anatomy at the Royal College of Surgeons. It became a world-seller for Mason's, then known as Opticians and Mathematical Instrument Suppliers.

And so to the fateful third generation of Masons. Seacome, Thomas's son, ran the business with his son Standish – and it went bankrupt: "asses out the window" as the current Stan Mason puts it.

Another of Seacome's sons, Thomas, was brought back from London in the 1870s to salvage things. A couple of guarantors moved in and the firm, with Thomas from London at its head, began to climb back to credibility and profitability.

"He was my great-grandfather," Stan explains, rounding the picture and moving it on towards today. Thomas Mason's son, Thomas Holmes, was born in 1877. The grandfather of today's company chairman, Thomas H. was a remarkable man.

He worked alongside his father in the company until the latter's death in 1913, at which point the company was called Thomas H. Mason. Stan explains how the company, under his grandfather's direction, made a "dramatic move with the technology of the time. In the late 1890s he introduced photography to the business in the form of picture postcards. We went on to become the biggest producer of picture postcards in Ireland, right up until the 1940s, when the price of silver, a major component in developing solutions, rocketed because of the war."

He takes a book from a glass case – Thomas H. Mason's *The Islands of Ireland*, published in 1936. "My grandfather was interested in archaeology, ornithology, historical sites on the islands off Ireland, interests which brought him all over the country with his full-plate camera. He built up a huge and very fine collection of pictures which, unfortunately, were destroyed by fire in 1963. There's a vast collection of his picture postcards in the Civic Museum, however."

Thomas H. Mason ran the company with energy and vision. By 1916 business had expanded to deal in optician/precision instruments, photography and laboratory supplies to the universities. It had also moved to 5 Dame Street in 1894. In 1914 they expanded further and bought the next-door building. A watercolour picture of the time shows the legend "Laboratory Apparatus Scientific Instruments. Estd. 1870" writ large on the façade with "Thomas H. Mason, Optician" precisely lettered over the door.

Thomas H. Mason married Meta Gray; they had four sons, Standish, Alexander, Barry and Dermot. Standish would grow up to father today's chairman and ensure a seventh generation of Masons ran the company.

In 1932, the company became a limited one and Thomas H. Mason & Sons Ltd was formed. "After the war the instrumentation area of things grew," Stan says, "with the development of valves and such, forerunners of electronics."

Fire tragedies struck twice in the 1960s: in 1963 a fire in the company's stores destroyed Thomas H. Mason's photographs; the second, in 1965, "took out the whole Dame Street building", Stan says, adding that it was "fairly dramatic at the time. I remember them as terrible. But we survived.

"My father took over the optical end of things and my uncle Alex, who was more the businessman, the scientific end. We used Crane Lane, which had been rebuilt, as a laboratory/works and opened a retail outlet at the top of Dawson Street. I was a trainee accountant at the time. My father died in March 1969. He was 59. I came into the company on 6 August 1969. I was 27. Alex, who was running the business, recruited me. I've never regretted joining. Never. Alex and I worked exceptionally well together. He died in 1987."

The company moved to Parliament Street in 1977 and in 1989 to the Greenville Hall building at 228 South Circular Road, which houses today's company. Streamlined, modern and with wonderful light from stained-glass windows, it was once a synagogue.

"I bought it from the Jewish community," Stan says with clear affection for the building, "and levelled out the balcony. It's a lovely spot with offices, seminar and showroom areas, as well as a purpose-built 400 square metre technical service centre. We shift in excess of one million microscopes per year.

"Things have changed dramatically in recent times. When I joined we'd 23 employees: now we've 73. We've Cork premises now, too, where 14 of those employees work."

There's another change — the eighth generation of Masons in the business is represented by a woman: Stan's daughter, Jean, who works in customer care.

Derek and Justin Leonard at their outlet in the Dublin Corporation
Fruit Market. *Photograph: Alan Betson*

Jackie Leonard & Sons

Fruit and Vegetable Importers, Cuckoo Lane, Dublin 7

Coming up to the end of the nineteenth century in Dublin the city authorities decided, with what time has shown to be wisdom, that its fruit and vegetable traders deserved a proper enclosed market from which to operate.

By 1892 the Smithfield markets were up and running, Victorian red brick with a glass ceiling giving shelter to those who'd sold in the streets around Dublin 7 for years out of number. Kate Leonard was one of those traders, and one of the first to move into the new market buildings. She couldn't have known she was starting a business which, at the beginning of the twenty-first century, would be still growing, faithful to its roots and reaping the benefits, as her great-grandson puts it, "of being versatile and open to change".

Jackie Leonard & Sons of the Corporation Fruit Market and The Old Schoolhouse in nearby Cuckoo Lane is run these days by Kate's great-grandchildren – Derek, Thérèse and Justin Leonard. Schools and schooling, as the story unfolds, are something of a theme in the family.

A lot has changed, and a lot has stayed the same, in the 112 years since Kate Leonard moved into the market buildings. Tastes are different these days and the availability of fruits and vegetables infinitely so. But the buzz is surely much as it always was, the early morning urgencies as demanding, the camaraderie a way of life that has always fuelled the markets.

Justin Leonard says he's steeped in the history, life and business. So too are Derek and Thérèse. But for all three, working in the family business was a conscious decision, not an inevitability.

Their father, Jackie Leonard, was the third generation to run things and believed in education, and choice. He died in 2003 and Justin speaks for him when he explains: "He always told us that learning was no burden, that we should have an education first and then, if we really wanted to, go into the business." Justin wanted to, as soon as he left Belvedere College. So did his older brother, Derek. Thérèse came on board after time spent in TCD and as a merchant banker. The company is thus well-equipped and directed for the future.

Justin, with a passion for detail, tells the family, and company, tale while we sit in a once-upon-a-time schoolroom, now his office. "The markets were given the same design as Covent Garden in

London," he says. "The original market hall had a glass roof to catch the light of the cool, early morning sun and a slate roof on the other side for when it moved around and got warmer; the Victorian way of keeping heat off the produce. The Corpo replaced the glass with Perspex in 1988–9."

Kate Leonard's son, John, who was Justin's grandfather, took over from his mother in the early 1920s. He had three sons: Thomas, Michael and John Jnr. Tom became a Dublin North Central politician for Fianna Fáil and Mick worked in the company until he died in 1983.

It was John Jnr who grew up to marry Patricia Eustace (whose mother was also a trader and a customer of John Leonard Snr) and to father Justin, Derek, Thérèse and their older brothers, John and Gary. In time, and to distinguish him from his father, John Jnr became Jackie. The company became Jackie Leonard & Sons in 1983, when Derek joined his father in the markets. Justin came on board in 1986 and Thérèse more recently.

Derek looks after the wholesale end of things in the market buildings while Justin, in a rounding of life's circle, is based in the school building they now own, where Jackie once went to school and from where Justin and Thérèse organise deliveries and the expanding company. "Dad went from the NS here to Brunswick Street Christian Brothers," Justin explains, "but left to go into the business with my grandfather when he was 14. He worked in the markets until he was 66 and died in February 2003, when he was 69."

Justin's mother worked alongside her husband until the mid-1990s, when she "took a back seat and looked after her grandchildren!"

In the early years the Leonards sold only home-grown produce – turnips, parsnips, carrots and cabbages from north county Dublin. "Cabbage arrived in horse-drawn carts driven by the farmer growers, 140 dozen heads at a time," Justin says.

"My grandfather would auction it off, as all produce was auctioned then. There were no sacks and boxes, so the cabbages would be in pyramids on the carts. The farmers would drive on afterwards to deliver to villages like Rathfarnham, which were outside the city limits. That's the way things were until the 1960s."

Until the 1960s, too, a lot of fruit came into Dublin by ship and was auctioned. The Leonards only came to fruit-selling in the late 1950s, when Justin's father bought a pallet of Jaffa 105 oranges. "My grandfather said 'you'll be burned with them' but my father made a profit, started to buy in French apples and to build up the fruit side of things."

Justin, when he joined in 1986, brought with him his conviction that the company should have the independence of directly importing their fruit.

His father, believing he was right, "let me go with it and we moved to importing from France,

Spain – wherever the source was. In those days, too, we'd sell between 500 and 600 dozen cabbages a day but the whole business turned on its head in the mid-1980s and the likes of iceberg lettuces and aubergines became big business. Cabbage became a thing of the past."

In the 1980s, too, the company took over the market stands of N.J. King. "Myself and my brother Gary, who now lives in Wexford, took over the running of them and specialised in selling exotic fruit. It was a great business and we ran it for a good while. In 1991 this building became available and we bought it. I'd always been at Dad about us needing a store but he'd held out, saying 'there's only one space for a store and that's my old school'. It's only a football pitch away from the markets. We deliver from here to restaurants, caterers, the defence forces in Dublin, the Curragh, Dundalk and Meath. We supply about 14 hospitals too."

The building's also on the way to being developed for another use, with an entire area nearly equipped for the pre-preparation and packaging of vegetables. "You have to look ahead and the way people live now they want things prepared," Justin says. "We were affected by what's called central purchasing, which means supermarkets buying from one source and cutting out independent wholesalers like ourselves. We supply a lot of the better greengrocers still, but it was logical to look at other avenues of sales. We found that the way to grow the business was to do the preparation of vegetables ourselves."

Other changes have had nothing to do with market factors. "I used come in at 7.30 a.m. and finish about 5 p.m.," Justin says. "Now, because of traffic congestion, we have to start at 5 a.m. to get produce out to customers. Our first van leaves at 6 a.m. for St Michael's hospital in Dun Laoghaire. The lads go home at 2 p.m. but I'm still here at 5 p.m. We work Monday to Saturday, never Sunday."

Luas is yet another factor. "It runs right down the bottom of the markets and, with market container trucks measuring 40 feet and the Luas trams measuring some 50 feet, no one knows how things will work out. They're talking about scaling down wholesaling in the markets to deal with the clash," he grins, philosophical, "but when I came to work here 17 years ago they were talking about the same thing."

Today's company has five vans on the road, employs up to 14 people (more in the summer). Van deliveries are necessary, since "customers who used love to come into the market can't any longer because of traffic. Our wholesale customers still come in from the country however."

Justin Leonard is more than a little cheerful about the future, assuring that "there's a line of young Leonards to come! Derek has two children and I've three. Margaret, my young daughter, is already a natural for the business. She's very wide, forgets nothing and has a photographic memory like my grandfather and myself. We've plenty of ammunition to send in between us."

Owner David Lyster (right) and head chef Eamonn Ingram in the restaurant of The Lord Edward.
Photograph: Frank Miller

The Lord Edward

Seafood Restaurant, 23 Christchurch Place, Dublin 8

As buildings in the city go, that on the corner of Christchurch Place and Werburgh Street is better known than most. High on its hilly site, distinguished from the newer, burgeoning Dublin all around by a large and lively mural of Lord Edward Fitzgerald and by bay leaded-glass windows, it has an obvious sense of rightful belonging.

Number 23 Christchurch Place has overlooked a lot in its time. The city's thieves, vagabonds, rogues, patriots, short-weight butchers and bakers all received justice at the ancient pillory when it stood at the corner of Castle Street and Werburgh Street. These days, and for more than 30 years now, the building has housed The Lord Edward, the city's oldest fish restaurant and, on the two floors below, one of Dublin's older pub and lounge bars.

David Lyster, owner of The Lord Edward, runs it with an old-style, elegant precision and an acute attention to detail. He may well be, as he says himself, "a newcomer to the area" but, together with his staff, he's more than served his time in the business of food and hospitality. Served his time in a Dublin publican family too – his father opened Lyster's pub in Stoneybatter in 1923.

Newcomer, in this instance, means David Lyster's been running things in Christchurch Place since September 1989, when he and his wife Maureen bought The Lord Edward from previous owner Tom Cunniam.

"This was a very old dwelling house which was refurbished, done up and opened as a pub in 1901," David Lyster explains on a sunny morning before the lunch-hour rush begins. "Several generations of the Cunniams lived here. The present building dates from 1875 but there's said to have been a licensed premises on the site in the late 1600s. Tom Cunniam owned the building when I came along. His father had died a young man, dropped dead coming up Dame Street."

The Lord Edward fish restaurant was born in 1969 out of the closure of another landmark Dublin eatery and of Tom Cunniam's desire to run a restaurant as well as a pub in the building. "Tom took over from The Red Bank, which closed in D'Olier Street and more or less relocated here," explains Lyster. "The staff all moved over, the chefs Mr Gerry Ferns and Mr Eamonn Ingram, the latter still here, and the waiters, including Mr Tom Smith, who is also still here."

David Lyster brought a fair amount of experience to the business himself. In the course of a long career in catering he's been food and beverages manager in Jurys Intercontinental Hotel, Ballsbridge, and general manager of Jurys in Cork. He worked in New York "for a number of years" and, for 14 years, "ran a little place in West Cork". In a reversal of the more usual trend, the Lysters decided to sell up in West Cork and open in Dublin, and so came to The Lord Edward.

The Lord Edward building is all narrow stairs, small crannies, hidden corners. In the lounge bar there's a dark beamed ceiling and banks of red, worn plush seating. The bar itself is a small affair, with wood and beaten copper surrounds and decorative painted glass overhead. Profiles of Robert Emmet and Wolfe Tone hang over the fireplace. "It's a very solid building," David Lyster assures. "When the developers were building next door they put in monitoring equipment and were surprised at just how solid it was. We've consciously kept it as it was, wouldn't dream of doing otherwise. It's got loads of atmosphere, lots of history.

"Lord Edward Fitzgerald is lying across the street from here in St Werburgh's Church, alongside Major Sirr, the man who shot him in 1798. He was taken prisoner in Thomas Street in what was meant to be a safe house. This place is named after him, of course."

Long before the restaurant achieved cult status, The Lord Edward bar was known and loved. When the nearby Iveagh Baths were in use, it was a meeting place for male bathers. "Before that, going right back, it would have been well known," David Lyster says. "It was adjacent, too, to Werburgh Street Labour Exchange, which was a busy place in the bad times of low employment. But any corner house like this, by virtue of its very location, becomes well known. It was the same with my family place in Stoneybatter."

The building has a rambling style and takes a lot of keeping in order. It has a basement, ground-floor bar, first-floor bar, restaurant floor, kitchen above that and, on top, the offices. The first-floor bar was the family dining-room when the Cunniam family lived there; the rooms above were bedrooms.

Most of the restaurant staff who came from The Red Bank are still *in situ*. Chef Eamonn Ingram trained in the old Russell Hotel and is "a very good saucier chef," David Lyster says, "very, very good." Waiter Tom Smith tells how, when The Red Bank closed in April, and The Lord Edward opened in September, "we came *en masse*. It was very small here when it opened first, just seven tables. It looked almost the same then as now."

The restaurant has a black cast-iron fireplace, bay leaded-glass windows, lots of the red plush found in the bar, a large period drawing of the murder of Lord Edward Fitzgerald and, in a glass case, a smooth hound shark caught in Carlingford Lough in 1927.

Tom Smith explains the link with The Red Bank when he says that "Tom Cunniam used go there to have his oysters in its oyster bar."

The Lord Edward restaurant didn't take off immediately after it was set up in 1969. "It took a while," Tom Smith says, "though it was visited from the beginning by the men from the Four Courts. You'd rarely see a woman here in those days; it was like a club for the very powerful men. You had to watch who you'd put together at tables! But in the last 10 years, as they began to come into high positions, we've seen ladies coming up from the Four Courts too."

The Lord Edward was witness to the dramatic ending in 1989 of Dublin's long-lunch culture. Tom Smith explains. "Charlie [Haughey] did away with expense-account dining in his budget of that year. We lost big expense accounts and long lunches became short ones. A lot of restaurants closed because of it.

"I'm not telling you a word of a lie when I say we were so busy up to then, we'd 11 tables up here and an emergency table for when someone important would arrive who hadn't booked. All of a sudden it became empty. A few people continued to come and after four years it picked up again.

"Tom Quinn, who worked here for 40 years as manager of the bar, remembers people queuing up the stairs from 5.30 p.m. Tom had a lot of relatives in the US and they got the word out and we've always had a lot of American customers."

In those early days of the restaurant Tom Cunniam bought the fish from Dunne's fishmongers in Manor Street.

"To overcome the Monday situation he used a contact in Wicklow to bring up fresh fish," Tom Smith says. "The menu was almost the same then as now."

What about scandal and dining stories of the famous down the years? "I'm not telling," he laughs and is adamant. Discretion is another old-time quality in The Lord Edward.

With two of the Lyster offspring, James and Maeve, working in the pub and restaurant, the future of The Lord Edward is looking secure. David Lyster throws an affectionate eye round the restaurant. "I retired to this," he says, cheerfully. "When you do something you like doing it's not work."

Richard Pender in his shop on Manor Street. *Photograph: Brenda Fitzsimons*

Richard Pender

Richard Pender sees what he does as a service to his country. He'll continue until it's no longer viable. The Penders, tailors for five generations, have been making uniforms for the officers and NCOs of the defence forces for three of those generations. The tradition is likely to end with Richard.

"There's a decline in the uniform business," he says. "I used to have 10 people working here. Now there's myself and one chap who does part-time. But I'll go to the end. I made a conscious decision to do what I did and I've made another conscious decision to stick with the defence forces until it's no longer viable. Then I'll have a rethink. The forces have given us the work over the years so I'll continue to give the service. I'll be sorry, of course. I'm a fifth-generation tailor, after all."

His shop and workroom on Manor Street are the essence of meticulous craftsmanship, the walls hung with paper patterns, old uniforms, new military jackets in the making and mementoes. The mementoes, mostly photographs, tell the Pender tale. The oldest framed photos show the premises in 1922, then a draper's and tailoring establishment, side by side at 5 Manor Street, Dublin 7. The Penders and their business came to Manor Street when Richard Pender's grandfather (another Richard — all three generations of tailors in Manor Street have been called Richard) moved there from 44 John Dillon Street, the Liberties, in 1922. Grandfather Richard's son, Richard, was a tailor in Manor Street until 1992 and his son, today's Richard, came into the business in 1972.

The premises has changed with the times. Photographs chronicle how it has alternated between use as a single unit and two shops. Today's tailoring establishment is in what was once the draper's shop, while next door is now used by Richard Pender's sister for her physiotherapy and acupuncture practice.

A fascinating photograph shows a nineteenth-century tailors' workroom in which everyone sits in the traditional cross-legged position. A metal clock used in the old Manor Street workroom hangs on the wall, as do plaques brought by army customers from Lebanon, a bronze plate and Richard Pender's tailoring certification from the College of Fashion and Clothing Technology in

London. Cavalry figures on shelves represent a passion of Pender's: he's been a member of the 11th Cavalry Squadron, FCA for 18 years and says he sees this as serving his country also. A waist-level cutting counter in polished wood has a central position in the shop.

In the small workroom there's an old-model Singer flat machine, electrified now and the "best of its kind ever made", according to Richard Pender. A Reece button-hole machine "cuts work hours in half"; an overlock machine is "a bit of an antique but for reasons of sentiment I don't throw it out". An old boiler boils water and sends it through a pipe to an iron; a fusing press generates enough heat to ensure that canvas fused to cloth will never separate.

Until 1916 Richard Pender's grandfather worked as a tailor for Johnson's of Henry Street, makers of British army uniforms. They're still in business, these days in London's Savile Row, but had to get out of this town after 1916. "With all the upheaval it wasn't until 1922 that my grandfather set up here," Richard explains. "The area suited because there were a lot of army barracks all around: McKee, Collins, Clancy, Griffith. My grandfather did civilian suits as well but in 1959, when he died, my father decided to concentrate on uniforms alone, making it a speciality. The move coincided with the availability of off-the-peg suits for civilians, so while the civilian trade decreased, army uniform work increased. Army numbers built up with the trouble in the North and our peak years for business were 1975 to 1985."

Change, inevitable as bad times, came for a number of reasons. "The first thing that caused the drop-off was pullovers becoming part of the uniform for officers. They're comfortable and the cause of jackets being worn less and so lasting twice as long. This brought about a barely noticeable but steady decline. Then there was the Voluntary Early Retirement Scheme, which cut numbers back quite a lot, and the Celtic Tiger economy, which affected officer numbers too, offering them opportunities outside the army."

He's most vehement of all about the damage done to the business by EU regulations which allow army uniforms to be made anywhere in the EU and claims Irish army uniforms are being made in London, Belgium, Lebanon, China and Jerusalem. Explaining the non-EU element, he cites the example of combat gear, now a regular part of the uniform. "An Irish company got the contract to make it and sub-contracted it out to China. All of this has brought about a decline in numbers working in the army uniform business."

The way to survive, he says, "is to own your own property and be in business for yourself. If I was renting a premises I couldn't do it. I stick at it out of loyalty to customers who stayed with me after my father died. These days, as well as defence-force officers and NCOs, I make Health Board officers' uniforms and Garda Síochána officer uniforms. I make the likes of tails and waistcoats for members of the judiciary too. We used to retail shirts and slacks up to three years ago, too, but stopped when they put a bus lane outside my door and destroyed the passing trade."

Over the years Penders have seen their uniforms worn by winners of the Aga Khan trophy, by the aide-de-camp and guard of honour at the inauguration of President McAleese and by the chief of staff inspecting the Scots Guard in London. The first blue uniform for the Air Corps was made by Richard M. Pender, Tailors, as were the uniforms of Col. Brennan, aide-de-camp to President Éamonn de Valera.

Irish army uniforms haven't changed much over those years, according to Pender. "The style of the standard officers' uniform has stayed the same. The only real change was when the Air Corps uniform became blue and its rank marking moved to the arm from the shoulder. Cloth quality has deteriorated. The army Superfine, a Barathea for the health boards and the dress-uniform material are the only ones of the same quality these days."

Richard Pender, tailor, lives above his business, in the rooms which have been home to his four children. He moved to the country once, to Navan. "I spent two years there and no one came to visit me. I broke my leg and still no one came so I decided to move back. I built an apartment over the shop." None of the young Penders – twins Helen and Richard, and Orla and William – will be going into the business. "It's a pity," their father admits, "but it's a free world and I wouldn't try to coax them into it."

Kevin Connolly in The Winding Stair Bookshop and Café. *Photograph: Bryan O'Brien*

The Winding Stair Bookshop and Café
40 Lower Ormond Quay, Dublin 1

The Winding Stair Bookshop and Cafe's place in this book has nothing to do with age, longevity or a place in the city's history. It's here because in the short time since its founding in 1982 it has taken on the essence and kudos that are the usual consequences of age, longevity and a history. The Winding Stair has become an institution.

Venerable, an Ormond Quay landmark, sought out by native and visitor alike, it's a regular location for film and TV people seeking to represent an older, authentic Dublin and a constant venue for readings, launches and music gigs.

Owner Kevin Connolly takes a modestly baffled view. "I don't know at what time the place became an institution, part of the fabric of the city. It's quite interesting how people know the place. Sometimes we can have three generations of the same family here: past, present and ongoing customers."

On the other hand, and less modestly, he says that "in a madly spinning Dublin it's still a haven of peace, espousing simple old-fashioned values, overlooking the Liffey, along which, traditionally, books have always been sold. We're the last booksellers on the city quays in a city that once boasted bookshops and bookstalls in much the same way that Paris does today. We're a living and thriving anachronism – a second-hand and antiquarian bookshop as well as a prize-winning café set in the bustle of city centre development."

His own haven within this haven is on the fourth floor, where the paperwork, antiquarian books and technology that makes the shop's web site possible are spread over low rooms with arched windows overlooking the river and city's rooftops. Of the three floors below, accessed via that winding stair with its nineteenth-century banisters, two are taken up by the café, while the ground floor is where the bookshop-proper resides. The entire building is securely rooted in its early twentieth-century origins: wooden floors, uneven stone walls, quirky dimensions and, because it used be a textile factory, floors supported by steel girders and concrete-reinforced floors built to bear the weight of heavy looms.

Kevin Connolly might have found his life's calling, and be himself the essence of what The Winding Stair is all about, but it wasn't always thus.

He was born in Swindon, England, the eldest of a family of seven who all moved to Bailieborough, Co. Cavan, in 1971, when he was 16 years old. The leap from a large English secondary school to a small convent in Bailieborough – where he was one of six boys in a class with 50 girls – was a "terrifying ordeal" but the ultimate making of him. He was teased out of an early shyness, "left it behind with a vengeance", and developed an enduring love of Cavan.

The idea of his own bookshop took root when he was at university in Liverpool, studying law and spending a lot of his time in the small, ideal world of the Atticus Bookshop. He was the longing child with face against the window, admiring but not a part of the inner-coterie activity around the colourful, eccentric, book-loving owner couple. "Browsing and watching it all sowed the seed of the wonder of working with books," he says. "I became totally besotted with the concept."

The practice of law no longer a runner, he headed for Berlin, where he spent a couple of good years before coming back to Dublin to "give the Atticus idea a try. I began spending my time at auctions, buying book lots for as little as 15p, selling from an outdoor stall. Then I saw an ad for office space on the first floor in this building. It was a small room but I thought it huge and sub-let part of it to an architect friend. Based on the Atticus ideal I had a table with my mother's home-made fruit cake as well as the books. I used make sandwiches too."

It was 1982 and The Winding Stair had begun its climb to institutional status. In 15 years it would move from a one-room bookshop with table and coffee pot to four bustling floors with bookshop, café and web site selling internationally.

In its earlier life, 40 Lower Ormond Quay had been home to Largey's Woollens and Worsted textile factory, with a weavers' shed out the back. But by 1982 the building's occupants were *In Dublin* magazine, a ground-floor picture gallery and a top-floor artist's studio. Kevin Connolly says: "little by little *In Dublin* got smaller and the shop and café got bigger. Without being aggressively driven or anything I got a long lease on the whole building, which has just been renewed – so I'll be here for the foreseeable future anyway."

He says it's "quite strange being this stumbling anachronism in a city which seems to have been consumed by brash superpubs and all that. Still, I'm not terribly critical of the way things have developed around here. There are a lot of good things – Ormond Quay and Bachelor's Walk used to be all gaping cavities and decrepitude. This building itself was burned down in the 1920s and had the steel girders and reinforced concrete put in when it was rebuilt. Textiles were produced here until the 1970s."

The Winding Stair gets its name from the title of a 1933 Yeats collection of poems. Kevin Connolly talks about plans involving the ground-floor bookshop being renovated, a false ceiling being restored to its original dimensions and the construction of a mezzanine. All the books will be on that floor because the café, which is very busy, will continue on the first and second floors.

He's very involved with the structural work himself and has "a fantastic staff, between 12 and 15 people altogether, though a number of them are part-time. My brother Brendan looks after the day-to-day bookshop and my own main function is the buying of books" – he won't entrust this to anyone else – "and the web site, which occupies most of my time. We sell all over the world with most of our antiquarian customers in the US."

He's to be found anywhere there are books for sale. He travels regularly to the UK but will just as often be heading out, as he was the day we met, to meet a man he's done business with for years, looking forward to the cakes and muffins which are part of the ritual of their working together. Bookselling's all a bit like that, he says, personal and idiosyncratic and definitely something you need to be a bit obsessive about. "We mainly sell books of Irish interest, as well as a lot of modern first editions, including international literature. We're interested in quality, basically, and though I'm not averse to Mills and Boon it doesn't fit on our shelves. We can't compete with the likes of Eason's and Waterstone's so we decided a few years ago to concentrate on what we do well."

He loves the "incredible relationships which develop with customers around the buying and selling of books". His son Benedict is extremely knowledgeable about the business and books – "but I think music is his thing and would expect him to develop his own uniqueness". He talks about the "raw dream" many people have of opening a bookshop, and about the reality of it as a business and how it really tests the resolve.

"To survive, you really have to know what you're doing. I'd hate to be starting now. I was given the opportunity in the early eighties and able to go at it at my own pace." Not long at all to establish a landmark by the Ha'penny Bridge.

Breda Roseingrave with Colm Byrne (left) and Gareth Lawlor at Mackey's Garden Centre, Sandycove. *Photograph: Matt Kavanagh*

Mackey's Garden Centre
Castlepark Road, Sandycove, Co. Dublin

Mackey's Garden Centre is the place to go for anything from seed potatoes to imported mature plants, from garden pottery to herbs and pâté. Which is to say that the once-and-always seed merchants are as acutely attuned and relevant as ever to the changing needs of the ever-growing gardening/horticultural community in this land.

The spacious, green and pleasant world of growing things on Castlepark Road, Sandycove, Co. Dublin, is testament to a business that's kept pace: this was where, in 1964, the country's first ever custom-built garden centre opened its gates. Mackey's was then just 13 years short of its two hundredth birthday.

Breda Roseingrave, a woman of vision and horticultural commitment, has been managing the centre since 1977. She tells the Mackey story from the beginning, going right back to its 1777 roots, detailing its growth and offshoots since then without resort to a single pun.

It started with "Stephen Mackey, a professional gardener, when he came to Ireland from Scotland in the late 1700s," she says. "By 1777 he was working with the nurserymen who owned Toole's Nurseries in Shankill, an area of wild countryside at the time with big estates and quite a few nurseries. In 1818 he moved in to Westmoreland Street with two of the Toole brothers, where they set up the Charles & Luke Toole & Stephen Mackey seed company. They sold farm and garden seed, agricultural and garden plants, as well as farm and garden tools." Things went so well that by 1860 Stephen Mackey had moved on to trade on his own.

Mackey family fortunes took a significant upward leap in the business and cultural life of the city with Stephen's son, James William Mackey. Twice lord mayor of Dublin (in 1866 and 1873), he was made Sir James William Mackey and by 1878 was proprietor of the sole-trading seed company carrying his name at 23 Sackville Street.

Sackville Street, in the days before it became O'Connell Street, was the place to be in business. "It was a stylish, fashionable place," Roseingrave says. "Mackey's was nicely outfitted with shining dark mahogany counters. Customers were given lots of personal attention and many would have had personal accounts. The basement was used for storage and for mixing grass and other seeds. Many of their customers were farmers but they sold a lot of interior plants too. Kentia palms were very much in style at the time and they would have dealt a lot with gardeners coming in for employers. They used to pack and sell seeds in specially designed packets with the company name on it."

In 1896, the business trading as Sir James William Mackey was incorporated under the Companies Act and became a limited company, with shareholders and directors. "Quite a forward step," Breda points out, "and one of the oldest companies around with only four digits in its registered number."

The premises escaped damage when the Rising broke out in the street in 1916 but was badly damaged in 1922. Rebuilt and reorganised, it continued trading as Sir James William Mackey for another 66 years. In 1962 the company modernised, dropped the title and became Mackey's Seeds Ltd.

"There was a lot happening in the country at the time," Breda says, "and business was changing everywhere." In 1969, Mackey's acquired a long lease on the premises occupied by an old seed company, Hogg and Robertson's, at 22 Mary Street. They sold the O'Connell Street premises to the Gresham Hotel and debunked to what had become the more commercial area of Mary Street. She recalls how the Mary Street property belonged to the Quinn family and how "their landlady, and the person who used collect the rent for the Phibsboro stores, was the mother of Ruairi Quinn, former leader of the Labour Party".

The manner of the company's trading changed with the move, and the times. "It became more self-service in style but with a well-informed staff," Breda recalls. "That same year the company acquired an old store in Phibsboro. It had a drive-in frontage and a loft for grains and cereals. They continued dealing in farm seed for another seven years before giving up that side of the business; by then farmers were being catered for in their own communities. They went into the wholesale seeds and sundries market, mixing and selling their own brand of Mackey's Lawn Seed.

"This meant they now had the retail shop in Mary Street and the wholesale distributors in Phibsboro. In time, however, they stopped packaging their own seeds and became the first people to import the UK brand Sutton Seeds to Ireland."

In between times, Mackey's were responsible for another first too. In 1964, on Castlepark Road, Sandycove, they set up the country's first custom-built garden centre. The idea came from managing director Jean-Pierre Eliet.

"It was part of Mackey's modernising plan and took some inspiration from the French garden company Truffaut," Breda says. "The garden-centre movement was already happening in the US, too, and in England they were way ahead of us. Jean-Pierre went to England for ideas and architects Robinson Keeffe and Devane designed the centre and shop on the basis of what he'd discovered. The site had been a market garden/nursery, so already had an association with horticulture. Watson's Nurseries in Cabinteely were in existence but they were wholesalers and exporters and not a garden centre in the sense of being there for the public."

It all coincided with an expanding economy and the building of more houses with gardens. In the years since then, with a newly affluent Ireland discovering the social cachet and pleasures of gardening, Mackey's in Sandycove has been constantly on hand to supply to needs.

These days the garden centre is the company's sole concern: the wholesale business in Phibsboro was closed in 1990 and in 1995, when Mary Street closed to traffic and parking became impossible, trading ceased there.

Breda Roseingrave takes a justifiable pride and delight in the garden centre she's moulded and overseen since the late seventies. She came to Mackey's via the Botanic Gardens and UCD, "where I studied horticulture in the heady days of the early 1970s. I saw this job as a challenge. I was young and green and grabbed the opportunity to put the place on the map. I feel I've done that!"

Some 70 per cent of the company shares are owned by the Mackey family and three of the four directors are family members. (MD Jean-Pierre Eliet married into the family.) Breda Roseingrave, who works with a staff as dedicated as she is herself, says she's been given "terrific support by the directors. I like to work without people breathing down my neck and they appreciate that. They assist and support – and give me tremendous freedom.

"There have been major changes but the core of the business is still living, plant material. I inherited a business which was still selling greenhouses, paving slabs, bare rooted plants. It ran from October to February because so few of the plants were potted. They're almost all potted now so we're open all year round. There's been a lot invested and the original shop has trebled in size. Pottery has become a huge seller and we get it from all over the world, even Vietnam, as well as quality Irish. Mature plants are big too: we bring them in from Italy and Belgium."

There's more: Mackey's will sell you French pâté, herbs, fertilisers, children's gardening tools, bedding plants, baskets – a stock which Roseingrave says reaches "from the sublime to the ridiculous, basic to exotic". All a very long way from the dreams of the Scottish gardener who started it all.

Fionnbarr Kennedy at M. Kennedy & Sons, Harcourt Street. *Photograph: Cyril Byrne*

M. Kennedy & Sons

Artists' Supplies, 12 Harcourt Street, Dublin 2

The elegance of Harcourt Street makes it an ideal location for what is arguably the city's pre-eminent artists' suppliers shop.

M. Kennedy & Sons has been carrying on its business at 12 Harcourt Street since 1918 – and its customers didn't always come from the painterly community; its stock didn't always include easels, paints, canvases and the like.

Things began, in 1887, with brushes. That was when Michael Kennedy, a Kildare man in Dublin, set up a brush-manufacturing company he named, fairly obviously, Kennedy Brushes. He was located at 87 South William Street (now a multi-storey car-park) and his company hand made brushes of all kinds, all from natural fibres. The strongest of these was hog or boar hair, for which bristle is now the generic term.

Kennedy's range, in the days when brushes were to housekeeping what the mobile is to today's handbag, included sweeping, scrubbing and glass-bottle brushes. By the early 1900s they were a household name.

In 1918, an expanding Kennedy Brushes moved into the fine late-eighteenth-century building that is 12 Harcourt Street. Outbuildings to the rear housed the brush factory, while the long-renowned Reed School of Piano occupied the first floor over the shop, which then, as now, was on the ground floor.

Michael Kennedy married Margaret Ryan and two of their sons, James Thomas and Michael, took over the company in time. Kennedy Brushes supplied the early Dublin Gas Company and even designed the ubiquitous circular logo with the letters "g-a-s".

Fionnbarr Kennedy, great-great-grandson of founder Michael Kennedy, sits in the gracious high-ceilinged first-floor Georgian rooms which today house a gallery to tell the family and business story. With his father, Ultan Kennedy, uncle Conor Kennedy and a staff of 10 he runs today's three-tiered company.

The Harcourt Street building, bought up by Kennedy's over the years, now houses a shop, a gallery and an educational suppliers to schools section.

Fionnbarr Kennedy remembers his grandfather James Kenneth, something of a towering figure in the family story, with affection. "He was a wonderful gentleman. I remember wonderful times in his company."

The company was going strong in the 1940s under James Kenneth Kennedy's stewardship when the first shift in emphasis, and an easing towards today's business, happened. Kennedy's began importing a small quantity of brushes from Winsor & Newton in the UK. Normally makers of artists' brushes, the firm had been directed by the British government, as part of the war effort, to make yard brushes and the like. "My grandfather, James Kenneth, was a good artist," Fionnbarr says. "He studied under Sean Keating, but was needed in the business so didn't become a professional. When the war ended and Winsor & Newton went back to making artists' brushes, my grandfather, because of his strong liking for painting, decided to take on a small stock of artists' supplies."

His decision was the acorn from which today's company grew. The demise of Kennedy Brushes came in the 1950s, with progress and changing work practices. The advance of machine-manufactured goods made it harder to recruit apprentices who would become skilled brush makers. A brush-making apprenticeship lasted seven years; the apprenticeship to become a machine operator lasted two weeks.

Regretfully, and sadly for staff who had been with the company for many years, as the 1950s came to an end James Kenneth Kennedy made the decision to end manufacturing and concentrate solely on the work of artists' supplier.

James Kenneth Kennedy married Marie Louise Hayden from Bray and they had five children. Ultan, father of Fionnbarr, was the first born of these and Conor the last. The artists' supply business, Fionnbarr says, "was built up through my grandfather's links with the artistic community. As a good painter in his own right he empathised with both students and struggling artists. He painted all the time, mostly dramatic landscapes; he saw everything in vivid light and made strong use of colour. He painted all his life." James Kenneth Kennedy died in 1984 – just three years before the 1987 opening of the first-floor gallery to mark the centenary of the company.

"My father, Ultan Kennedy, joined the company in the late 1950s," says Fionnbarr, "and went out on the road actively seeking business. That was when the advertising agencies were starting up and there was a whole new market for art supplies. He chased this market and was very successful.

"One of our best customers at the time was RTÉ, which got all its materials for graphics and the like from us. The company grew through the efforts of my grandfather and father, who constantly expanded the range. The premises were extended internally as we acquired more of the building over the years. Today's shop is much longer than it was originally and the buildings at the back are now used for stretching canvases.

"Pretty well all of the country's artists would have come in here over the years. We've Orpen's paint-box in the family. He gave it to my grandfather." He tells an anecdote which places their position in the business. "When, in the early 1980s, Winsor & Newton celebrated its 150th anniversary, it launched a special edition of the number 14 Series 7 Sable brush (watercolour). It cost 700 punts and we had one. It was sold within weeks to a leading Dublin artist who used it constantly." No amount of prodding will get him to reveal the artist's name.

Kennedy's moved into the business of educational supplies when the advertising agencies moved towards use of commercial products such as Letraset and computers. "At the same time," Fionnbarr points out, "increasing prosperity in the country meant art was becoming a larger part of the school curriculum. We've noticed, over the years, how budgets available for art supplies in schools have grown. We're now one of the leading school art-room suppliers. We also notice that, in general, girls' schools use more art supplies than boys'." This side of the business grew steadily through the 1980s and 1990s.

Another change came with opening of European links and a decision to trade more with the continent. "We went from stocking almost exclusively British brands to also stocking all the major continental brands, such as Sennelier, which is French, Maimeri, Italian, and Schminke, a German brand. It made a huge difference because it enormously increased the variety available to our customers."

Fionnbarr Kennedy grows more enthusiastic by the minute, admitting he could talk all day on the subject: he tells of oil colours in student quality and separate artists' quality (the former made to a uniformity of price, the latter for the higher end of market).

"We've four different brands of student oils and five different brands of artists' oils," he explains, "all of them slightly different to suit customers' needs." He feels that the two-room James Kenneth Kennedy Memorial Gallery makes "marvellous use of the two first-floor rooms. We show mainly representational-style Irish artists, which was the sort of work my grandfather liked and my father still likes."

Fionnbarr Kennedy carries on the family tradition in more ways than one: he has inherited a talent for painting from his father and grandfather – in his case, in watercolours. He's very definite that the company will "continue as artists' suppliers. The gallery is a very nice addition to what we do but the primary business is the shop." The father of two children, he says his eldest, Ciara, "is determined to come into the business with her dad." Son Cian hasn't expressed a view as yet. One way or another, the future is secure for M. Kennedy and Sons Ltd – though perhaps with a vital change in the name if Ciara has her way.

Ian Davis, managing director of Davis Recycling Ltd at Pigeon House Road. *Photograph: Alan Betson*

Davis Recycling Ltd
Pigeon House Road, Dublin 4

Ian Davis's office and working day overlooks a sprawling, Beckett-like landscape of low scrap-metal mountains, unruly coiled copper, transformers by the sackful and another lot of (higher) mountains – this time the piled detritus of aircraft parts, WCs, fridges, aluminium window frames and unrecognisables. There are some three acres of this, a magpie appeal to the bath taps and metal cut-offs glinting in the sun, a grandeur to the giant, poised cranes over it all. Not bleak at all.

The yard thus spreading below his office doesn't belong to Ian Davis, third-generation MD of what is now called Davis Recycling Ltd, and was for years Samuel Davis Ltd, Metal Merchants. But the fact of the company not having a yard of its own any more doesn't make the industrial-waste scenario any less his business and heritage.

The yard, on Pigeon House Road, belongs to the Hammond Lane Foundry and Ian Davis, ex-chairman of the Metal Merchants Association of Ireland, has his eyrie-like offices thanks to a six-month trial arrangement with the foundry – made 18 years ago.

All a bit like the story of the Davis family business, which grew from random beginnings to today's venerable status via hard work, adaptability and an ethos which decreed that a Davis would never ask an employee to do a job he hadn't done, or couldn't do, himself.

Ian Davis is casual about the family history, almost diffident about the long road travelled since Philip and Minnie Davidovics arrived in Ireland from Riga, Latvia, in the early 1920s. Full of a restless energy, the finer details escape him. But his pride and loyalty to family, creed and the company are embedded. He loves what he does, even if he came to it by accident (or could it have been fate?) and is excited by the dramatic changes to the business of waste metal, which have latterly made it "essential to the world we now live in".

There's lots of family detail about the office: wedding and other pictures of his son and daughter, of his grandchildren, one even of a meeting with de Valera. Wall clocks telling the time in New York, San Diego and Dublin have nothing to do with business, all to do with the fact that his son and daughter live in NY and San Diego. He makes a few family phone calls, checks a salient fact and, bit by colourful bit, we put together the story of Samuel Davis Ltd.

Philip Davidovics, Ian's grandfather, came first, a refugee from the early twentieth-century pogroms against Jewish people in Latvia. His grandson leads me to a large world map on the wall and we study Philip's journey, the same route taken by the ancestors of many of this country's Jewish community. "Zada [the Jewish word for grandfather] got off at Cobh thinking it was New York," Ian Davis explains. "He worked at all sorts of things, including selling photographs, and made his way to Dublin, where he had relatives. Then he brought Bobba [the Jewish word for grandmother] over and became a butcher in Clanbrassil Street." The Davidovics lived in Clanbrassil Street too, had two sons and two daughters and abbreviated the family name to a more easily understood Davis. "In about 1940 Zada decided to go into scrap and set up in Mill Street, The Coombe," Ian Davis continues. "In those days you didn't just deal in metal: it was everything from feathers to jam jars to rags as well. It all had to be segregated. If it was rags the whites had to be separated from the colours and so on, the way you'd separate green from coloured glass today."

Philip's son Samuel, Ian Davis's father, came accidentally (fate again?) to the business. "He wanted to be a doctor," Ian says, "and had been studying for six-and-a-half years and working in the Meath Hospital. He brought 41 babies into the world and came home one day and said he was sick of the sight of blood and seeing people in pain and was going into the family business." By then the company changed direction to a concentration on non-ferrous metals and its name to Samuel Davis Ltd.

Philip (Zada) Davis died in 1964 and when Samuel Davis had a heart attack in 1967 Ian joined the company. "I was 18 and had wanted to do law but my father needed someone in the business and when he got out of hospital he sent me to Holland, to a refinery in Middelburg, Zeeland, to learn about metals.

"The business then was mainly in non-ferrous metals, about separating copper, lead, aluminium, zinc, all of them, then sending them to refineries Philips and Lion in London and R. Easdale in Glasgow for melting down and recycling. We didn't have a refinery in this country until the late 1960s."

The company was still based in The Coombe and Ian Davis talks about long hours worked, about leaving Dublin at 4 a.m. to drive a lorry to Cork or Galway, where he would unload and load up again before driving back. "They were tough times," he says, not regretting a day of it.

He drove the lorries "for years. I thought my father hated me, keeping me on the road like that, and when he told me to stop one day I asked him why. He said it was so as I'd never have to ask anyone to do anything I'd never done myself. And he was right and it was all to my benefit. He was a good man, my father."

The company, in time, took over another in Pleasants Street, Dublin 8, and moved operations there. When Samuel Davis died, in 1977, Ian Davis became the company. "Times were changing," he says, "and parking and yellow lines in Pleasants Street made unloading difficult. I approached David Frame of Hammond Lane and told him I'd like to come down here, and we came to an arrangement for me to move in on a six-month trial basis. I'm still here."

In the years since, he's been chairman of the Metal Merchants Association of Ireland and, proudly, been responsible for bringing the Bureau of International Recyling to Dublin for its 2001 world meeting.

The business has "changed dramatically over the years. We've diversified a bit and deal mainly in steel. We're an approved packaging-waste collector for Repak. We deal in the recycling of white and brown goods too. You have to move with the times and Samuel Davis is about recycling these days. Everything is legislated for now. Last year I diversified and deal a lot in steel now, which I sell to Hammond Lane, which in turn sells on to Spain and the Continent."

He turns on a large-screen TV and on Ceefax demonstrates the global dimensions of the business, with a look at lead prices that morning (£2 a tonne) and copper (down $6 since the day before). On a calculator he works out the state of new lead ingots. Someone's on the telephone from Galway, someone else from London. Business is busy and business is good.

"With all the new EU legislation, everything has to meet environmental standards. We're dealing in a service which is essential to the world we live in. It's changed in other ways too. You don't meet the same fantastic characters you used meet, the personal touch isn't what it used to be, loyalties aren't the same."

He loves it, even so, and doesn't miss "the old ways. The hassle is less and the future's looking good."

Ken Ryan, managing director of Abbey Stained Glass Studios. *Photograph: Brenda Fitzsimons*

Abbey Stained Glass Studios

18 Old Kilmainham, Dublin 8

The Abbey Stained Glass Studios is over 60 years old, spends most of its time working with stained glass 100 and more years old, employs craftsmen and artists who continue through generations and operates from studios in Old Kilmainham that fit happily into an ageless ideal – flaming kilns, long tables in long workrooms and an ordered chaos of glass, lead, paint and drawings everywhere.

The company has its roots in The Dublin Glass and Paint Company, set up in Abbey Street in the 1920s by Tom Ryan. Tom's nephew, Frank Ryan, joined the business in 1944 and proceeded to set up Abbey Stained Glass, a company within a company, which flourished and grew and is today managed by Ken Ryan, son of Frank and the third generation of Ryans to run the business.

Work in the 1940s came fast and beautiful on the heels of a nationwide church-building programme and subsequent need for stained-glass windows.

The Ryans lived in Clontarf and Ken Ryan remembers his father working on the windows of St Gabriel's Church in that part of the city, as well as the churches in Donnycarney and Raheny. It was Frank Ryan too, along with the studio craftsmen, who put Evie Hone's *Four Green Fields* (made for the New York World Fair of 1945) into the storage from which it was subsequently resurrected to take its glorious place in today's Government Buildings.

Today's company is mostly involved with restoring stained-glass windows in older churches. "Three-quarters of our work would be in restoration and the rest new work," Ken Ryan explains; "largely we'd work on churches 100 or more years old, so the requirement is for the traditional. New works are often in older buildings, in response to people leaving bequests for new windows."

Ken Ryan is not a stained-glass artist himself – his training is as a quantity surveyor and his pre-Abbey Glass years were spent in Africa – but the company's senior artist, Kevin Kelly, has been with the company for more than 50 years. "We use other artists from time to time on various projects," says Ken Ryan, "as on restoration and repair work. We're sometimes asked to do repairs to vandalism."

His background in quantity surveying comes in useful. "I'm able to offer other advice, for example, on construction ideas a stained-glass man mightn't be aware of."

His African adventure ("seeking fame and fortune!") began in 1967 in Malawi, where he worked on contract with Sisk. Later, in what was then Rhodesia, he and two Cullinane brothers set up a construction company which, prior to the country's war of independence, worked at everything from building churches to setting up civil-engineering schemes. Post-war, the company rebuilt mission stations for the Carmelite Fathers in remote parts of Zimbabwe.

Abbey Stained Glass had moved to Old Kilmainham, via a stop in Inchicore, by the time Ken Ryan returned and joined forces with his father Frank in 1984. Father and son worked together until Frank's death in 1987, at which point his son took over as MD. Ken Ryan's wife, Muriel, is also a director.

Ken Ryan, steeped in the lore and expertise of stained glass, explains the difference between stained and leaded glass: "In stained work the artist paints details onto glass which is then fired in a kiln up to four times to give depth, colour and texture. Leaded is purely coloured glass joined together with lead. Stained-glass work can be absolutely traditional or completely abstract — we're very much in the traditional mould, but every sort of job we get is a challenge."

The Abbey Stained Glass Studios is responsible for most restorations on the work of artist Harry Clarke RHA (1889–1931). Ken Ryan is precise about the artist's life, work and the company's involvement.

"Clarke was only 41 when he died but worked at a frenzied pace and built up a group of top quality artists around him so that, even 20 years after his death, his students were producing work of quality in his technique and style. We restored his *Stations of the Cross* in Lough Derg [for which Clarke was paid £721 in 1929]. They'd become buckled over the years, largely because of the heat of the sun. Darker colours in stained glass attract more heat than paler ones and the lead becomes pliable when it gets warm; its weight makes the window sag and buckle. When this happens on a regular basis over 100 years, the pressure causes individual glass pieces to break."

The Studios are responsible, too, for restoration of the masterpiece east window in St James Church, Dublin 8, sucked out in an accidental explosion in 1987. An example of the mid-Victorian revival in stained glass, it was fitted in 1859 by the renowned Michael O'Connor studios, whose windows are to be found in Pugin-designed churches around the country.

Ken Ryan explains how the job was done. "Our guys went down and collected the stained glass in buckets and had to put it together in jigsaw fashion. Fortunately for all, Dr Michael Wynne, keeper at the National Gallery at the time, had a record of the original window in slides, which he blew up and which helped us piece it together again. There were voids, of course, and inscriptions missing, which Dr Wynne was able to help us with."

The company's work-force varies between 15 and 18, eight of whom are craftsmen who assemble the glass – the likes of Willie Malone, the fourth generation of his family to work for the company. "We do work all round the country and outside too," Ken Ryan says. "We're currently working for the Augustinians in Hammersmith, London, and doing another job on St Ninian's Church in Scotland. We do some work in the US also, but nothing like in my father's time, when we did a lot."

Stained-glass techniques today are much as they were 100 years ago. "The glass will last forever if minded," Ken Ryan says, and goes on to talk admiringly about Chartres Cathedral, with its on-site studio where craftsmen and artists carry out periodic restoration.

A tour of Abbey Stained Glass's own studios reveals a 100-year-old window from Carlow Cathedral being put back together by Paddy McLoughlin; he's worked in the studios since he was fourteen-and-a-half and adamantly won't reveal the number of years he's clocked up since then.

Studio foreman Willie Malone, younger, and a fourth-generation craftsman, says the work is slow, time consuming and needs patience. Today's kilns are worked by both gas and electricity to reach temperatures of 600 degrees centigrade. "In the old days," Ken Ryan says, "guys would have used bellows to make the heat come up." Some things have changed in the business, but only some. The traditional, for this stained-glass company, is the way forward.

Christy Plunkett of Simon Dental Laboratories, Blackhall Place. *Photograph: Dara MacDónaill*

Simon Dental Laboratories

6 Oxmantown Lane, Blackhall Place, Dublin 7

When Christopher Simon Plunkett was 14 he left school and found himself a job. The year was 1952, work choices were thin on the ground and he was glad to become an indentured apprentice to Archibald Vinson, a dental surgeon who ran his own dental laboratory.

Christy Plunkett has been in the dental business ever since — though these days, and for the last 30-odd years, he's been running his own place, Simon Dental Laboratories, manufacturers of dentures, crowns and chrome cobalt. The latter, to you and me, are metal dentures.

High-precision sculpting and concentrated work is going on all round as we talk, with a touch of the mediaeval about the instruments of the trade — sandblasting units, polishers, furnaces, even in the ultra-sonic cleaners and automatic mixers. He looks younger than his years and tells the story of his working life with clarity and humour. Even tragedy, and there was tragedy, has a positive side in Christy Plunkett's telling.

"I'm in the business since I was a child," he begins. "I started work in October 1952. That was when secondary school fees had to be paid; my brother's were paid but, by the time it came to pay mine, my father was on strike. He worked for the City of Dublin Working Men's Club and the strike there became one of the longest running ever, ending in the High Court. He was out for 12 months. I went knocking on doors, literally, and ending up in this business was a pure accident."

Archibald Vinson's laboratory was in South William Street and the young Christy Plunkett lived in Whitehall. Until he was 23 he cycled across the city every morning, home for lunch, back again and home in the evenings.

"There wasn't a lot of traffic then," he says, "and we didn't put on weight in those days either. We burned off the fat."

He says he learned "a vast amount" from Archibald Vinson, that when the company closed he thought about taking it over but that "things were different in those days and it wasn't possible".

He did get married, though, to Kathleen Coleman when he was 23. He worked for two different companies during the next five years and, after that, in the Dental Hospital in Lincoln Place, where he did the London City and Guild exams in practice and theory of dental laboratory work. By the time he'd finished these, he and Kathleen were parents to two daughters, Lorraine and Caroline.

An admitted thirst for knowledge and learning has been a constant ever since. Over the years it has taken him to East Greenstead Hospital in the UK, on to Chicago, to Connecticut and further. He started Simon Laboratories in 1968. "I saw an opportunity to open a dental laboratory and set up in 15 Montague Street, off Harcourt Street. We were there 30 years until our landlord decided he wanted to redevelop the site and we had to move."

We digress into a short history of teeth, beginning with the Egyptians. "They developed what we call the lost wax casting technique," Christy explains, "an excellent system which gives great accuracy and precision. It was itself lost to us for about 1,800 years but came into use again in the seventeenth and eighteenth centuries, when dental men of the time picked it up. It's still being refined today." He reveals other odd and fascinating facts: how wooden pegs were used for teeth in the eighteenth century, as well as ivory, animal teeth and teeth from cadavers.

"In 1952, when I came to the business, we were still in the Vulcanite era for dentures," he says. "Vulcanite was a rubber which had to be processed. We went from there into the plastic. When I started, too, porcelain teeth accounted for about 90 per cent of all dentures. At present it's nearly all plastic teeth because plastic has been refined so well."

The digression takes him into a discussion of the value of porcelain for crowns and bridges (better for colour and strength in the mouth) to the excellence of the shade guide produced by Vita Lumin Vacuum – German made and used all over the world.

"It has 16 shades of teeth, which cover practically every nationality in the world," he says, in tones of wonder, "or you can mix colours to make them exact."

Christy Plunkett's tragedy happened in 1973, the year of the Dublin bombings; the latter the reason he sees the hand of God in what happened to him.

By 1973 the laboratories had 13 employees and was doing well. Christy was part-time teaching in Kevin Street College of Technology and was a member of ANCO's Dental Advisory Board. Then it happened.

"A fire started with molten beeswax in the lab in Montague Street," he explains. "In my stupidity I tried to save the premises from going on fire. I would advise anybody now to get out when a fire starts. You can rebuild buildings but you can't rebuild people when they're dead." Christy Plunkett was rebuilt, but then he didn't die.

"I tried to shift the beeswax container," he says, "but it caught on the side of a bench and the whole thing fell over my head and hands. People tell me there was a scream that could be heard at the end of Stephen's Green. There was a dentist called Dr Andrew Woolfe standing behind me. He put my head and hands into water immediately. I ended up with a face mask of beeswax. I was taken to the Meath Hospital and from there to Dr Steevens, both of them gone now."

His face took six months to rebuild in Dr Steevens. "I was under the care of a man called Prenderville and was probably his worst nightmare because I knew a little about maxillofacial," Christy laughs, "which is the rebuilding of the face artificially. I look younger than I am because the rebuilding means I don't have the wrinkles I might have!"

And the hand of God? Christy Plunkett had arranged to meet his wife and daughters in Leinster Street the day of the bombings. "Because of my accident they weren't there," he says. "It probably saved their lives."

After the accident, he says, with a degree of understatement, that he probably wasn't "mentally attuned" to changes in the world of the dental laboratory. "In time we went back to having just four people working in the business," he says. "We're still four today and quite comfortable with that."

The company moved to its present premises, at 6 Oxmantown Lane, Blackhall Place, Dublin 7, in 2000. The company employees are all dental technicians: his daughter Caroline Redmond ("who runs me and the company!"), his nephew Paul Coleman, who does most of the metal casting, and Sean Gallagher, whose expertise comes from almost 17 years spent working in Germany.

Christy says that, nowadays, "if you've got money you can get anything done with your mouth! For €30,000 you could get your whole mouth reconstructed. The full upper and lower dental market still exists but is decreasing. People are looking after their natural teeth a lot better and going for crowns and bridges, and so on."

Simon Laboratories has recently overhauled its accounts system and, after 30 years using the Kalamazoo System, has installed a computer accounts package.

Christy Plunkett says he's supposed to be retired and is going to cut back on work, a bit. He intends playing more golf. He will also continue with the prayer guidance work he's been doing for years in All Hallows and with the course in Bereavement Counselling he's already started. "People are too busy to listen to the bereaved any more," he says. He intends listening.

Peter Butler-Bateman, proprietor of Edward Butler Antiques on Bachelor's Walk, with a shop sign from his great-grandfather Michael Butler's shops in London and Dublin in the 1880s. *Photograph: Frank Miller*

Edward Butler Antiques

14 Bachelor's Walk, Dublin 2

There's more than a whiff of the real thing about the business being conducted at 14 Bachelor's Walk. Old polished wood, aged nautical instruments, elderly leather furniture, air of calm appreciation – everything fits with the selling of antiques.

Peter Butler-Bateman fits too, like the proverbial glove, and with the rock of family tradition behind him. He runs Edward Butler Antiques, with his son John, from a premises as familiar to Dubliners as the slow flow of the Liffey outside its window.

The shop's been there since 1916, Peter Butler-Bateman (his mother was the Butler) since 1959. John came on board more recently but is set to make his life's work in antiques too.

Peter Butler-Bateman knows well what he's inherited. "The rules and integrity of antique selling are set by previous generations," he says, "so you do your best to maintain them." The rules are basic, and two. Father and son confer and agree that honesty is prime. "The buyer has to be able to trust the description given by the seller," Peter says. "There can't be any covering over of cracks! You must say everything there is to say about a piece." The second rule has to do with the customer too. "He or she must be looked after," they agree. "We have generations of families coming here to buy. People won't come back if they can't be sure of the provenance and truth of a piece." Buying antiques is not simply a pastime for the rich, or even the moderately wealthy. "Many customers," Peter points out, "are building a home and have an appreciation of antiques and this hasn't changed over the years."

He knows what he's talking about. To his own years on the job can be added family experience going back to 1841, when Patrick Butler won a medal for craftsmanship at an RDS furniture exhibition. The family's renown as furniture makers grew – the time would come when Michael Butler, Patrick's son, would be the one to make the furniture for a 1903 royal visit to the Vice-Regal Lodge (now Áras an Uachtaráin).

Discursive and gentle, Peter Butler-Bateman puts together the family story, telling how their renown in the furniture-making and antique business grew throughout the nineteenth century.

By 1855, Patrick Butler was a "furniture broker" in Liffey Street and by 1880 his son Michael was running a gallery and workshops around the corner in Upper Abbey Street. The company made a name for itself reproducing furniture in the Chippendale style, as well as in the styles of Adam and Sheraton, and opened another shop in South Molton Street, London.

When Michael's son, Edward, came into the business, he went for a while to the London shop. Described as a "true Dub" by his grandson Peter, he returned, married Pollie in 1915 and in 1916, a month before the rebellion of that year, opened his own place at 14 Bachelor's Walk.

Somewhere around this point in the conversation, a grandfather clock chimed the hour and brought us, sort of, back to today. The clock, bought by Peter Butler-Bateman just months ago in the UK, dates from 1720, still keeps perfect time and epitomises his continuing, antique dealer's love of "a bit of quality".

The small office behind the shop has a couple of comfortable chairs, a single-bar electric fire and walls replete with framed memorabilia. A letter dated 1902 indicates that the Duke of Connaught paid E.M. Butler the princely sum of £1,619 for furniture. The Countess of Aberdeen sent a note and payment of £160 in 1908. A framed photograph shows the workers in the Upper Abbey Street workshops in 1902. Later in the century, Dame Nelly Melba was a customer and later still (in 1938) a newspaper cutting shows Edward Butler holding the stone that was the Turk's Head, when it was taken down from the Parliament Street "beef steak and chop house" it had adorned since 1758.

Edward Butler died the year Peter Butler-Bateman left school. "This opened the door for me to come into the business," his grandson says. His grandmother, Pollie Butler, went on working in the shop for many years and now John, after seven years in Australia, has come on board. All to the good, they both believe. John feels his time in the southern hemisphere has given him "a knowledge of what's out there, an awareness of different tastes. Our business tends to be conservative, something I'm coming to appreciate more and more."

John used to come into the shop as a child. So did his father; there's a 1949 picture of him looking through the window at his grandfather working inside. "It was like an Aladdin's Cave to me," he says, "with treasures from all over the world." It was the same for John. "I came in as a child too, saw things from all over the world, even took some of them home with me!" He laughs. "Still do!"

Peter acknowledges that, in a changing world, the antiques business has changed less than most. "There's no supermarket in this business," he says. "Even the furniture my grandfather made is still in the Áras, hasn't disappeared with the upheaval of times."

Bachelor's Walk, "a very special part of Dublin", has changed too. "The antique galleries and auction rooms are mostly gone," Peter says. "All the businesses around me either closed or moved out, leaving us on our own. It's a very special location, right on the riverfront, and the quays here have become a living street again with apartments and the boardwalk. Once O'Connell Street has the work done on it, and the tunnel is finished, I wouldn't be surprised if Bachelor's Walk became pedestrianised."

Their conservative stock and style won't change much. "We've found that by being conservative we don't go far wrong," Peter admits, "while realising at the same time that if you want to keep trading you have to move with the times. The conservative ground is still the safest and it's where I'd guide people to put their money." Conservative, in Dublin, equals Georgian furniture for the most part, and sources haven't changed a great deal over the years. "Old customers moving house come to us with things to sell," Peter explains. "I go through the auction system both here and in England. It's getting harder and harder to find things of quality, and good items are going to become dearer. New items are coming on the market, which I won't be queuing up to sell! But as long as a thing is hand crafted and hand made, in 100 years it'll become an antique. The self-evident quality and time makes the difference. The mass-produced product doesn't have the skill and labour of love which makes that difference."

The future, they agree, is in antiques. "There's a future for quality antique items but defective pieces, or those described wrongly, are losing value. Pieces of quality with Irish provenance will keep their investment value."

They love what they do. "As the world becomes more streamlined it's becoming more incongruous to be an antiques dealer," Peter says, happily.

"That," his son assures, "is part of its appeal."

Jessie Supple (right) and Amy Luke, Glenageary, Co. Dublin, with ice-cream from Teddy's. *Photograph: Eric Luke*

Teddy's

Ice-Cream Shop, 1A Windsor Terrace, Dun Laoghaire, Co. Dublin

Teddy's is much more than an institution. Dun Laoghaire's best and original ice-cream shop is also a repository of memories without number, the place to go for an enduring summer experience in a changing world.

Teddy's, through the decades since it opened in 1950, has been selling ice-cream from a small shop overlooking the wide expanse of Scotsman's Bay at the end of Windsor Terrace. It also, now as then, sells boiled sweets, iced caramels, clove rock, acid drops and chocolate satins by the quarter pound from jars. On summer Sundays you can get strawberries and ice-cream there – but they don't do flavourings or syrups.

"We try to stick with what people got here when they were young," says Yasmin Kahn, who runs Teddy's today, "to keep things as traditional as possible. We still use the original weighing scales. We do Cadbury's ice-cream as well and a couple of Italian ice-creams. I was told when I took over that if it wasn't broken, then I shouldn't fix it, that I should do things the way they were always done in Teddy's."

Yasmin Kahn has known Teddy's all her life, began working there when still at school. Her father Brian has been intimately acquainted with Teddy's for even longer. Rita Shannon, behind the counter on the day I visited, has worked in Teddy's for more than 40 years.

Teddy himself, real name Edward Jacob and the man who started things in 1950, now divides his time living between Morocco and the south of France. Gone he may be, but certainly not forgotten. Edward Jacob made Teddy's the small seafront empire it was and the team behind today's smaller, but no less vital, outlet are aware and careful of this. "He was a nice person," Brian Kahn says, "a very nice person. He worked here himself all the time."

Brian Kahn, Yasmin's father and a man who admits himself indebted to ice-cream and the "nice life" it's given him, bought Teddy's from Edward Jacob 10 years ago. "I always loved the place," he says, "even before I came to supply Teddy with ice-cream. It was real ice-cream, quality stuff – not like today when they use maize instead of egg yolk to bind it. Quality, not watery, rubbishy stuff. Real ice-cream – when you bit into it you felt you were eating food. And that's been passed on."

Teddy's, in the beginning and for many years, was an ice-cream shop, tea rooms and souvenir boutique taking up the first stretch of Windsor Terrace. The Kahns are happy to own the landmark ice-cream shop only, and may even build over it to bring back the tea-rooms. "A place where we could serve afternoon tea and cakes, the way they used to," Yasmin says, "where people could sit and just look out. We don't have a lot of space but it could be done. I'd spend all of my time up there myself!"

Teddy's has a way of inspiring loyalty, devotion even, from customers and workers alike. Rita Shannon arrived in Teddy's to do a two-week holiday stint more than 40 years ago. She's still working there, youthful-looking evidence that Teddy's has something of Tír na nÓg about it. "I just stayed on," she says, "I liked it so much. We had such fun! In those days you could walk from one to the other of the businesses. The awnings were red and white and the shop red and blue. The boutique sold all Irish handmade stuff – Aran sweaters, jewellery, that kind of thing."

Bridie, who died in 1990, was another Teddy's employee who has gone into history. Her devotion was such that she even slept in the place, Brian Kahn says. "People say she's still here, in fact, that they can hear her in the night when they pass by," he says.

Brian Kahn's connections and devotion to Teddy's go back an equally long way, his journey to ownership of Dun Laoghaire's own and original ice-cream event as circuitous as it now seems inevitable.

Born in South Africa, he came to Ireland to study medicine in 1962, gave it up in 1967 and joined Cooper Bros to study accountancy instead. He married and joined the accountants T.P. O'Neill, where he found himself doing the books for "an ice-cream man. He wanted out of the business so a friend and myself bought his vans and machinery and started making ice-cream. Ice-cream's given me a nice life. I've never liked wearing a suit and tie, always enjoyed meeting people."

The links with Teddy's were there before Brian started supplying him with ice-cream. "My late wife lived next door to old Mrs Jacob, Teddy's mother, in Dalkey. There was another son, Michael, too. They were all involved in the business but Teddy was the main one. It was said he got his name from dressing like a Teddy Boy in the 1950s, winkle-pickers and all that. I bought Teddy's after my wife died. I loved it. I used stay open until about 2.30 a.m."

Brian Kahn "retired" in 1999 – though Yasmin says that semi-retired is more accurate, since he comes into Teddy's most days. "I took over but have to do things his way," she says. "He still likes to keep his finger in the pie." Some things have changed though. "Up to when Brian retired we were open late but now we close at 9.30 p.m. For a while it just wasn't safe; people didn't go walking after 9 p.m. It's changing, though, getting safer again. We're hoping that, with the lights going up along the sea-front, the evening walkers will come back."

She won't discuss the secret of Teddy's especially good-tasting ice-cream, won't risk de-mystifying a legend. Brian Kahn says it's all to do with quality. "Ice-cream has to be fresh every day so you must clean your machines every day," he says. "Especially in the heat. You'd be surprised how even a little drop left in a machine can affect the taste of things."

The ice-cream business runs from April to October. Yasmin says that they've "managed to keep a steady business through the Celtic Tiger years. We haven't put our prices up for two years and hope to keep it that way."

She'll go on running things, with the help of her brother Haniff, partner Craig Macintosh and Rita. "Haniff may take over in time," she says, "but that's up to him. If he doesn't I'll keep it going. I've been working here since I was 17, before Dad even bought the place, and really love it, the regulars, seeing the kids who come in grow up."

Brian says too that Haniff might take over one day. "He's got a good business head on him. He's like my father and grandfather, even to his gestures." He falls to remembering. "How I've loved the place! I used sit outside Teddy's on the wall in the night and talk and laugh and joke. You could go on all night, there are so many lonely people about. Still are. I see them all the time.

"When we're not open we still get phone calls to the house, people saying they've come home on holiday and want to give their kids the experience of a Teddy's ice-cream!"

Aidan Robinson and Ron Consenheim in the Robinson Surerest showroom at Bow Lane East. *Photograph: Matt Kavanagh*

Robinson Surerest

Bed Shop, Bowe Lane East, Dublin 2

For more than 80 years, through the thick and thin of the nation's march and over three generations of the family, Robinson Surerest has been supplying handcrafted beds to discerning sleepers. Orthopaedic beds are a speciality but they do a full range of traditional beds too, custom-made with natural materials and pocket sprung.

The great and the good go to Surerest: actors, politicians, designers and the diplomatic corps, all seeking the imperative of a good night's sleep on a good mattress. So do the descendants of decades-ago clients – Surerest has been serving many of its customers for several generations. The company offers a personal service it's proud of and has moved only twice since being set up by John Robinson in 1922.

The Surerest story is one of an early-nineteenth-century triumph over adversity, proof that fact really is more interesting than fiction.

John Robinson was born in England in 1900. His father was a member of the Royal Army Medical Corps and his mother, Emily, an Irishwoman, came home to Dublin with her three small children when her husband died.

John Robinson's great-grandson, David Robinson, tells some of his great-grandfather's story. His mother, Gemma, adds her memories and so does his aunt, Pauline. David's father, Aidan Robinson, chips in on the end of a phone line. We drink coffee and eat Gemma's home-baked scones. It's all very convivial and relaxed. Customers get the same treatment. Sometimes, they even get the coffee.

"Things were horribly tough for Emily, my great-grandmother, when she came home," David says. "She had no pension and there was no social welfare. My grandfather, her son, John, told me he remembered her putting cold tea on her eyes to keep herself awake while she sewed buttons onto army shirts, just one of many things she did to make money."

Things reached a stage when the only way to manage was to put John in St Vincent's orphanage in Glasnevin. "He had nothing but good things to say about it and about the education he got there," Gemma assures. John Robinson's education got him a job in O'Dea's Bedding in Mary Street, where he worked on the accounts. Things were still tough for his mother and sister, living in Cabra, but now he was able to help out.

John Robinson liked camping and Sutton, then a place of green fields and sand dunes, was his preferred location. It was also where he met and fell in love with another camper, Polly Tutty from Drumcondra.

"He wanted to marry her but couldn't afford to," Gemma says, "so he went to Berkeley Road church to pray and look for guidance. The idea of setting up a bedding company came to him there."

John Robinson opened his bed-making factory in Hardwicke Lane, off Dorset Street, in 1922, when he was 22 years old. He called it J.R. Bedding and he worked day and night producing hog- and horse-hair mattresses. Hog hair makes the better mattress, David explains, the hairs being shorter, shaped like a coiled spring, and providing more bounce.

The object of the exercise was more than achieved when John and Polly married and, in 1930, expanded the business, moved to Mercer Street and changed the company name to Surerest. John and Polly Robinson had five children – Damien, Aidan, John, Paul and Marie. In the fullness of time, in the 1940s, Aidan became the one to join his father in the business.

In the 1940s, the company had a staff of 20 and was run by John Robinson senior, his son Aidan and Polly's younger brother, Roy Tutty, the accounts manager. "He was a gentle, gracious and courteous man; people still talk about him," Pauline says.

Other workers are remembered too. Women like Edith (Edie) Worley of Shielmartin Terrace, Fairview, and Christine Smith from Kelly's Corner, SCR, seamstresses who earned £6.5.0d a week in 1964. Mick Berkley, Joe Glennan, Paddy O'Connor and John Farrell were all long-time bedmakers; hard and patience-demanding work involving hand teasing the heavily compacted flock apart, cutting materials, hand stitching mattress and tufting. "A massively arduous handcrafting industry," is how David describes it.

Jack Kenny drove a van for the company for many years. Before that, local deliveries were made by horse and cart and before that again a handcart was used. Time was, too, in the 1940s, when beds were delivered by canal barge from Broadstone to Limerick, when hair mattresses that rolled up into canvas sail bags went to lighthouses, ships and yachts and others were specially made for monasteries and caravans and, famously remembered by many, the penitential Lough Derg. Today's beds are delivered by van, by the company's excellent Dutch courier, Ron Consenheim.

Designer Sybil Connolly was a customer; Surerest has always had a definite design edge. Then, as now, Surerest beds were designed in-house to a time-tested specification. All of their models, David points out, "are called after the lighthouses around the Irish coast; they look after you in the dark hours".

"We don't do built-in obsolescence," David says. "We've customers who bought beds during the war and are still using them. And they still work. We make to order, to customers' own designs — we've made circular beds and seven-foot square beds."

The company worked out of Mercer Street for 43 years, "across the road from the house where Noel Purcell lived", David says, "and where another local industry at the time was cutting sticks into bundles of firewood for sale by the local kids".

In 1973, a compulsory purchase order was put on Surerest's Mercer Street premises because of the development of the St Stephen's Green Shopping Centre. "No one really wanted to move," Gemma says. "Everyone was used to the old place."

The idea of closing was mooted but then they moved to where they are today, a stone's throw away to a premises which had once been a stables on Bow Lane East, just off Mercer Street in Dublin 2. John Robinson senior, Aidan Robinson, Ray Tutty and Seamus Thornton got things up and going again, albeit in a smaller way.

Through the 1970s and 1980s, Surerest sold directly to customers and to shops like Carrolls of Bachelor's Walk and, later, Switzers and Clerys. Medical referrals built up and so did the numbers of physiotherapists recommending Surerest beds. In the 1990s, interior designers looking for uniquely designed beds grew customer numbers even more. John Robinson senior died in 1988 when he was 88 years old, the age of the century through which he'd cut such a swathe.

Through all the years, word of mouth and repeat business have been at the core of the Surerest business story — along with a quiet assurance about the quality of its product.

"We'll continue as we are," David Robinson says, sage and sure and echoing the confidence of his parents and aunt.

Maura McDermott and Grace Halpin at Flora, Exchequer Street. *Photograph: Cyril Byrne*

Flora

Florist, 34 Exchequer Street, Dublin 2

Time was, in the world of flowers and fashion, when carnations, chrysanthemums, freesia and lilies were what choice was about, with tulips and daffodils added in springtime.

And then there were violets: cut ones with tiny leaves in a beautiful purple colour which were worn as a buttonhole. Or used as a posy. They were grown in the hills around Glandore, Co. Cork, and posted twice a week, in boxes of 36, to Flora, one of just three or four flower shops in Dublin in the 1940s and 1950s. The empty boxes had to be sent back to Glandore and the violets, which imbibed through the flower not the stem, had to have their heads kept wet at all times.

Flora began life in South King Street. In time, and with a developing Dublin, it moved to Exchequer Street. It's still there, and it's blooming.

Yvonne Good became Flora's second owner when she took over the South King Street shop from Mrs Norah Sherrard, the woman who started the business.

Norah Sherrard, *née* O'Sullivan, came to Dublin from Ballylickey, Co. Cork, and was married to a TCD professor of horticulture. "He used give the topical talk on the radio after the news," Yvonne remembers.

"The original shop was between Sinnott's pub and an antique shop. Mrs Sherrard was a keen gardener and had a partner called Dorothy Sinnott, who was a great flower arranger."

Another Cork woman, Yvonne Good's early 1960s journey to Dublin and Flora was circuitous. "When I was at the stage of deciding on a career, a woman from the Constance Spry School of Floristry in London arrived in Bandon, where I lived. Bandon had one of the first flower clubs in Ireland, run by Eva Jeffers, who was a wonderful and natural flower arranger."

All of this influence propelled Yvonne to Dublin and a year's study of domestic science at Alexandra College, followed by a year in the Constance Spry school in London. She was working in Harrods, "doing the flowers", when she met her Irish husband.

She was 20 when she married and, back in Dublin, discovered her cousin was about to leave her job with Mrs Sherrard in South King Street. She took the job. Five years later, when Flora was put up for sale, her father helped her buy it.

The year was 1969 and the auction made headlines. "I fully expected to get it for £5,000 to £6,000," Yvonne explains, "but the developers had just moved in and we were bidding against them and it went up to £10,000. The whole area was going to the developers anyway, for the St Stephen's Green Centre and all of that, and I knew I would have to move before I was put out. In 1972 we bought Exchequer Street, in 1973 excavated the basement there and in 1974 sold South King Street. In 1975 we refurbished 34 Exchequer Street, putting in a cold room and mezzanine floor."

It was hard work and she had a growing family. "I was for years thinking of getting out of the business. Christmas, Easter and especially Valentine's Day were becoming more and more nightmarish. But I had great people working for me and when my husband moved, I offered it to two of them, Maura McDermott and Grace Halpin. We did the deal and they took over and we were all very happy. Still are."

Flora is like a small and intimate corner of the Botanic Gardens. Flowers and greenery dazzle with choice and the mood is relaxed, as happy as Yvonne promised.

Grace Halpin, selling flowers in Flora since the late seventies, arranges an intricate basket of greens and white blooms. She remembers the violets. Remembers too how "men who bought flowers used to hide them.

"They'd ask for a black bag so's they wouldn't be seen carrying them, or stuff them under their coats. And that was only back in the 1980s! Hard to believe. Nowadays men know everything about flowers, down to the individual names of red roses. These days too they're proud to walk down the street with a bunch. It's not like when people used come in and ask for a nice bunch of Friesians for a wedding!"

Men buy a lot of the flowers sold these days. More even than women. Maura McDermott says she would "put men ahead of women in the passing-trade stakes". Especially for Valentine's Day. "February we can have up to 30 people working for us, have to use a variety of premises all around here to store and arrange roses and make up to 800 deliveries of red roses on the day itself.

"Time was when you'd have maybe 20 orders for Valentine's but in the late 1980s things escalated out of control. We're here all through the night before Valentine's Day." And then there's Christmas ... "We dream about having a Christmas off."

Maura was in catering when she met Yvonne, who asked her to help out in South King Street.

Grace was a florist in Limerick who was passing through Dublin, *en route* to foreign parts, when she stopped off in Flora's. "I liked it and stayed," she says, then grins. "I'm still optimistic about getting away. One of these days I really will go abroad."

Flora's current owners changed the front windows of the shop some years ago, going for curved glass and a door in the middle.

"We'll have to get fridges in some time soon," Maura says, "the sort they use in the US." She doesn't envisage much else changing.

Flower selling reflects social change in a big way – and it all puts up the price. "Most Valentine's buyers are loving and caring, some want to remain anonymous, others are "stalker types" and a few "plain weirdos, guys who send flowers to eight or ten women."

Chrysanthemums are coming back. The word on carnations is that they're are making a comeback too. But for now "People are still horrified when they get carnations in a bouquet," Grace says, "even though the reality is that they last for weeks."

The more delicate flowers now in fashion last only a few days. Have we become affluent, or what? Today's fashion-statement flowers include Anthuriums, Proteas and other South African flowers, orchids of all kinds, Nutans (also called Pin Cushions) and Agapanthus, an old and lovely flower which has come back in both shops and gardens.

"In the old days we went to the markets," Maura says. "Now the Dutch guys come up to the door with everything you could want in articulated lorries and containers. You can see the quality and don't have to order over the phone and it's all very good.

"But we'd like to do the same business with Irish suppliers. We've an Irish supplier for freesia, lilies and Alstroemeria. His name's Brendan Goodman; he grows in Co. Meath and he supplies to select shops only," she laughs modestly. "He's the best there is.

"Tony Lefroy is a fine Irish grower too. He brings us our Monday-morning flowers."

There are nine full-time employees in Flora, including drivers and a bookkeeper. Elaine Foley, the shop's senior florist, is "brilliant" and has been with Flora since the mid-nineties.

Driver Joe Humphries comes from a family of street vendors in the Grafton Street area. His mother, Connie, sold at the corner of South William Street and Exchequer Street.

"The granny sold on South Great George's Street," he says, "and my Aunt Sally still sells on Grafton Street."

Maura says he's the best driver you could have, that he knows his city and that she doesn't know "how he gets around. We go hand-in-hand with street vendors – they create the buzz for flowers. Our big competition comes from Marks and Spencer's. But Grace and myself would prefer to maintain what we have and give a personal service."

Peter (left) and Stephen (right) Caviston, with chef Noel Cusack, at Caviston's Seafood Restaurant, Glasthule Road, Co. Dublin. *Photograph: Eric Luke*

Cavistons

Food Emporium, 59 Glasthule Road, Sandycove, Co. Dublin

Peter Caviston tells the story of the night's drinking that gave birth to Caviston's fish shop with some reluctance. "Everyone knows it," he protests. Everyone does: but every good story deserves a retelling too.

It was 1948 and Peter's uncle, James Augustine Caviston, was studying medicine. He was, by his nephew's account, "some man to go!" and a lover of life and books. The day came when, after buying a pound of fish, Jim Caviston crossed Glasthule Road for a pint with the fishmonger in The Eagle House. He woke next morning to find he'd bought the fishmonger's shop for £300. When he tried to stop the cheque it had already been cashed.

By such means was a legend born.

The Caviston fish shop, grown to become an institution and epicurean force way beyond its Glasthule location, is as much a cultural phenomenon as anything else. It's a drop-in centre and meeting place, a restaurant, deli, fish and poultry shop and bakery.

There's flamboyance and *joie de vivre* and lots of hard work going on in Cavistons. There's also, in the early morning air, the smell of great coffee and fresh fish. Today's business employs 30 people – chefs, fish filleters, fishmongers, deli staff.

Peter Caviston *is* Cavistons. He was born to it, grew up with it, worked in the shop while going to school and, finally and seamlessly, made the full-time move into the business when he was just 16.

Before that, his uncle Jim Caviston had got it all up and going, selling fish, eggs and poultry before deciding, when he was 40, that he wanted to tour the world. So his brother John Caviston – father of Peter, Stephen and Paul – took over with his wife Margaret in the mid-1950s. Peter, their eldest child, was 11 years old and, even then, had his heart set on going into the business. He was not, by his own admission, "the best student the Presentation in Glasthule ever had". At 16, after much pleading with his father, he'd finished with classrooms and was behind the counter and filleting fish full-time.

He remembers when four herrings cost 20p, when cooked chickens were 15/-, 12/6d and 10/-. "My father was the life and soul of any party and a great ideas man," Peter says. "He began to diversify with olive oil, then came duck eggs. Cooked chickens were a huge seller, and unique in the mid-1960s. We used sell and deliver them. Then my father bought a coffee machine. I said to him 'Jesus, we're never going to sell coffee!' But of course we did, and do."

It was always a sociable place, customers helping behind the counter in the early, and not so early, days. "You relied on friends and customers to help," Peter says; "we couldn't afford to pay staff then. My brothers and I would take turns minding the shop; I remember filleting boxes of fish before going to school. The rule was that we never handled smoked fish – the smell is strong. If you did, the roar would go up in class, 'Caviston! the smell!'"

He's an unstoppable font of memories and stories, a lot of them involving personalities public and private. "I remember us buying from John Clark and Son on Wellington Quay – he was the first to import Primrose Caviar and such epicurean goods. His son, Derry Clark, now owns l'Ecrivain restaurant."

He remembers, too, the late and lamented media cook Monica Sheridan coming in to discuss recipes in the shop with his uncle, and how the poet Monk Gibbon fell into a fish box, having "the craic" on a Sunday-morning special opening for Ted Kennedy and his sister Jean Kennedy Smith.

He recalls with special affection his great buddy, cookery writer Theodora FitzGibbon. "I got on like a house on fire with her! She did an interview with me here and at the time there were only about six Irish cheeses available – now there are hundreds.

"The most important people are those who come in every day, however. They're all great, just great." He stops, words uncharacteristically and momentarily failing him. "You get great fun out of them, out of this business," he says at last.

The diversification at Cavistons went "on and on and on. Just mushroomed and kept going. I remember Geoff Read coming in and telling us he was selling water. I said to my father that we'd never sell it, so my father, of course, ordered two cases and of course we sold it. That was Ballygowan and of course it's blossomed too."

In 1989 Cavistons bought the shop next door, number 58 Glasthule Road, and in 1994 "knocked the insides out of it and turned it into a restaurant". Today's elegantly busy premises has a full deli, fish counter, two kitchens, filleting area and restaurant.

"The backbone is still the fish business," Peter Caviston says, laughing. "We're going to put in a bakery in a few months' time and will be baking and selling our own bread. We want to have a tasting counter at the back too. We've lots more ideas. Lots, lots more."

He's full of wisdom passed on by his father. Top of the list is never trying to be something you're not. His energy is formidable and renowned. He rises at 6.30 a.m. on Mondays for a day of "planning and meetings and buying fish – I might end up in Kilmore Quay".

Tuesdays see him out of the bed at 4.20 a.m. "I've programmed myself and don't use an alarm clock. I'm in here by 5 a.m., having met Mr Fox sniffing his way along the road to meet the truck which brings the fish from down south.

"I unload the fish and check the fridges and go to the market to see the lie of the land there, buying vegetables. I'd love to be behind the counter all the time. I've great fun with the customers."

Wednesday, when he doesn't get up until 9 a.m., is "a day of rest, though the brain's always working. I'm trying to take up golf but the temperament doesn't seem to suit."

Thursday is a 7.30 a.m. wake-up, more planning and thinking and into the shop by 10 a.m. Fridays is a 5.30 a.m. rise and "a bit of wheeler dealing in the vegetable market. I'm more than 30 years going to the market and I love it." Saturdays are "hectic, the busiest day of the week. I get up at 5.30 a.m. and open the deli and restaurant at 8.30 a.m."

He loves Sunday. "We put a lot of food on the table and people come and gather around. We always set an extra place because you never know who'll arrive."

They're a close family, the Cavistons. Peter's brother Stephen has a restaurant in Monkstown Crescent. His other brother, Paul, works as a "shrink" in the UK. Peter and his "lovely wife Maura, who puts up with me, is my adviser and keeps me on the straight and narrow," have three children. Mark, who has a degree in marketing, is already in the business and will, his father assures, "carry it to a new, high dimension".

David, "a computer whizz", is still in school. Daughter Lorraine worked in the business for a year before taking off around the world. She's on her way back "to help out again".

Caviston's success, Peter insists, has to do with the "great people who've worked here and who still do. We'd be nothing without them. Great people, really great.

"And, of course, there are the customers and, most of all, enjoying what you do, having a bit of fun. Customers should be a joy, not a nuisance. They pay our wages, after all."

Dance World at Parnell Street. *Photograph: Cyril Byrne*

Dance World

163 Parnell Street, Dublin 1

Secure and indispensable, between the Bank of Ireland and Itchy Fingers (specialists in Afro-Euro hair styles) Dance World continues to trade from the Parnell Street premises which generations of Dublin mothers and daughters have come to know and love.

This is the shop the Royalettes and a fledgling RTÉ television depended on; it's where the Bolshoi and Kirov ballet and Ruby Wax shop when in town, where Twink shops regularly and where dancers worth the name shop all the time.

More than all of this, it's the shop where, since the early 1970s, small girls have come to dream about being dancers, leaving only when their mothers had spent more than they could afford.

A modest Aladdin's cave for many years, it had a makeover in 2000. Today's Dance World is definitely twenty-first century: it has a new logo, with a slogan claiming it is "the first step to stardom", and a web site. But the essentials haven't changed: pink and glitter still dominate the decor.

A second Dance World shop opened at 16 Sandford Road, Ranelagh, in 1988 and has established the same sort of customer loyalty.

The Dance World shops are owned by the Rock Family. Noel Rock, who started the business in Parnell Street as Charles Stewart Fashion Shoes more than 30 years ago, says he's happily handed the running of things over to son Stephen and daughter Sinead. Stephen Rock, a TCD business graduate, is managing director and was responsible for the revamping, logo and introduction of technology.

Sinead, a UCD graduate in Irish and music, is marketing manager. Their father's pride in them is boundless. "Stephen's enthusiasm is everywhere," he says. "The business is fine tuned today with technology and all that; in the old days I took it on as an adventure."

Rock senior is no slouch himself when it comes to enthusiasm for the business: "I love it," he admits, "it's so different. It's lovely. When the little girls come in and their eyes light up … it's magic." A Dubliner born and bred, he began his working life in Arnotts, went on to spend 14 years in the UK and came back determined to "get out on my own".

Charles Stewart Fashion Shoes Ltd, which he opened in 1972 ("in those days the big thing was to call your shop after an Irish patriot …"), came into being and was doing well when, in 1978, Noel Rock heard the Harcourt Shoe Store in Harcourt Street, which had been selling dance shoes and wear for some 40 years, was about to close.

"It was owned by an old couple called Silverman. They were in their eighties and such lovely people. I went and chatted with them and bought their stock. They sent letters of introduction to their dance suppliers in England so I went over as the new dance person in Ireland.

"Because the Silverman's were so highly regarded, I was immediately welcome. I put the dance stock side by side with my own shoe stock and the dance stock quickly became the real business. I sold off my shoes and became Dance World."

Luck continued to smile. The television series *Fame* hit the small screen at about that time and Dance World "just rode along on all of the hype. It was terrific, absolutely amazing." But what he calls "the real biggie" happened when the Kirov and Bolshoi ballet companies came to Dublin.

"Eighty-five of the Kirov dancers arrived to the shop. I had to close for three hours and give them the run of the place. That was the old shop, before we changed the look of things, and they loved it. The Bolshoi came twice. Maire Mac an tSaoi used come with her two daughters and President Hillary and his wife with their daughter."

Dance World, in the 1970s and 1980s, with Noel Rock in charge, was "run very much as a privately owned business, when knowing your commodity was what counted. But now it's technology, the Internet, dot.com and being on line. It needed the new ideas Stephen has brought to it."

Noel Rock says he's never felt any kind of threat from other shops selling dancewear. "It's an extremely specialised business and being so specialised means there are very few people willing to take a chance. The dance pie is so small that two people couldn't slice it without going down the Liffey. I'm not being smug or self-gratifying when I say that we know the business. It's great that Stephen and Sinead have the business acumen as well as the knowledge passed on over years of talk at the dinner and tea table."

When he started he catered solely to dancers. "Now dance wear is a fashion item. Girls come in for cross-over cardigans like these" – he produces a peach-coloured number – "or jazz pants. We've even got our own T-shirt now."

We go through the rails and he holds up velvet and lace, glittering Lycra, tutus in every colour. These days, Dance World deals in gymnastic wear too, and in the accessories very young aspiring dancers might need for a party – balloons, paper cups, books. They sell ballroom and ballet shoes, Irish dance shoes and lace collars, videos, socks, party wear and even rabbits in tutus.

"When the little ones come in, they don't want to leave," says Noel Rock. "They're lost."

Their mothers don't want to leave either. Ruby Wax came in one summer. She bought outfits for herself and her children. She came back twice and bought some more.

"Twink is always coming in. She says if she buys any more she'll have to be made a share-holder. Of course all of the Billie Barry youngsters have come in over the years. Billie Barry opened the refurbished shop for me four years ago."

The graceful young women who work in the Parnell Street and Rathgar shops are all dancers. Summers, with schools closed, bring a lull but during the dance high season, the company employees up to 12 people. Noel Rock is adamant about one thing.

"Dance World wouldn't be where it is but for Stephen and Sinead. Stephen has taken it on to a new plane."

Louis Copeland (centre) with his brother Adrian and their sons Adrian Jnr (left) and
Louis Jnr (right) in the Louis Copeland shop on Capel Street. *Photograph: Alan Betson*

Louis Copeland & Sons

Master Tailors and Gents Outfitters,
39–41 Capel Street, Dublin I

The Capel Street premises of Louis Copeland & Sons, Master Tailors and Gents Outfitters, is a retreat in mahogany and Canadian oak with good light, great mirrors, celebrity photographs, fine clothes and a lot of discreet class. It wasn't always thus. Hyman Copeland started what has become a dynasty in the tailoring business of the capital in a much smaller shop seven doors down the street in 1908.

A Latvian Jewish trouser maker, Hyman quickly lost his heart to and married Harriet McCarthy, a Dublin Catholic trouser maker. They had a son and a daughter. Their son, Louis, born in 1914 in Ormond Quay, went to work with his father in Capel Street as a young teenager. By 1933, before he'd yet reached 20, he'd set up his own cutting and tailoring business in the Capel Street premises. The rest is a history of hard work and the triumph of experience.

As well as the flagship premises in Capel Street, today's business has outfitting shops in Pembroke Street (opened 1980), Wicklow Street (opened 1985) and, most recently, an outlet at Dublin Airport and a shop in Galway. The Pembroke Street outlet is run by Adrian Copeland, brother of Louis (son of the original Louis); the one at Dublin Airport by his son, Louis Jr. (Another brother, Carl, is a bank manager and a sister, Jacqueline, is a hairdresser). There are two Copeland workrooms: one over the Capel Street shop, another in Strand Street. Adrian Copeland's son, Adrian Jr, is gearing up to move into the business. With the dynasty thus secured, things are looking good for Copeland tailoring in the twenty-first century.

"Experience is what counts," says a dapper Louis Copeland, a suit man if ever there was one, buoyant and unconvincingly diffident, "and it's why we're still in business. We don't always get it right but we do try to give the best service we can." Then there's the hard work and great staff. "My father was a very good cutter and had a very good staff and so have I," Louis says. "They're all long-term; people don't just come and go. They don't retire either. There's only one way people go out of here. Some people in the workrooms are there 50 years." When his father set up the business "it was all made-to-measure suits. Nothing off-the-peg then. Now 90 per cent of what we do is off the peg. Our main suit brand is Canali and I go abroad a couple of times a year buying. We do hand-craft tailoring, of course, but it's only about 10 per cent of the business."

Louis Copeland went to school in St Patrick's NS, Drumcondra, but started coming in to help his father in the shop when he was about 10 years old.

"I've been in the business since then, you could say, since about 1960." When he was 14 he went to the then Technical School in Parnell Square to study tailoring and textiles. He left there when he was 16 and went to work in a clothing factory in High Street – "cutting and tailoring and sewing and sitting at a machine. The result is that I know what's what under the bonnet of clothing. I left there after three years and came into the business."

He's famous, of course, for clothing the bodies of celebrities. The photographs and letters, nicely framed, nothing flashy, bear testimony.

Tony Byrne, droll as they come and working with Louis for about 16 years, gives me the tour. There are White House letters, from Ronald Reagan (thanking Louis for the "handsome suiting fabric" in 1984) and two from Bill Clinton (in 1995 thanking him for the "lovely wool suit material" and in 1998 for a tweed jacket).

There are photographs of Louis with his measuring tape ready for such bodies as Kevin Spacey, Tom Jones, Terry Wogan, Gay Byrne, Richard Harris, Daniel O'Donnell, Liam Cosgrave, Frank Carson, Christy O'Connor, Ken Doherty and Van the Man Morrison. Pierce Brosnan, a particularly well-liked customer, is there in triplicate. "Louis met him at 6 a.m. in his hotel," Tony says, "and that evening on the *Late Late Show* he was wearing the suit we made for him during the day."

Then there's Taoiseach Bertie Ahern, a neighbour growing up in Drumcondra. Louis says modestly that he's only partly responsible for getting Bertie out of the anoraks. On a mahogany mantel there are the 1998 *FHM* awards for best overall retailer and best classic retailer in the UK and Ireland. Louis is particularly proud of beating the likes of Harrods and Debenhams to the post for that one. In prime position there's an oil of Louis Copeland senior. He died in 1984 but is still, Tony Byrne assures, "watching over the business".

The Louis Copeland shops open at 9 a.m., six days a week, except for the airport where young Louis is open for business seven days out of seven. "We stay open," Tony Byrne says, "until the last customer leaves. Usually about six-ish, but no one's ever thrown out." Young Louis, arriving in from the airport, has his father's relaxed enthusiasm for the business. You'd be surprised, he says, how many suits people buy when passing through the airport. Delayed flights allow plenty of time and often business people seize the hour to purchase. The airport shop does alterations and delivers free of charge.

The Copeland retail selection is carefully made. Louis makes twice yearly buying excursions abroad and says that his background in making suits and knowing how clothes go together helps. "When I go into Italian or German workrooms I know what to look for. I could still, if I had to, go from designing a pattern to cutting and making it up. Fashions come and go but quality is the thing for the moment. Years ago people bought a suit just to dress up in for a special occasion. Now they want one to feel well in as well as look well in. Lapel and trouser widths come and go."

Louis Copeland's mother, May, is a "hale and hearty woman with a good singing voice which she'll use if called upon. If not she'll push herself forward." His daughter Avril, "who was a hockey player and a bit of a singer", works as a roadie in Nashville, Tennessee. Rachel, his youngest, is "into sport". He pays special and caring tribute to Mary, the nurse from Waterford he married in the late seventies, there through good and bad times and "who does all the background work".

Elaine Williams, director, Michael K. Williams (left) and Jim Milligan, manager, of the Fogarty Lock and Safe Company, Dame Street. *Photograph: Dara MacDónaill*

Fogarty Lock and Safe Company
80 Dame Street, Dublin 2

The Fogarty Lock and Safe Company was set up in 1834 by a Mr Joe Fogarty, lock and gunsmith. He knew the business, which at the time involved working with guns, bell ringing, locks and safes. He knew how to run it, too, and the Fogarty premises in Crane Lane, off Dame Street, became a key part of the city's life.

The company was still in Fogarty-family hands when Edward Williams went to work there in 1916. It would take a while, but taking on that new, young employee was the beginning of the end of the Fogarty dynasty.

Edward Williams worked well and learned even better and, in 1929, opened his own place in Gardiner Street. By the time he closed down there in 1981 (on foot of a compulsory purchase order and following a fire) he'd already, in 1952, bought out the goodwill of his first employer's business. The Crane Lane premises and Dame Street shop, opened in 1981, became the hub of all his activities.

Today's company, still, and very deliberately, called Fogarty Lock and Safe Company, is owned by Edward's son, Michael, and his wife Elaine. Has been, in fact, since 1990, when Edward Williams finally retired. He died in 2000, aged 94, devoted to the end to the delicate and complicated intricacies of locks and their place in business.

Michael Williams inherited his father's enthusiasm for the world of locks. He admits to starting work "when I was about seven years old. We lived in Cabra West and I used to go into Crane Lane after school and deliver keys all over the place for my father. I knew the city inside out. Crane Lane was different in those days. It was cobbled and a horse and cart from CIÉ, Broadstone, what we called the "Heavy Crew", used arrive once a fortnight to collect safes. They had a terrible time on the cobbles; everything had to be manhandled – there were no vices or aids like today."

Fogarty's, he says, was the city's main locksmith for "at least 30 years. Locksmiths from all over Dublin would deliver keys to my father in the morning and collect them in the evening. He was a workaholic, working seven days a week and enjoying what he did. In those days a lot of keys were made by hand using very small files and ranged from large church-door keys to those for small safes."

The precision required took up a lot of his father's time but Michael Williams says it was a pleasure to watch his father at work. "He passed the skills on to me and I've likewise passed them on to my own three sons."

Michael Williams started working full-time for his father's company when he was 13 years old. "We were operating out of one small, upstairs room in Crane Lane at the time, paying 10/- a month in rent. My father was happy enough with that but I persuaded him and we got a second room for a rent of £1 per month. By 1969 we'd bought up the Crane Lane premises. My father, and Fogarty before him, had concentrated on cutting keys and repairing safes. I wanted to supply safes and move on to other things."

Fate, and a fire, was to play another role in the company's expansion. "In 1987 there was a bad fire in Crane Lane," Michael Williams explains. "We got temporary premises behind the original building and in time were able to buy that too.

"This gave us a huge space in which to do all we wanted to, as well as which we had the frontage on Dame Street. It just all came together nicely."

Aspirations are high in the family for a final rounding of the circle. Crane Lane itself was de-cobbled and has now been cobbled over again.

The Crane Lane premises were sold for development purposes in 1999 but the hope is, according to Elaine, "that we can keep the old tradition alive" by reopening the original, now revamped, shop in the lane.

The company also has a showroom, offices and workshop at Damastown Industrial Estate, Mulhuddart, Dublin 15. This is where Elaine Williams is mostly to be found, though she admits to "hopping between the two premises". A director of the company, she looks after the business of credit control. The Williams' sons, Michael Jr, Wesley and Keith, are all locksmiths with other specialities – Keith is a safe engineer, Wesley a sales representative and Michael works in accounts.

Three grandchildren, two girls and a boy, will ensure, Elaine Williams says, "that a fourth generation is on line to continue the business. They're showing an interest already."

In the late 1960s, Michael Williams began taking on work for the Gardaí and insurance companies. "I became involved with *Garda Patrol* and later the crime-prevention programme, looking at new locks coming on the market and, when the guards were interested, mounting them on a display unit to be used for showing how the locks worked and to give advice on security."

Fogarty Lock and Safe Company moved smartly, too, to take on the IT world. They introduced the Mul T Lock hi-tech master key stem here and their present workload includes looking after the security needs of banks, hotels, pubs and households, supplying everything from bullet-proof doors to IT Fall-Out Rooms – bomb-, fire- and bullet-proof rooms used to safeguard data of all kinds.

Michael Williams Snr says he's never thought of doing anything else. "I was born into the business and every day I look for something new on the market that we can do. We've come on a lot. We're big into safes, fire protection cabinets, data protection cabinets and master keying systems for licensed premises, hospitals and museums.

"We also do exports: systems to South Africa and safes to west Africa, Scotland, Paris and the Congo. We've a name in the business internationally – we're not just known around Dublin any longer."

Dermot (left) and Tony Healy of James Healy (Brass Founders Engineers) Ltd, at their workplace in Pearse Street.
Photograph: Dara MacDónaill

James Healy (Brass Founders (Engineers) Ltd

51–54 Pearse Street, Dublin 2

Brass and bronze are on a downturn, their decorative place in our lives taken by other metals, by plastics, by the disposable.

Down but not out, not by a long way. James Healy (Brass Founders Engineers) Ltd, located at 51–54 Pearse Street, know a thing or two about brass and bronze and other metals. The company is where those seeking the best have been going since the middle of the last century for handcrafted stair rods, mat frames, hand rails, candlesticks, church, hotel, airport and office fittings. James Healy Ltd is the firm which made the cross for the top of Knock Cathedral (it has a steel core), racing's Power's Gold Cup (brass-plated in gold) and the Abbey Theatre's aluminium canopy. More recently, it was responsible for the much-admired ornamental lights in Cork's Aula Max and the reredos in Armagh Cathedral.

Though the path to their door is well known, the numbers travelling it are less than they used to be. Things have changed, though this is more a question of emphasis. James Healy Ltd are still actively involved in general metal fabrication and restoration, the old part of the business. But they are increasingly concentrated on their role as non-ferrous-metal distributors and stockists of engineering materials.

The company is also on the move, consolidating and heading for the JFK Industrial Estate off the Naas Road.

Traffic's at the root of it, as it is for so many fleeing the city centre; traffic, parking and the difficulties people have getting to Pearse Street. James Healy Ltd will "keep a presence" in their time-worn location, probably in the form of a showroom. "We'll feel the loss," Tony Healy, doyen of the eight family members in the business and company secretary, admits. "We'll feel the loss … but it's not practical any more."

Time was there was another, more intimately vibrant, life in the company's part of Pearse Street. It had its hey-day in the 1850s, when the area's great Georgian townhouses were built and when, according to Tony Healy, "there was a hive of industry in the area generally — small shops and businesses and craftmakers".

By the 1870s McLoughlin's, an older and equally renowned brass and bronze casting and crafting company, had amalgamated and adapted 51–54 Pearse Street for their own needs. Behind today's Georgian facade there's a vast and cavernous workshop and storage, atmospheric and cluttered and with more than a hint of times past about it.

James Healy Ltd, by a circuitous route, arrived in the Pearse Street buildings in 1969. Tony Healy, wryly humorous and with some help from his brother, Dermot, tells the story of the family business like it was.

"My father, James, started the business in Cumberland Street in 1948," he says. "He lived off Meath Street and had served his time in Dockrell's in Ship Street. In the early days he did a lot in the ironmongery trade. Gradually he made a way into the building trade, into a broad cross section of work involving brass, steel, aluminium and such. The 1950s and 1960s were good for us because the building trade was expanding. I came into the business in 1964 after doing accountancy."

But change was on the way, even then. McLoughlin's moved from Pearse Street to Jamestown Road — then fell victim of Vatican II and the subsequent decline in church demand for elaborate casting in bronze and brass. The place had been empty for a while when James Healy, according to his son, "took a gamble which proved good and bought it. We moved in 1969. My father died the same year."

Tony Healy, for a while, was on his own with about 20 employees. He's been joined, over the years, by his siblings: Dermot, who has an engineering background; Brian, who manages the warehouse on the Naas Road; Barry, who looks after the workshop and liaises with architects and foremen on site; Rita, who does the accounts; Jim, in sales; and Cormac, also involved in the Naas Road depot. A third generation of Healys is represented by Dermot's son, John, who has come aboard to look after the IT and computer end of things.

James Healy Ltd also, over the years, was responsible for landmark brass and bronze works: the ambo in Galway Cathedral, the brass-clad pillars at the entrance to the IFSC, the AIB eagle, the bronze lights, stairs and brass panelling in the Treasury Building.

Along the line there was diversification. "The jobbing end of things became too labour-intensive and competitive. There are smaller, specialised firms who can do it cheaper so we diversified from fabricating to the metal supply end. We had been making everything – even manhole covers for sewers – in brass and bronze because steel would have rusted. It all changed in a short space of time, galvanised steel and such taking over. The future lies with small, specialised business – some of the bigger names in the building trade are setting up their own fabrication plants."

A man who calls a spade a spade, Tony Healy says that, though the company was "reasonably buoyant" in the early 1970s, they didn't want it to become too big, so "began cutting back on the employment level".

Today's company has a work-force of 20 people, including family members. "We've been cutting back on the fabrication end of things since the 1980s and expanding the supply end," Tony explains, "the likes of brass tubes, axles, flats, sheets sections and so on. We didn't want to get too big, wanted to keep the firm small, compact and specialised. We're more interested in doing the job well than going into the mass production end."

James Healy Ltd opened a Cork depot in the 1980s and one in Limerick in the 1990s. In the mid-1990s they set up the depot into which they are consolidating off the Naas Road.

For all this, Tony Healy insists, wryly humorous, that "we didn't see the Tiger. He didn't even pass up the road. We were doing better in the 1960s and 1950s than in Celtic Tiger Ireland. Even though we're smaller than we should be, comparatively speaking, I see great hope for the future."

As a family, and as workers together, the Healys get on. "We have frictions and disagreements," Tony says. "We're all directors and, when Dermot and I leave, our younger siblings will take responsibility. I can't see either of us retiring, however."

Barry Healy is the company's craftsman and has three craftsmen working with him as well as a craftsman/polisher and driver/helper. Private individuals still come looking for stair rods (out of fashion since the 1970s but making a comeback) as well as for mat frames. Tony Healy says he's got "very little" brass in his own home, says he sees enough of it every day.

James Healy Ltd, he says, "will always cater to restoration and preservation projects, always be interested in quality craftwork in specialised areas."

He also says of the eight family members involved that "we're Jacks (and a Jill) of all trades and masters of none. We're all willing and able and don't strictly segregate responsibility."

Joe Murtagh with his son Colin at their city centre hardware business. *Photograph: Alan Betson*

Murtaghs

Over the years since 1887, Murtaghs, for generations in Blackhall Street, Dublin 7, and now based in Ashbourne, Co. Meath, have grown, diversified and kept their roots firmly in their beginnings. Originally corn merchants, they've moved energetically into agricultural hardware and the supply of stable equipment.

The twenty-first century has brought the greatest change of all. The recent expansion to Ashbourne means Murtaghs are now the proprietors of a retail/office park and residential development on Main Street, of which their hardware and DIY superstore is the lynchpin.

All a long way from the day in 1887 when Stephen Murtagh set up corn merchants Stephen Murtagh & Sons in Middle Abbey Street. A long way, too, from the company's move to Blackhall Street in 1930 and its acquisition, in the same year, of premises in Ashbourne. The style of things thus established, growth continued until, in 1969, Murtaghs moved into the agricultural hardware business. For more than 20 years now the company's been building up the stud and stable equipment and hardware supply side of things.

Colin Murtagh, great-great-grandson of the founder, fills in the historical gaps. "We were simple grain merchants to begin with," today's managing director says, proudly immodest. "Then in 1915 the original Stephen's sons, Joe and Stephen II, joined the company. They were the ones who engineered the move here to Blackhall Street, to what was then a stable, in 1930."

"The company was doing well but the move was necessary for reasons of space, transport and expansion. They were flying back then, relatively speaking. You can see it in the accounts. I've got every set from 1919 on." He produces these casually, spreads them on the desk. "We've also got a book with the old recipes for animal feed and such."

We take a look at both, lamenting together times when a horse could be sold for £20, when the income tax bill for the year amounted to £94.9.3d, the net profit was £1,033. 10. 11d and a horse and dray could be bought for £140.

"We began as provender millers and grain merchants," Colin Murtagh explains. "We made up feed for poultry, dry food for beasts." Murtaghs had a particular and special renown for their Murvita product, a chicken and hen feed which they began manufacturing in the 1920s and sold nationwide. Murtaghs' MD produces another historical document, running a finger admiringly over the drawings for the suction trunk and aperture for hand feeding on the blueprint for the machine responsible for making Murvita. It has the look of a Heath Robinson contraption about it and was in use until the late 1970s.

Colin Murtagh goes back to tracing the family and business history. His father's generation, he says, "hit the company in 1940 when Brendan Murtagh became managing director. He remained so until 1995, when he died. His brother, Donal, had come into the business in 1943 and my father, Joe, had joined in 1950. My father took over in 1995 and retired in 2001 (after 51 years) and that was when I became MD."

He explains how the emphasis changed in the business "in the early 1980s. Before that we were doing 80 per cent grain and 20 per cent hardware. That balance has totally flipped and we're now doing 20 per cent grain and 80 per cent hardware. We supply all of the parks around Dublin with tree stakes and so on, and general hardware to such as the Law Society and Dublin Corporation. We also supply stable equipment to Coolmore Stud in Tipperary, which is the biggest stud in the county."

He grins and simultaneously gives an apologetic shrug. "Foot and mouth was good for us, gave us a huge turnover in disinfectant and foam mats. It's an ill wind, as they say; these things happen every 20 or 30 years and you get a hit on sales."

Today's MD joined the company in 1998 to give his father a helping hand after the death of his uncles (Don died the year before Brendan, in 1994). "I'd been a printer for 10 years before that," he says, "and hadn't really thought about coming into the business."

But come into it he did, wholeheartedly. In 1999 he devised the plan for the Ashbourne development and, since taking over in 2001, he's upped the marketing of the company, producing glossy brochures.

Some things don't change, however. Employees incline towards the long-term on the Murtagh payroll. Of the dozen or so office, sales, management and truck-driving staff, at least three have given a lifetime's service: accountant Brendan Barry has been with the company since 1974; hardware manager Paddy Gorman has been there since 1968; and Damien White, the manager in Ashbourne, has been there since 1973.

Brendan Barry's memories are evocative of an earlier Dublin. "We used sell to every pigman in every street in the city at one time," he says. "They were known as swill men, and piggeries, as well as the cattle market, used be located all around this area. Pigs, cattle, sheep, we had the whole lot around here. We used get beet and pulp nuts [for feeding cattle and sheep] from the sugar company and tractors would be waiting the full length of the street to take them from the truck when it arrived.

"The piggeries around would have supplied all the butchers before the EU regulations came in."

Part, at least, of that specialised area of the company's business lives on – Brendan Barry says that "Murtaghs stock the widest variety in Ireland of dog food."

Customers stay with Murtaghs too. Micky Sheridan, one of the last of the city's pig farmers, says he's been coming to Murtaghs since shortly after they opened in Blackhall Street.

"I was the youngest farmer on the streets of Dublin. I started life very early," he laughs, "when I went, underage, to work as a carter for Dublin Corporation."

He moved on to pig farming, remembers the Emergency and "what a great minister Sean Lemass was; his self-sufficiency plan opened up things for us. For a four-mile area around here there used be 5,000 to 6,000 pigs, all needing to be fed. Murtaghs would give you the best of pig meal.

"The pig business was going nice until it started to wither out about 20 years ago with the new EU regulations. I've only one sow at home now in Bohernabreena and 17 pigs. When they're gone," he says ominously, but not meaning a word of it, "I'm gone."

The move to Ashbourne was dictated as much by the changing city as it is by the company's growth and needs. "It became very difficult to work in Blackhall Street," says Murtagh. "Building and the new road system meant we were, to a degree, driven out of the city.

"It was difficult to get trucks in from Ashbourne and load and unload. It was also difficult for customers to get to us – the one-way system was disastrous as far as we were concerned. Consolidating to Ashbourne won't, hopefully, change the business too much.

"The contract work we do supplying the likes of the county councils, Garda headquarters and the prison service is predominantly done on the phone. There was a population of about 200 when we first moved into Ashbourne; today it's more like 20,000."

Sean Burgess (left), mum Noreen and brother Padraig in the Burgh Quay
headquarters of Lafayette. *Photograph: Bryan O'Brien*

Lafayette Photography

11 Burgh Quay, Dublin 2
(now at Sandyford Industrial Estate, Co. Dublin)

The 150-year-old Lafayette story is best told in pictures. Sepia-toned subjects gaze into the middle distance: there's the elegant, posed hauteur of Yeats and Countess Markievicz; a frisky G.B. Shaw; a dour Queen Victoria and her better-humoured son King Edward.

Lafayette was the company which snapped the only, and famous, profile of Patrick Pearse, as well as the best-known portraits we have of de Valera, Lady Gore Booth, Dan Breen, Cathal Brugha, Mrs Patrick Campbell, James Connolly, Count John McCormack – the list goes on and on.

Not just portraits either. Lafayette Photography was on hand to record the scene in the GPO just before evacuation in 1916.

The glass negative of the Pearse photo, a corner broken off, still exists, along with many others. So do customer books with famous signatures and comments, business records and advice, frames, furniture and references in *Ulysses*. It's a living, working museum, the business of taking photographs still fuelling its existence.

Sean Burgess, who runs and is today's Lafayette Photography, deeply and affectionately appreciates the company's past and glory days. He knows, too, how to ensure it has a present and future.

In the first-floor studio and portrait room at 11 Burgh Quay, looking over a Liffey as complacently snot-green as ever described by Joyce, he tells the Lafayette story – with more than a little nostalgia, as the company was preparing to move (and has since moved) to a new premises.

He's ably abetted by his mother, Noreen, a retired schoolteacher and no mean wielder of facts.

It's a lush room, all velvet-draped screens, blue brocaded seating and ancient (as well as modern) tripods. "The chair I'm sitting in is hundreds of years old," Sean pats carved wooden arms appreciatively, "and the couch you're sitting on, 100 years old." The chair is visible in the corner of a portrait of de Valera, itself hanging opposite a glorious 10-foot by 5-foot picture of restaurateur Patrick Guilbaud contemplating an egg. History meeting the contemporary, without a clash in sight.

The Lafayette story began in 1853 when pioneering photographer Edmund Lauder opened a daguerreotype studio in Henry Street. Things went well. So well that his eldest son, James Stack Lauder, opened a second studio at 30 Westmoreland Street in 1880, trading under the name "Lafayette, late of Paris" and using James Lafayette as a professional name. (The company later moved to 22 Westmoreland Street.)

As a marketing ploy, the "Lafayette" name worked, helping when James put his work and prize-winning medals on show around the world. Lafayette soon became Ireland's premier portrait studio and when Princess Alexandra visited Ireland in 1885 it was James who took her picture.

A couple of years later, when he snapped Queen Victoria in Windsor and at the same time got himself a Royal Warrant as Her Majesty's Photographer in Dublin, business was nicely consolidated. By 1900, he'd opened branches in Glasgow, Manchester, Belfast and, most prestigious of all, New Bond Street, London.

The early Lafayette portraits which made the company's name were highly glossed, chocolate-brown collodion prints on decorative mounts. Lillie Langtry got the treatment in 1902 and so, in a commemorative album in 1897, did the Devonshire House Fancy Dress Ball. At the height of its fame the Lafayette studios photographed kings, queens, emperors, empresses, viceroys and vicereines.

Full of appreciative glee, Sean Burgess shows a 1930s handbook on how to run a successful business, Lafayette style. There are no margins for error or for humour. "The problem of profits is altogether in the hands of the branch to give away, lose or make," it declares, advising against, "giving out work without payment to people of no credit" or "accepting cheap orders from monied people". Sean, with humour, says: "it explains why we lasted so long. I follow the advice. We get prepaid or paid on the day we do colleges. If you don't get paid on a person's graduation day, you won't ever get paid."

Just 100 years on from its beginnings in Henry Street, when Lafayette closed its studios in Britain and decided to close down in Ireland too, employee John Anthony Burgess entered the picture. John A. — whose passion for photography was such that it was said of him that he slept with a tripod — made his employers an offer. They accepted and, together with his sister Kathleen and Kathleen's friend Mary Froggatt, he bought Lafayette's lock, stock and barrel. "He bought the names, goodwill, negatives — the lot," says Sean.

The post-1952 Lafayette Photography continued to take portraits but also, Sean explains, "did a huge amount of copy work, as in making pictures from old prints. Dad did huge business too with all the religious organisations and schools. Blackrock College, Wesley, Rockwell, Clongowes, St

Michael's, 30 schools in all. And with the seminaries, every one in Ireland. And the IRFU. It was a good business.

"Dad was a superb portrait photographer but had no interest in money. Kathleen and Mary looked after that end of things. He had to get as close to perfection as possible with every picture. I remember him reprinting 800 prints taken in Rockwell College at five in the morning because of a small flaw."

Noreen Burgess, rearing a family of five children (two girls and three boys) in the Mount Merrion family home, took no part in the business but Sean and his younger brother Padraig helped out as boys growing up. It was Noreen who found Joyce's reference to Lafayette in *Ulysses* for me. There it was, on page 573 of the Penguin edition, a description of Lafayette of Westmoreland Street as "Dublin's premier photographic artist".

Kathleen Burgess and Mary Froggatt moved on in time and John A. bought them out. When Sean left school (officially) at 16 he joined the company. "That was in 1970," he says. "Padraig, who is younger than me, joined in 1974." An earlier attempt of Sean's to join the company had been thwarted. "I ran away from boarding school in New Ross," he admits, laughing, "because I wanted to help my father photograph Ireland playing England in Lansdowne Road."

In 1986 Sean opened his own place in Baggot Street. "The idea was that I would take college pictures," he says. "I set up as Sean Burgess trading as Lafayette. My dad retired in 1993 – he was taking pictures until he was 81 years of age. He died in 1995. Padraig took over and ran the place for about three years and then, when I bought the name, Padraig took some lines of the business and I took others. The move to Burgh Quay happened in 1988. We now run our own businesses: he's Padraig Burgess Photography; I concentrate on portraits and on the contracts we have for third-level colleges. We never have a complaint. We spend a fortune doing the job properly."

UCD, in 1973, was its first, and still main, contract, a development from the days when that college's students used come in to be photographed. Things are going "really well," Sean says, becoming rhapsodic about a business high point on 15 November 2003. "I'll never forget the date! We did seven different college graduations on that day, from Letterkenny to Carlow. We'd up to six photographers in any one college at a time, plus admin staff, dressers, make-up, sales, scroll-framing people. We'd 130 people working altogether. The phones started at 6.15 in the morning and I finished work at 2.15 the next morning. We take on between three and five new college contracts every year. Education," he beams, "is the most important thing in the new Ireland. That's why I left school at 16! I've been in the university of life ever since."

The Pen Corner, College Green. *Photograph: Bryan O'Brien*

The Pen Corner

12 College Green, Dublin 2

For John FitzGerald the "nicest things" about his line of business are the personal contacts and customers who tell him things he doesn't know.

He meets quite a few of the latter: people who are particular about the kind of pen they use tend to be enthusiastically involved with life around them. A bit like John himself, the third-generation Fitzgerald to run The Pen Corner, that quietly enduring, where-would-we-be-without-it landmark oasis on College Green.

Pens, people and planning exercise John FitzGerald's passions. Pens and people because they're his business, planning because of what the lack of it has done to the medieval and commercial centre of city on The Pen Corner's doorstep.

The shop hasn't changed much, he says, since his great-aunt Florence FitzGerald set it up with her husband in 1927. Not physically, anyway, though pens and pen technology have changed.

The building which houses The Pen Corner has been on College Green since the late nineteenth century. Originally owned by life insurance companies, it went into private ownership in 1986. The first retail tenant was the AA, when it followed automobiles into Ireland in the early years of the twentieth century. When it moved out, John FitzGerald's Aunt Florrie and her husband moved in and set up The Pen Corner.

Florence FitzGerald and Paddy O'Brien met each other while working in Hely's of Dame Street. Encouraged by a benign Mr Hely, who saw an opening in what he saw as the new technology of fountain pens, they started their own business. When Paddy O'Brien died in 1933 his wife carried on; she did so until she died in 1982.

Long before that, according to John, she'd achieved definite *"grande dame"* status. He remembers her as "very sociable. Her milieu was the world of Jammet's and the old Brown Thomas. When her husband died his shares were dispersed to his family, who chose not to take an active part in things.

"Everyone knew my aunt as Florrie and she ran the business with the support of two people. One was her brother, George, who was my grandfather and an accountant and who gave her business advice. The other was a lady called Ms Dunlop, a really hard-working woman and interesting character, who managed the shop while my aunt, as director, ran things from her office."

He puts his mind to remembering how things were in her day. "This was a classic, old-style shop with a bell and a small door. All sorts of people bought their pens here. Lord Killanin was a regular and friend of my aunt. He brought Prince Rainier and Princess Grace shopping here in the 1950s. Oddly, it's not writers who're fussiest about pens – they'll use anything – actors are particular, though, and so, these days, are rock stars."

Like the musician Kurt Cobain who dropped in, in the late 1980s, to buy odds and ends of stationery. John didn't know who he was until he signed his credit card.

Before all that, in the late 1920s, fountain pens were very much the new technology. "I suppose now we'd call them a lifestyle accessory," John grins. "In those days the shop only sold inks and fountain pens and some of the original and traditional suppliers are still going strong – companies like Parker, Watermans and Sheaffer. There are many more which have ceased to exist, though – the likes of Swan, Conway-Stewart and Onato are all gone."

The war years offer interesting anecdotes. "Nibs were made of gold and there was an embargo on gold during the war," John produces a curled and tapering piece of glass, "so Murano glass became a solution for a while." He shows how the glass nib was fitted, how the ink circled and flowed, then tells how his Aunt Florrie came up with a supply solution of her own just after the war. "Parker and the other companies in the UK were unable to supply gold nibs but gold was available in America. She went there on the *Queen Mary* and smuggled Sheaffer pens back under her skirts. Only 20 or 30 of them but they would have been a high-value item. She was instrumental in setting up the distribution of Sheaffer pens in Ireland."

John FitzGerald's father, Maurice, came into the business in 1946, an almost unimaginable career change for a man who'd fought with the British 8th Army in north Africa, followed on to Monte Cassino and took part in the liberation of Greece. He died, too young, in 1987.

Maurice FitzGerald was 24 when he came home from war. "He went on the road," John explains. "Aunty Florrie stayed in the shop while he imported pens and sold them around the country in the 1940s and 1950s. There wasn't a lot of business in those years and a lot of pen companies went to the wall. The biro came in then too, the first ever made of sterling silver and costing a week's wages. It meant we were selling new technology again!"

While Elizabeth FitzGerald, John's mother, gave up working with Max Factor to rear five children in Glasnevin, her husband Maurice introduced the country to Mont Blanc and Cross pens. Her sister-in-law, Florence, and Miss Dunlop continued to run the shop.

"Over the years Dad became more and more involved in the day-to-day running of the business," John explains. "When Florrie died it made sense to buy out the shareholders, so that's what he did and ran the business until he died, aged 67, in 1982." He allows himself a personally reflective moment. "It's odd," he admits, "being in the same geographical situation as my father, doing the same job and facing the same business situations."

John took over the shop in the mid-eighties, after taking a degree in art history and archaeology in TCD. The 1980s were "bad times" and he didn't make any major changes to the company. "Businesses which survive as long as this are, to a certain extent, recession-proof," he says.

"Then, too, pens sell when people are flush with cash and signing-off contracts. A pen is a high-value token to give." He is voluble, and clear, about the effects of the lowering of EU trade barriers, something of which he was originally in favour. "It used be I could phone a distributor in Stillorgan and an order would arrive next day. Now most come through the UK and returns and repairs have to go back there. It means, too, that we no longer employ as many people locally."

The Pen Corner employs three to four people these days. Service technician Pat Martin has been with the company since the late 1960s, Aileen Morin manages the shop and Grainne McHugh is a sales assistant. Part-time employees are taken on for seasonal work.

John Fitzgerald unequivocally laments changes to the city too. "The Central Bank happening was new vision, I suppose," he gives a dry laugh, "but the heart's been taken out of the working environment and the rest left to die. Temple Bar is worse than death! I don't even go any longer to its excellent art venues and don't quite see what their context is within the city."

As for pens and selling them: Cross, Parker, Watermans and Mont Blanc are still fine, solid brand names selling to a traditional customer base of professionals, doctors, legal and banking people. "Pens," John says, "tend to sell as prestige presents at one end of the market, while at the other end there are those who just love using fountain pens. We sell roller ball pens too, propelling pencils, biros, a small range of briefcases, social stationery. But," he is adamant, "the core of the business is still pens."

The most expensive item they sell is a limited edition Mont Blanc costing €4,920. There are 888 of them in the world. The cheapest is a drawing pencil costing €1. The Pen Corner does not, John says, sell cheap biros. He himself varies between using "a nice Mont Blanc and an auld biro". His siblings, when they need pens, come to the shop.

"I would very much like," he says as I leave, "to thank all the customers who keep us in business — and who tell me things I don't know!"

John (right) and Richard Beshoff, at Beshoff's fish-and-chip shop on Harbour Road, Howth.
Photograph: Dara MacDónaill

Beshoff

Fish-and-Chip Restaurant, Harbour Road, Howth, Co. Dublin

Sitting on the sea wall in Howth, gulls squalling and dogs sniffing hopefully at my fresh prawn breakfast, John and Richard Beshoff tell the story of their family and business.

It began with the sea, in the nineteenth century, when one Ivan Beshov fell foul of the mutinous and historic drama on the battleship *Potemkin*. In the years between, the ocean and its bounty have been omnipresent in the Irish Beshoff scheme of things – happily in a manner more benign than it was to Ivan Beshov, grandfather of them all.

The shrimp, and a couple of portions of fresh cod, have been brought to us from the Beshoff Bros fish-and-chip shop on Harbour Road, Howth, 200 yards away.

There's another, older shop on Vernon Avenue, Clontarf, and Beshoff's retail and wholesale fish selling outlet (run by Alan Beshoff) is just down the road. Franchised Beshoff chippers are to be found in Westmoreland and O'Connell streets.

But for now, we're talking about the original and, the brothers would say, best: the fish-and-chip shop set up by their grandfather, Ivan Beshoff, in 1922.

Grandfather Ivan Beshov was born in the Ukrainian town of Odessa. His career in the Russian Imperial navy ended when he became part of the famously mutinous crew on the *Potemkin*. He didn't go home after the mutiny, moving west, instead, across Europe until he fetched up on these shores sometime around 1914. The turbulent times caught up with him again here and he was interned in the Curragh, suspected of being a German spy.

Free again and undaunted he set up Russian Oil Products (ROP) but with the changing times he was, John says, "squeezed out of business". A survivor and a worker, and with good friends in the growing Italian community, he set up his first fish-and-chip shop in 1922 on Usher's Quay. He opened a second in the North Strand in 1938 and, when the bombs fell in 1941 and put paid to that business, opened yet another fish-and-chip shop on Sundrive Road, Kimmage.

Beshov had by now become Beshoff, and the Ivan part "John" to his friends. Ivan/John Beshoff met and married Noreen Mulcahy from Ballyporeen, Co. Tipperary (daughter of General Richard Mulcahy), and they together reared five sons and one daughter. This first generation of Irish Beshoffs included Thomas, Louis, Freddy, Ivan and Anastasia. The youngest, Anthony, married Kathleen Emmet and the pair of them became parents to a second generation of Beshoffs, rearing a family of boys that included John and Richard, as well as Tony, Gerard, Gary and Alan.

The business expanded and diversified over the years. Of the five sons reared by Ivan and Noreen, two, Anthony and Thomas, chose to go into the fish-and-chip shop business. A shop opened on the Malahide Road in 1958 has been sold but one set up on Vernon Avenue, Clontarf, in 1967 is still going strong.

Along with the relative newcomer, the nearby, stylishly tasty shop on Harbour Road which they opened in 1997, Vernon Avenue is these days run by the John and Richard Beshoff partnership.

They come from sturdy stock, the Beshoffs. Grandfather Ivan Beshoff died in October 1989, officially 104 years old. "He may have been older," John says, "because births in the Ukraine weren't registered in his day until children were three-to-four years old. Charlie Haughey visited him on his hundredth birthday and Granda, whose own alcohol tolerance was very high, poured him such a stiff whiskey Haughey had to discreetly dispose of it into a flowerpot. Granda never touched vodka, only Irish whiskey. And he always had a glint in his eye for a pretty girl."

The fish-and-chip business is unavoidably a family thing. Their mother Kathleen's grandfather came from the island of Malta to own a fish-and-chipper in Derry. "She was, and is, a great cook," John says.

He himself came home to the business after years abroad, travels in Brazil, the US, Thailand, Cambodia, winding his way back until, in the mid-1980s, he returned to the job he'd been doing since helping out in the Malahide Road shop after school.

The business has changed, and the Beshoffs aren't sure it's all for the best either. Richard explains: "These days EU and government legislation take a lot of control away from the owner. There's endless paperwork, about how food is cooked and amounts and temperatures. Ultimately the cost has to be borne by the consumer."

John gives an example of customer preferences. "People prefer to get tartar sauce from a container but we're obliged to give it in sachets. It's to do with the 'best before' law. Yet people survived and ate well before all of the EU food laws."

The Beshoffs are proud of the characteristics they say distinguish their business. "We're slightly more expensive," Richard admits, "but that's because we believe in a good quality product and the proof," he eyes my breakfast, "is in the eating." There is absolutely no disputing this.

"We're distinguished in that we cook in vegetable oils," says Richard. "Either sunflower or groundnut. We don't cook in fats. This cuts down on the fat content and calories in our average portion. Our average cod and chips, for instance, has about 850 calories. A Chinese take-away has about 1,700 calories and a McDonald's Big Mac meal has 1,200 calories."

He's gloriously immodest about the value they give for money. "Our success lies in this use of best oil and the fact that our portions are bigger; our seven–eight-ounce fillets are skinless and boneless and we use a light batter."

There's also the fact that they use a great deal of fresh fish. "This of course depends on the weather," John says, "and is affected too by the way the Irish fish quota has been reduced over the years."

Richard takes up the tale of fish supplies. "It's become a more global thing," he says. "I got hoki in from Chile yesterday. It's a lovely white fish, a bit like cod, and becoming very popular. We get hake from Cape Town in South Africa. People are eating more fish than ever, since meat's been getting such a bad press."

Other things have changed too. "The traditional fish-eating day used be Friday," John remembers, "but Sunday's our busiest day now."

Beshoffs, in the 1960s, were selling wild salmon and chips for 2/9d. "Our father had a trawler for a while in the 1980s and a couple of retail fish shops too. We learned a lot from all of that — you could say we grew up with fish," John says. "We certainly know the difference between fresh and fresh." He looks enigmatic. "There's fresh and there's fresh, you know."

Italians buying in the Howth shop in the summertime favour salmon and calamari; French customers go for lemon sole and scampi; the English prefer haddock, chips and mushy peas. The Irish favour fresh cod and long ray. "But it's changing," Richard says. "There's a home demand growing for haddock and hoki."

The Beshoffs are unequivocal. Good fish and chips are the great staple food of all time. "We operate on the basis of simple, unpretentious food, well-cooked and value for money portions," John says.

"We're the most underdeveloped brand name around," says Richard. "A big disappointment recently was not getting a shop opened in the airport because of business complications. It's been a hard graft over the last few years. Working 10-to-12-hour days is not uncommon, with seven-day weeks over the summer. But we're planning to open nationwide in the next few years." John is more cautious about this, but doesn't disagree.

The cod and shrimps go down a treat. Old ways are proven in the eating — and the original is still the best in Beshoff terms.

Peter Flanagan of Flanagans of Buncrana, Mount Merrion. *Photograph: Dara MacDónaill*

Flanagans of Buncrana

Furniture Company, Mount Merrion, Co. Dublin

Flanagans of Buncrana has been charting the change in the nation's needs and taste in furniture and design for almost 60 years now. Since 1946, to be exact, when Derryman Jim Flanagan gave up working for Great Universal Stores and Woolworths in Northern Ireland and set up a couple of furniture shops in Derry and Buncrana.

From little acorns great things grow.

Flanagans of Buncrana these days operates best in large spaces. Its Mount Merrion furniture emporium has 1,858 square metres (20,000 square feet) of rambling split-level floors. The furniture centre in Buncrana has 8,732 square metres (94,000 square feet), the biggest such in the country according to Peter Flanagan who, as a director with his brother Brian, should know about these things.

They're also a company that likes to occupy buildings with links to the past. The Buncrana centre was once the home of Fruit of the Loom; their Dublin outlet was once the much-loved Stella Cinema.

Emporium is the only word for the Flanagan set-up in Mount Merrion – emporium in the grand and dazzling sense used by the Victorians for a centre of commerce. You can wander up, down, in and around the antique showroom and piano department, rug department and classic-furniture showroom, bed department, curtain gallery and more.

Peter Flanagan, the six-foot two-inch self-described "baby of the family", is a man who wears his roots firmly on his sleeve. His accent is pure Donegal, his philosophy securely based in a sense of continuity and on where he and the family come from. He tells the Flanagan story with an ear to detail and an eye to the future.

There is a business and entrepreneurial gene common to both sides of the family. "My grandfather dealt a little in antiques in Derry," he says, "and my mother's people were the Barrs of Buncrana, who owned the Plaza Ballroom, started the Lough Swilly bus service and had the White

Strand Motor Inn [one of the first motels around] as well as Barr's Construction. All of those businesses are sold now except for the Plaza Ballroom."

The good news about the Plaza is that Brian Flanagan has managed, at a cost of €1.4 million and with the help of a group of local people, to save it for use as a much needed Local Youth Community Project. But *sin scéal eile*, as they say in Donegal and elsewhere.

May and Jim Flanagan had four children. Brian was their first born. Then came Joan, Edward and baby Peter. Brian and Peter are partners in the business and Edward, an accountant, gives his expertise part-time. Joan lives in Navan.

It was Brian who began growing the company to what it is today. He'd been studying philosophy in UCD when, in the early 1970s, he started to buy and sell British Army supply furniture. "He bought bunk beds, silver-plated cutlery, RAF officer supply furniture," Peter explains, "all of it of superb quality but functional. My father came up to Dublin at weekends to help and, because the one thing furniture needs is space, they took over the old Stella Cinema which had closed and was lying idle."

Within a few years the family had bought the Stella Cinema premises and, in a few more years, Brian Flanagan had built up a team of restorers and craftspeople in Buncrana.

"Today, in Buncrana, we've a 25/26-person strong team working in upholstery, cabinet making, French polishing, wood carving," Peter says. The move into the ex-Fruit of the Loom factory was "a dream come true" for the company. "Everything under one roof and on one level," Peter Flanagan says. "I only wish my father was alive to see it, to see the scale his little acorn has grown to!

"Still, it's really the Dublin market which keeps us going," Peter says. "The local market in Buncrana couldn't sustain us. We've a lot of loyal customers who come from all over the country."

Peter Flanagan came to Dublin in 1982 to work in the business for the summer. He'd intended studying law but found, very quickly, that retailing suited him better. He married Yvonne, a Dubliner, and they have four children, sons Michael and John and daughters Ellen and Isabelle. Brian Flanagan, who lives in Buncrana, has five children, one of whom, Andrew, has already joined the company.

"In 1982," Peter goes on, "we were only using the ground floor, which was basically a slope without the cinema seats. We've now as great a diversity of goods in the building as there were once films. In 1982, about 90 per cent of what we sold was antique and second-hand furniture. Then it was those with most money who came looking for second-hand bargains, wanting an investment and long-term value. The people with least money bought on credit to get lesser quality.

"What has changed is that people are now going for a more coordinated look in their homes as property values increase. We now work with interior designers and architects, both on domestic and contract work.

"Back in 1982, customers came because they needed something individual, a dining-room table or set of kitchen chairs. Now we're being asked to custom-make a solid cherrywood kitchen table to match similar presses, perhaps with painted legs, and chairs with black leather seats to match black, polished granite worktops. Things have gone full circle to nineteenth-century times, when a wealthy merchant class would go to cabinet makers and have pieces made for their homes."

Trading in second-hand furniture really ended, he says, because of low-price imports from the Far East. "We can now get a walnut Regency-style circular one-leaf extension table which will seat eight people and sell it for €595. That's a lower price than we were able to get a second-hand equivalent in the late 1980s. We have leather couches that can be cheaper than the cost of recovering a couch."

Flanagans has developed the business in other ways too. Its designers have helped customers completely furnish homes bought in places such as Spain, Portugal and the south of France – and the company will ship the lot out so "people can arrive, walk in and start living in their new home. We find we're more and more involved in project-managing furnishing problems," says Peter.

For 20 years Flanagans opened for business on Sundays. "We found we were becoming slaves to the business, so in 2000 we went for a six-day week with a late night on Thursday. Our turnover dropped and it took us 12 months to catch up but it was worth it. The quality of life has improved for everyone involved with the shop."

Flanagans has two interior designers in its Dublin showroom who will advise on anything from a living-room to an apartment block. In its classic-furniture showroom, Flanagans sells reproduction furniture sourced in "the best furniture fairs in the world. We've such a diversity of choice here that our interior designers and sales team can customise any project to suit."

Peter concludes: "It's always a challenge to pass a business on to the next generation – they have to be inspired and enthused." For now, at any rate, neither quality is in short supply in Mount Merrion.

Dorans Barber Shop, Rathmines: pictured are owner Robert Feighery (left) and barber Malcolm Lewis (right) with Jimmy Doran (sitting), son of the original owner, who worked there for 68 years. *Photograph: Dara MacDónaill*

Dorans Barber Shop

38 Castlewood Avenue, Rathmines, Dublin 6

Jimmy Doran and Robert Feighery are an unlikely pair. A 60-year gap in their ages apart, they're as one on most things. Both have a passion for history and the continuity of things well done, a belief that business should be personal and that people are what matter. Most of all, though, they share a passion for a particular old-style barber shop in Rathmines.

Which is why, and how, Dorans, the traditional barber shop on Castlewood Avenue, has become the place to go in Rathmines for hot-towel shaves, a good cut and a convivial service second to none.

Dorans was opened in Castlewood Avenue on 2 January 1912 by James Doran, Jimmy's father. He paid £52 per year rent for the entire building and, for 20-odd years, before moving up the road to Oakley Road, he and Mrs Doran reared four daughters and two sons in the rooms overhead.

Today's shop has the sense, if not the reality, of that first establishment.

Not over-large, it has a polished wood floor, black painted wood, a scattering of historical memorabilia, a couple of wooden benches and a large window on to the passing world outside. With just two wash-hand basins, this is never going to be conveyer-belt hairdressing.

The hours of business too are fairly traditional: 9 a.m. to 6 p.m. Monday to Friday, and 9 a.m. to 5 p.m. on Saturdays – although Mr Doran points out that in his day opening hours were 9 a.m. to 7.30 p.m. on weekdays and 9 a.m. to 9 p.m. on Saturdays.

In 1930, a shave cost 4d and a haircut 10d. By the 1950s this had rocketed to 2/- for a haircut. A hot shave in 2004 costs €15.

Mr Doran doesn't work in Dorans anymore. He just visits a couple of times a week to chew the fat and see how new owner Mr Feighery is getting on. He's delighted with him and says the business couldn't be in better hands.

Mr Feighery, cutting heads, taking appointments and getting on with things, agrees. Dorans is a sociable place, a meeting point for men and big boys, where the chat is of football, old times, the state of the world and Rathmines – aspects appreciated widely enough for Dorans to be fast developing a fashionable cachet.

Mr Doran tells the Doran barber-shop story. "I was born upstairs in 1916," he says. "I'm not a Dubliner, though. I'm a Rathmines man. The oldest one around, they say, although I'm not saying it myself. Dublin didn't come in here, to Rathmines, until 1930. Rathmines Urban District Council used make its own electricity until then."

He produces a bundle of electricity meter reading cards, dated from 1912 onwards, requesting all queries to a Mr G.F. Pilditch M.I.E.E. at the Electricity Works in the Town Hall.

"I was 68 years working here," Mr Doran goes on. "Came in at 14 years and only gave up work in 1998. I started work here in 1930. I left school in Westland Row in the July and on 14 September, my fourteenth birthday, joined a hairdressing class in Kevin Street, where I learned how to do ladies and gents.

"My mother was a Rathmines woman but my father was a city man, came from Dublin. He often told me how Padraig Pearse got his last haircut here before he went to fight in 1916. His brother Willie, too. We've the chair they sat in at home."

He has the proof, too, in a picture of a large, old wooden barber chair. "There's not a mark on it," he says proudly. "My grandchildren sit on it to use their computers."

He recalls the hours he worked, "my God, they were long", how "a shave was a great thing in those days", the fun of his years on The Irish Hairdressers Committee and the cutting competitions in the Mansion House.

But he's keen to include Mr Feighery, "cutting the heads of the kids of the guys I cut 30 years ago," he says.

Mr Feighery took over Dorans barber's in 2002. He'd been in the business for 11 years at that stage and says "this shop and its history always attracted me".

He adds: "Jimmy and his brother sold up four years ago and when I heard it was coming up for sale again I jumped at it. It was fading a bit between myself and Jimmy but I did it up, changed the front — you couldn't see in before — and freshened things up and put a bit of life back into it.

"We only do two customers at a time and the hot-towel shaves are getting very popular. Wedding parties come in for them, groomsmen and the like. Guys like to treat themselves and often their girlfriends will buy them gift vouchers.

"It's the best hangover cure you can get. Clears the head completely! In Jimmy's day, of course, people had a hot shave every day.

"The main thing is this is a traditional haircut and shave, a traditional gent's barber shop. We don't do colour or anything like that."

Customers come and go and the chat — between them and old friends calling to see Mr Doran — is mighty. After a while Mr Doran resumes the tale of his days.

"When the Beatles came in all the fellas kept the hair long," he remembers. "We were lucky with the crowd we had coming in but over 200 hairdressing workers went out of business. We kept going and we came up again, by God.

"Robbie's doing well now. I was very glad to see a fella like him getting the business. He'll do well."

He remembers the rooms upstairs and the eight of them living there, how the number 18 tram used go past the door ("it's the 18 bus now") and that the cost of a journey from Terenure to the GPO was 3d.

"There were a lot of individual shops in Rathmines in those days: Findlaters, Magee's, Gilbey's and Lee's. Lee's was a lovely shop, lovely. I often think of it.

"I remember the Emergency years well. Tea and sugar were rationed and a terrible lot of people used come over from England and the North of Ireland for a bit of grub and that; things weren't great for them. We were all right in the shop. We kept going grand. It used be only number one and two blades but it's a different trade now, anything goes.

"There was a bit of trouble in the trade in the fifties and sixties when prices went up to 2/6 for a haircut in the big shops in the city, the likes of Prost at the top of Stephen's Green and on Grafton Street and in Jewels, which was opposite Prost on Kildare Street. They'd awful old snobs of customers who started coming here because we were only charging 2/-.

"We had such craic here over the years! The things we did! I missed it when I retired but I'm all right now."

His wife Cora died in the mid-seventies and he's got one son and grandchildren. He sees great changes in the way people live. "They have something now, they're well dressed. In the old days people had nothing. The old-age pension used to be 7/6d. When I think of it."

He's had enough of the telling and encourages Mr Feighery to tell his story. Mr Feighery says he was 16 when he started in a ladies' hairdresser's. "I went into gents' when I'd enough of the ladies, after working for a guy with shops in Fitzgibbon Street and in Finglas, Swords and Glasnevin. I went from there to the Merchant Barber's and from there to here.

"A barber shop suits me more. You can be more like yourself. You can't talk about football all day long in a ladies' hairdresser's."

He's married with one child and agrees with Mr Doran that they'll be having a Dorans centenary celebration in 2012. "That'll be some bash."

Mr Doran greets another customer. "Sometimes a fella comes in and says 'you cut my hair 30 years ago'. Some are fifth-generation customers and a number go back four generations. Famous people come and go but everyone's the same importance here. When a fella pays and goes out the door he's all the same!"

Mr Doran never wanted to do anything other than hairdressing. "I loved it," he says. "The way to a good life's in a sense of humour. Don't be a grouse … Some people are terrible cribbers and moaners. I've no time for cribbers."

Both he and Mr Feighery are unanimous about Dorans' future. People will always want haircuts: the prospects are good.

The Lansdowne Hotel, Pembroke Road. *Photograph: Eric Luke*

Lansdowne Hotel

27 Pembroke Road, Dublin 4

In 1948, when the B&B premises occupying 27–29 Pembroke Road became the Lansdowne Hotel, the going rate for a room with full Irish breakfast was 6d.

There were other differences from the way business is done today. Bathrooms and toilets were at the end of corridors and shared by up to four rooms; bedrooms were the original high, old Georgian ones; and breakfast (juice, bacon, egg, sausage, slice of toast and no choice about it) was served in the original dining-room. There was no choice about when guests might have their breakfast either; they were given a time the night before and that was it.

Margaret English, who deputy-manages today's Lansdowne Hotel, wasn't even born when all this was the norm. But she cares about what she does and has listened, and learned, about the earlier days and ways of the hotel business. "I came here in 1989 and things were very much as they always had been then," she says. "The really big changes, to this hotel and to regulations in the industry in general, have happened since then."

There was no restaurant in the early Lansdowne Hotel and breakfasts were cooked on a four-ring electric cooker in an everyday domestic kitchen. Margaret English remembers guests waiting, and waiting, for breakfast. She remembers, too, how Margaret Sherry, the long-time hotel cook, "refused to move with the times and use a proper catering cooker when it was installed. She continued on the old one, wouldn't use the new one at all. She just couldn't adapt and she left. It was funny in one way, and not funny in another. She was a lovely girl who just couldn't go with the change."

Frank Quinn, who owns today's Lansdowne Hotel, is interested in the building's past life too. He bought it in 1989 from the original Horgan family owners. Between them, he and Margaret English put the hotel's story together.

The building's real hostelry beginnings were in 1934 when the then owners, Comdt D.V. Horgan and his wife Mabel, set up a B&B. Frank Quinn tells how it happened. "The Horgan family originally owned number 29 and later bought the next door, number 27. When they began running their B&B there weren't many such businesses around. In 1948 they turned it into a hotel, adding a Co. Offaly licence to their existing Hatch Licence, so as to have a full hotel licence. Calling the place the Lansdowne was a marketing idea, because of the closeness to the rugby grounds. I bought it from them in 1989."

Margaret takes up the story. "Things hadn't changed a great deal from how they'd always been when I came to work as a receptionist in 1989," she says. "There were 22 bedrooms then, lovely, big old rooms with old furniture and a bathroom to every four rooms. When customers checked in and you told them their bathroom was at the end of the corridor they didn't even bat an eye. Most small hotels were the same; standards were so very different then to now. There was no grading, as such. Nowadays, of course, you have to have everything in place or you just don't get a grading."

The Lansdowne was always a good hotel, with a regular, return clientele. "The people who stayed here were well-heeled business types, most of them from Cork or Kerry. A charge of 6d for a room was expensive in 1948. The core business was corporate, still is. We've a man who has been coming from Cork to stay with us for more than 50 years. He's never stayed anywhere else. He was a commercial rep, as travelling salesmen were called. When they found a hotel they liked they stuck with it, never went anywhere else."

Contrary to mythological tales of wild and roguish salesmen, those who stayed in the Lansdowne were a sober lot. Margaret English remembers them "gathering in a room beside reception for a cup of tea and a chocolate biscuit at 10 p.m. every night. They went to bed early."

Every hotel worth its salt has had a long-time resident and the Lansdowne is no different. Margaret remembers Dorothy Browne well. "She was a local lady who owned a large house and had maids and servants attending her all of her life. As she got older she couldn't live on her own so she sold the house and moved in here and we looked after her. She was a nice lady with high standards. Her breakfast, dinner and tea had to be served at times dictated by her and if she didn't get them exactly as specified, she'd eat you! She was a very smart woman, investing in stocks and shares into her nineties and speaking several languages. She left here for a nursing home a few months before she died and was smart about that too. She knew she couldn't manage any longer when she couldn't get out of the bath one morning – but she'd the wit to let the water out."

Frank Quinn remembers how, in the way of things at the time, there was a large picture of Mabel Horgan in the lobby. "Comdt Horgan was quite a famous boxing referee. Their son Don Horgan was running the place when I bought it. Mabel Horgan told me how, at the time of All-Ireland matches, people used to come looking for cheap rooms, bring their own sandwiches and drink all night. Some things don't change. They're still looking for cheap rooms and drinking all night!"

Proving the customer always right, Frank remembers too what happened when a UK customer heard a ticking in his bag some years ago. "He was convinced someone had put a bomb in his case so we called in the army bomb-disposal unit and they blew up his case and wrecked the room. The ticking had been coming from his dictaphone! He came downstairs and said his room was a mess and could he have another. He got one."

Some 18 months after buying the Lansdowne, Frank Quinn set about a revamp, knocking the two houses into one at ground and first-floor levels and adding 18 *en suite* bedrooms. "Basically, I added a wing, opened up the interior floors and built new rooms," he says. "There's a preservation order on the façade so that's stayed exactly as it was. We're landlocked here, so can't expand any more. We added a basement function room and bar. The original dining-room has been extended and is now The Druid's restaurant. For some reason, the Lansdowne has always attracted both the famous and infamous. Bono is a regular in the restaurant and so is Van Morrison. We've had Nicole Kidman and Tom Cruise in here, as well as Jack Charlton, Alex Ferguson and Glen Hoddle."

Things have changed hugely in the hotel business as a whole, Margaret says. "Frank's way of running things is quite different to Don Horgan's, for instance. Don was quite traditional while Frank's style is to work with the staff. Frank's anything but traditional, and that's a compliment. Changes too in fire laws, in safety laws and to work regulations of all kinds mean we must be the most regulated hotel industry in western Europe. We pride ourselves on being a small hotel with a big welcome, with our bottom line a knowledge of the customer and what they want."

Gerald Kavanagh in Kavanagh's on Aungier Street. *Photograph: Cyril Byrne*

Kavanagh's
Sweet Shop and Newsagents,
10 Aungier Street, Dublin 2

Eddie Kavanagh, who knows a thing or two about it, says Kavanagh's in Aungier Street "may be the only real, loose sweet shop left in Dublin". It's the only one dating back to 1925, certainly, and no other comes to mind which sells, by the pound and from old-style jars, boiled sweets of a variety and suckable quality lodged in long-ago memories.

Kavanagh's sells chocolate satins, bulls' eyes, liquorice all-sorts, acid drops, clove rock, orange and lemon drops, jelly babies, jelly beans, cough tablets, sherbet lemons, bon bons (in toffee, strawberry and lemon flavours), aniseed balls. More than 150 varieties in all for a uniform price per quarter pound.

Sadly, Peggy's Legs are gone, discontinued in the early nineties.

Eddie Kavanagh is a young man with a purpose. He's determined, with his brother Finbarr, to keep and bring new life to the shop and business started by his grandfather, Joseph, in 1925. "The shop has come full circle and I've come full circle," he says, energy formidable and good humour constant. "I started behind the counter here, went off and learned more about retailing and now I'm back. The shop, which used to have tea rooms at the back and sweets in front, will in the future have convenience foods and sandwiches in the back and sweets to the front. A small convenience shop specialising in loose sweets, which is what it always was. The sweets will always be here too; they're the heritage of the shop."

His father, Gerald, and mother, Catherine, in their seventies now, will continue to be involved too. The shop has been their life. The building is listed and has a preservation order on it. Work in recent years has changed the floors and, somewhat, the counter, but has kept a huge, original beam and the windows. "The walls and ceilings can't be touched either," Eddie says. "We've just done a general renovation without changing the structure."

Together we admire the original glass case for displaying the sweets and the wooden trays which hold them. "They're like jewellery," Eddie says, and they are, the cough drops and bulls' eyes all shining and differently coloured. "My mother used to call the shop an adult paradise for sweets," Eddie says.

When Eddie Kavanagh's grandfather, Joseph Kavanagh, opened the Aungier Street shop in 1925 he already owned two other sweet shops, one in Moore Street and another down the road from Aungier Street, in South Great George's Street. "This one and the shop in Moore Street had tea rooms in the back," Eddie says. "Women weren't allowed into pubs at the time so tea rooms were where they could gather together socially. There used to be Irish-dancing lessons in the back too, and dance competitions were held there during the 1970s and 1980s."

Joseph Kavanagh came from Edenderry to Dublin. He married and had six children, a girl who died young and five boys, Desmond, Edmund, Albert, Tadgh (now deceased) and Gerald. "They all worked in the shops," Eddie says, "and all, in time, went their own way except for my father, Gerald, who was interested in the business. My grandfather passed on in the early 1960s and my grandmother in the late 1960s and the business came to my father."

The tea rooms lasted from the mid-1920s until the early 1960s. Eddie Kavanagh was born in 1968. Sweets, and retailing, were what he was born to and all he ever wanted to do but by the time he was born the shops in Moore Street and South Great Georges Street had gone.

"Things were not good during the 1940s, with the war and everything, so they closed," Eddie says. "Aungier Street was more viable so it was kept on. The back rooms here were used by various Fianna Fáil *cumainn* in the late 1920s and Eamon de Valera used to plot campaigns and election strategies there. Evidence of this and other events were found in the building in 1999 when workers were peeling away some of the walls. Old guns were found and different outfits from the time — they're all now in the National Museum. My mother also found an old convict outfit in the attic. It was in a tin box, wrapped in plastic.

"The Kavanagh family must have been Fianna Fáil because Sean Lemass used to come here in his time too."

Gerald and Catherine Kavanagh reared eight children in Crumlin while running the Aungier Street shop. Eddie is the fourth youngest. "I went to Synge Street and from the age of six worked behind the counter after school. The shop used to open from 9 a.m. until 8 p.m., Monday to Saturday, and I'd be here from 4.30 p.m. until 8 p.m."

Eddie's older brother Finbarr worked with Gerald and Catherine Kavanagh in the shop over the years and will work with Eddie developing the Kavanagh's of the future. "In the 1970s and earlier all of us worked in the shop, so as to keep costs down," Eddie says. "I remember my Uncle Tadgh, who lived upstairs, singing and entertaining customers in the shop. There was a bus stop outside the door then and people would come in simply to be entertained. Some of the customers would sing along with him."

He shakes his head at the wonder of it all. "Things have changed so much. People are flying around all the time now, no time to spare. The essence of life for me comes from here, from this shop. I'm very much aware of its traditions and very much want to keep the Kavanagh name going. To be realistic about this we've had to diversify."

He's learned the business well: nine years as a manager with SuperValu and before that working in fruit and vegetable stores around Leinster. He relishes having full-time responsibility for the family shop. "I've been in retailing since I was six years old and it's changed a lot in that time," he says. "This will be a return to the real routine of buying and selling and meeting people and building a business." He says he's seen the plans for the area, the redevelopment on the cards for Wexford, Aungier and South Great Georges streets and across to Grafton Street. "The mistakes that were made in Temple Bar won't be made," he assures. "The pedestrianisation there is a good thing but a lot of the quaint old shops there were weeded out. It's become a tourist attraction but is not true to itself."

Where do the sweets come from? "They're not buried out the back, anyway," he laughs, "which is what some people think. We buy, as we always did, from Waverley Confections who used to be in the Moore Street area but make the sweets off the Naas Road now. They're still a family business and so are one of our other suppliers, Shelton. They've moved out to the Robin Hood Industrial Estate off the Long Mile Road. Trebor supplies us too – they used to be family but have been taken over by Cadbury's."

The jars which used to be glass are now plastic, though are the same shape and size. When they were glass people used to come in to buy the jars themselves.

Eddie Kavanagh's father has lived through three currencies, worked a lifetime of six-day weeks. "In the 1920s, 1930s, 1940s, 1950s and 1960s people could buy everything here," Eddie says, "sugar, milk, tea – even snuff. The sweets then were sold in cones made out of newspaper. Over the years of working here I know the customers want a loose sweet shop. They like to see sweets weighed in front of their eyes and put into a brown paper bag. This is our niche in the market."

Oliver McCabe, manager of Select Stores, Dalkey. *Photograph: Alan Betson*

Select Stores

Time was, and it wasn't long ago either, when the staple national diet was based on the virtues and availability of carrots, parsnips, cabbage and potatoes.

All's changed, as our digestive systems and cookery columns and a certain fruit and vegetable shop in Dalkey village will attest. For a long time now, according to the McCabes of Select Stores, the staples have been selling side by side with the new basics – broccoli, avocados, peppers and salad in variety. "People want all sorts of fruits and exotics too," says Leo McCabe, "but they still want their fuel delivered and potatoes and onions to go on being a solid part of the family diet." His brother Oliver agrees, adding that, these days, Select Stores is looking at the nutritional value of certain popular fruit and vegetables.

Select Stores has an enviable spot from which to chart the social and dietary changes in Dalkey village. Central to the junction at the end of the village's main thoroughfare, it overlooks that main drag, as well as having shop fronts onto the vital arteries of Railway Road and Tubbermore Road. It's been there, growing all the time, since Paddy and Margaret (*née* Brady) McCabe opened in 1959.

It takes time to extract the word on Select Stores from the McCabe brothers, who run today's business. Customers come and chat and purchase and go. Everything's personal and nobody's rushed. Their sister Hilary, who helps on a part-time basis, flits through with her baby son. The story emerges at a Select Stores pace and while fruit and vegetables, eggs and briquettes fill customers' baskets and car boots.

Oliver, Leo and Hilary are three of the five children born to Paddy and Margaret McCabe after they bought the place in 1959. Oliver, the youngest, tells their story as he heard it. "My father came from Ballybay, Co. Monaghan, and my mother from Monaghan too. They met in Dun Laoghaire. My father had a newsagent's in Glasthule and my mother worked in a newsagent's on York Road, and my Dad, who was keen on my mother, went in there to buy a paper. They dated and got married and bought this place.

"There were three shops here then: a Gilbey's wine merchant's, a butcher on Railway Road and a fruit and veg shop. You can still see where the butcher hung his meat."

You can too — high along the ceiling of the part of the shop now selling lawn seed and garden needs, firelighters, briquettes and plant food. Select Stores, nothing if not eclectic, is also the place to go to stock up on home-made marmalade, sweet potatoes, fresh lemongrass and earthy-looking organic parsnips and carrots. It's not all that far removed from the original store run by Paddy McCabe which, according to Oliver, "sold everything. He even repaired and sold bikes" — we view another set of hooks, this time once used to hang bikes — "as well as moss peat, horticultural things and turkeys and ducks at Christmas. He supplied local hotels too, the likes of the then Dalkey Island Hotel."

The store expanded when Paddy and Margaret McCabe bought first Gilbey's and then the butcher shop. "We ended up with a substantial piece of land," says Oliver, "with the shop on the ground floor and my parents and the five of us living upstairs. Leo and myself still live over the shop with my mother; it's like a long bungalow up there, with lots of stairs between sections. My father died in 1980 from cancer when I was four years old, which was a great shock to my mother, who had to take on the shop as well as rear five children. She put her heart and soul into the business."

So did Leo, eight years older than Oliver. Leo stayed with the shop, looking after things while his siblings spread their wings. "If it wasn't for Leo, we wouldn't be here today," Oliver freely admits. "I would have come back from my travels and there would have been nothing."

Oliver spread his wings in Australia and the US, spending three years on the hoof after studying TV and radio production. "When I got back, Hilary, who'd been running things with Leo, was having a baby, so Leo trained me and I got to know the customers and Bob's your uncle, here I am."

The brothers work it so that Leo looks after the buying and deliveries while Oliver is the hands-on person in the shop.

Leo is to be found in Dublin's fruit and vegetable market on Tuesday and Friday mornings at the crack of dawn. The other three weekday mornings, he's in the fuel yards on Tolka Quay at the later time of 7.30 a.m. His day is a long one. "I'm out quite late in the evenings on fuel deliveries," he says, "which I start when I come back from the markets and do on six days a week." For leisure he says he "crashes out in an armchair".

With a workload like that, you're inclined to believe him. He genuinely likes what he does, says he used to spend every evening after school helping his father "stack shelves and get things in order. As you would in any family business."

Dalkey was different then, he says. "When I was going to school, the streets were full of kids kicking football and playing. That's all gone now. It's become so expensive to buy a house here in Dalkey, only professional couples can afford to move here and they're often not interested in rearing children. A lot of the old community spirit is gone, but that's not only in Dalkey."

Oliver gives his view of the place in which he grew up. "There's a good cross section of people here, the wealthy and not so wealthy, all sorts – it's a good community. There's a high percentage of older people and not so many young couples with babies and children.

"They're a very friendly people; they've taken me in very well since I came home, even seem to like me being here in the shop! They like things to go on the way they always have and we certainly intend maintaining the tradition of personal service and supplying fresh fruit and veg."

For the future, he says there's "lots of potential" ahead for Select Stores. "I'm very much into studying the nutrients of fruit and veg and into organics too. We've a small supply of these at the moment, but people are asking for more. I want to bring something fresh and new into the business, marry it to what's traditional and here already.

"There's a lot of trust between us and our customers; it's not like a supermarket. We look people in the eye and offer personal service and a chat. In this kind of business, conversation is very important. There's always something to learn from people and customers tell us what they want."

He talks about his father, whom he barely remembers but who was "well loved in Dalkey village. He was a great man for trying things out. A customer said to me recently that during the Christmas rush of business, my father didn't get to sleep until Christmas Day afternoon.

"The McCabe Swimming Cup is presented in his name by my mother every year."

Talk of Christmas reminds them of the hard work involved with trees, wreaths, hollies and mistletoe. "We still do turkeys for regular customers and fruit baskets as gifts."

They're a close family, the McCabes, and they stick together according to Oliver. "I've been away and, now that I'm back, I realise Ireland, and Dalkey, is not such a bad place. Running a fruit and vegetable store is not such a bad thing either.

"In fact, I think it's a fine thing and Dalkey's a fine place too. When you're a sole trader, running your own business, you're involved in sales, marketing, PR, buying – what more could you ask for in this lifetime?"

Tea Time Express, Chapelizod. *Photograph: Brenda Fitzsimons*

Tea Time Express

Bakery, Chapelizod Industrial Estate, Dublin 20

The Tea Time Express story is all about more than 60 years of making cakes the traditional way, of real eggs and hand finishing, of a staff and customer loyalty which have garnered the company an old-style exclusivity and cachet which any amount of latter-day marketing campaigns couldn't buy.

Time was when Tea Time Express was most famously known for its Dawson Street shop and the cakes were baked in Usher's Island. All's changed: the shop is gone and today's cakes are made, the way they always were, in Chapelizod. They may be on the move again however; expansion's on the way, the taste for Tea Time Express cakes unwaning.

The company was founded by the Arigho family on 16 December 1938. Managing director Donal Hogan, a man who has given his working life to the company, knows the date and tells the story. John Tarrant, another (almost) lifer with Tea Time Express and these days a production consultant, adds fact and detail as we go along.

The original shareholders, along with founder Jack Arigho, were James Kearney and Norman Judd. The original bakery was in Usher's Quay and the company, originally, operated a daily door-to-door delivery service, on bicycles with sidecars, of freshly baked cakes. Things went well, even during the Second World War years, and the cries of the cycling delivery boys gave the company its name.

Things went even better and the shop at 51B Dawson Street — which in time would become almost as famous for its queues as for its cakes — was opened. In time, too, a small teashop opened in the shop. In 1954 the Arigho family bought out the other two shareholders.

Founder Jack Arigho died in the 1960s, of a heart attack while at work in the Usher's Quay bakery. His son, John, just finishing school at the time, took over the company.

John Tarrant, with Tea Time Express since he came to Dublin from his parent's Killarney bakery in 1978, remembers how things were: "John Arigho took a great interest, was in the bakery every day. Miss Teresa McDermott was the manageress of the bakery when John was the owner. The company was small, about nine employees, and the range only ran to layered cakes, a few speciality cakes and morning goods."

Morning goods — custard and cream slices famous in their day but no longer an item — were

Dublin's long-time equivalent to the croissant. Their demise was part of the company's march towards the end of the twentieth century.

The Lydon House group bought the company from the Arigho family in 1972. "The company had grown significantly by then," Donal Hogan explains, "and Lydon House – whose base was very strong in Galway and Mayo – saw the potential for expansion into the Dublin and east-coast market. John Arigho stayed on during the transition and for quite a while afterwards. In 1978 Lydon built a state-of-the-art bakery in what is now the Sandyford Industrial Estate and Tea Time Express moved out from Usher's Quay and the city centre."

The new owners went on baking the same line of cakes, although, thanks to modernity and EU directives, they were obliged to use new mixing and baking processes. Cakes continued to be hand-finished – "just as we do today", Donal Hogan says. "We may well be the only people left who really hand-finish cakes." Things went well enough for the company to open outlets in the Dun Laoghaire Shopping Centre, Irish Life Mall, Nutgrove Shopping Centre and a popular shop in the bakery.

The company, along with many others, went through difficult times in the early 1980s. Donal Hogan joined in 1985, straight from school, to work in the accounts department, and stayed. He became an accountant and, in time, one of the most youthful-looking MDs around.

When Donal Hogan joined, the company employed 35–40 people and still traded on a certain exclusivity. "There was a much bigger product line then too," he says, "but we weren't dealing with the multiples, the supermarkets and such. Only with high-class delis. It was policy not to supply shops within half-a-mile of each other."

He shakes his head. "I don't know … it had to do with exclusivity. I think it was the reason the company was struggling."

A couple of years on a management buy-out was led by John Sherry, who is still the company's owner. "He was MD of Lydon House," Donal Hogan explains, "and saw potential in Tea Time Express so bought it out along with Chris Kenny, John Tarrant and Marie Mullaney."

The new management team "grew the company", Donal Hogan says, "by moving away from exclusivity and supplying the multiples like Dunnes Stores, Quinnsworth and Superquinn. They also broke into the gift market, such as the hamper business."

There were other changes too. The traditional red box with its circular cut-out had to go. "It wasn't tamper proof," Donal Hogan explains. "Kids would stick their fingers through and into the cake."

The new management also decided that the shops had to go (the only one left is in the Irish Life Mall) and cut production to what the company excelled at: the original layer and sandwich cakes.

The company moved to Chapelizod in the millennium year, a move which brought it full circle and close to its origins in Usher's Island. A visit to see Tea Time Express bakers and confectioners in action enlightened: cakes are iced, creamed, decorated and finished off with dexterity, all amidst the soft, sweet smell of warm madeira and fresh baking. John Tarrant points out that they still use 100 per cent eggs while other companies, he says, use 50 per cent. "We're also obliged to use hi-ri-ratio flour these days," he says, "but otherwise the recipe is exactly the same as it was when I joined 25 years ago."

Management changes, the departure from the company of Marie Mullaney and John Tarrant (the latter is now involved on a consultancy basis) and the sadly early death of Chris Kenny meant that at the time of the move to Chapelizod the company was being run by John Sherry, with Donal Hogan as finance director, Clare Dolan in sales and Fiona O'Sullivan looking after quality assurance. Clare Dolan has since been replaced by Nikki Murphy and Fiona O'Sullivan by Siobhan Reilly.

"We've a low turnover in staff," Donal Hogan says, "with some people 23–24 years with the company. John Sherry has huge loyalty to Tea Time Express and that philosophy of loyalty and tradition runs through the company. We've gone for new packaging, and a slight change of logo, and we're looking at the UK and US markets now. But the cakes aren't going to change. We've decided to stick with what we're good at, making quality cakes. We won Great Taste Awards in the UK last year, two gold and two silver medals. Our Chocolate Orange Sensation 2003 has been a huge success; so has our Coffee Mocha Sensation 2004. We've a new one on the boards but I'm not telling! We're at full capacity and are actively looking for a new site for the bakery, one which will be double the size."

Jackie Larkin in A.C. Taylor's, Upper Sandwith Street. *Photograph: Matt Kavanagh*

A.C. Taylor

Glass Company, Upper Sandwith Street, Dublin 2

Glass has never had a brighter future. Ask anyone in A.C. Taylor, the venerable glass company in Sandwith Street, and they'll recommend you look around, take note of the amount used in new buildings, how easy a substance it is to maintain and install and what a boon to light – whether reflecting it or letting it in.

Glass has a history too, but they don't talk about how it's existed, in its natural form, for billions of years. A.C. Taylor is a relative newcomer. The company was started in 1923 when one Arthur Cyril Taylor, an English schoolteacher, left his homeland for reasons unknown, came to Dublin and set up a glass-making company in the Christchurch area.

Jackie Larkin, a present-day director of the company and daughter of the man who worked for and took over the company from Taylor when he died, remembers Arthur Cyril. "He was an entrepreneur, a man with a hugely inventive mind who was always dreaming up things.

"We don't know why he came to Dublin. After a while in Christchurch, he moved the company to Percy Place. He had a factory there, made signs and aeroboard and manufactured mirrors."

All this despite health difficulties posed by his diabetic condition. In 1954/55 Jackie Larkin's father, Kenneth, came to work for him.

"My father had served his time in Brook Thomas, where he was a manager in glass," says Jackie. "He came to work for Mr Taylor as a manager. Mr Taylor was married but had no family and suffered ill health on and off. Even when he went blind he was determined to continue mowing his lawn and I remember him working out a way he could do so by using a piece of string to guide him. He was full of inventions and ideas – before his time in many ways."

By the time A.C. Taylor moved to Upper Sandwith Street in 1974, Kenneth Larkin was a director of the company. When Arthur Cyril Taylor died in 1975 it was Kenneth Larkin – another man cut from the inventive/imaginative mould – who took over building up and running the company until he died in 1998. "Though he was semi-retired for the last few years of that period he still came to work," Jackie says.

"He was always thinking ahead and planning. Years and years ago he saw a bevelling machine at a trade fair, came home and made one. We were using his bevelling machine here long before they came into the country."

"I joined the company in the early eighties and my brother Donald, who worked here during his summer holidays from school, came in about the same time. Donald and myself, along with our mother, are now in charge of things and the directors of the company."

Back in 1923, when A.C. Taylor first got going, the company made its own mirrors using glass from the factory, silvering it (applying the thin layer of reflective silver to the back) themselves. Glass these days arrives already silvered but, Jackie Larkin says, "we still do silvering and also re-silver if people want old mirrors repaired. I think we're the only people doing re-silvering at the moment, certainly in the Republic."

She talks about the techniques and skills which are still part of the everyday job in A.C. Taylor. "Hand silvering is doing very small pieces," she explains, "and is a very old trade. Donald can silver and we've another man can do it too. These days we've got automatic bevelling machines, which put a sloping edge on the glass – though we also do hand-bevelling, which is done on a stone. The glass is ground down and polished. We do 'brilliant cutting' by hand – 'brilliant cutting' is when you cut designs into the glass and polish it. It's like Waterford but using smaller wheels."

She says that a lot of this work can be done by machine. "But machines only tickle the surface, don't go as deep – and there's no craftsmanship in a machine!"

Talk of craft brings foreman Paddy Hyland into things. Working for A.C. Taylor since the mid-sixties, he was reared to it you might say, since his father before him worked for Dublin Glass "all his life; God, the work he had to put into it in those days".

Paddy Hyland started his working life with City Glass in Thomas Street, still going strong but now located in Dolphin's Barn. He moved to A.C. Taylor to serve his apprenticeship. That was when the company was in Percy Place and he remembers glass being delivered to them "on floats drawn by horses from the docks. They were low loaders and we had to have lads on benches to take the weight of the glass. They would only bring us two cases at a time, packed into heavy joints of timber. Now we get great loads of glass at a time, packed just with end caps and steel bands."

A.C. Taylor, in those earlier days, "did a great deal of fancy, bevelled mirrors for the likes of Roches Stores. We did spoon, oval, scallops and cross bevelling. They're styles which are mostly gone now, not the fashion any more."

Other things have changed too. EU strictures, metric measurements and safety consciousness mean safety laminated glass is *de rigueur*. The job is easier too. "The work would kill you years ago," Paddy Hyland says. He recalls fellow workers. "There was George Anderson, who used stoke the boiler and actually lived in Percy Place, and Dick Power, Matty Walsh, who went on to Dublin Glass and died a young man, a great spoon beveller, very talented. Then there was Paddy 'The Whack' Gordon, a real character."

A.C. Taylor did all the glass for the Burlington Hotel when it opened in the early 1970s. Paddy Hyland remembers the "massive floor-to-ceiling mirrors and the really lovely fanlights in the ballroom. They were about 31 feet long. We bevelled every bit of glass, individually. "We did a lot of work over the years for P.V. Doyle — the Tara Towers, the Montrose, most of his hotels in fact. We did a lot of pubs too, some of them gone now."

He points out that glass was never actually made in Dublin. "Not float glass anyway. The Glass Bottle Company made sheet glass, which is a different, rougher kind. Some kinds of glass have gone. Bottle-end glass went because it's hard to make. Others, like the Miraflex used in discos in the 1970s, is making a comeback. Glass bricks, which we make, are very fashionable."

Latter-day jobs include work for such art-in-glass establishments as Ryan's of Parkgate Street, Dwyer pubs, Trinity Hotel in Pearse Street and Dawson Street's Cafe en Seine. "A lot of it's very intricate," Paddy Hyland reminds, "all of the cutting notches out of glass in different shapes and sizes."

Machinery has brought lots of changes to the business, with the safety end of things more emphasised these days. A.C. Taylor employed about 10 people when it was in Percy Place — and employs the same number today. It does artwork in glass, Waterford glass repairs, glass tops, engraving, display aids — the lot. "Glass is the future," Jackie Larkin says, with quiet certitude.

Sandra and Renato Fusciardi in Fusciardi's, Capel Street. *Photograph: Matt Kavanagh*

Fusciardi's

Fish-and-Chip Shop, 10 Capel Street, Dublin 1

Some names are forever associated with Capel Street: master tailor Louis Copeland, painter and gallery owner Gerald Davis, Romano's Italian restaurant, Lenehan's Hardware.

And, of course, Fusciardi's. Since 1937 they've been making and selling some of the best fish and chips in town. It was in the rooms over the shop at 10 Capel Street that the first Irish-born generation of Fusciardis, all nine of them, grew up.

Adults now, and parents to today's generation of Fusciardis, they're scattered across the land but still in the business. You'll find Fusciardi family fish-and-chippers in Tuam, Navan, Lucan and Bray, as well as in Dublin's Abbey Street. The original Capel Street shop, opened in 1937 by Elio and Louisa Fusciardi, is these days in the capable hands of Renato and Guido Fusciardi.

Elio and Louisa (*née* Macari) Fusciardi arrived in Capel Street with three small sons in 1937. Elio Fusciardi, born in San Andrea near Monte Cassino in southern Italy, had been travelling and working his way around Britain and Ireland when he met and married Scottish Italian Louisa Macari. The youngest of their three boys, Ernaldo, who was only weeks old when they arrived, is the father of Renato and Guido.

Elio and Louisa went on to have nine children altogether, seven boys and two girls. Elio has been dead since the early seventies, but Louisa was an integral part of the life of Capel Street for 50 years until she moved out.

"She loved Capel Street," her daughter-in-law, Sandra Fusciardi, affirms. "She used to do all her shopping in the street with a trolley bag and made midday dinner for the entire family, married and unmarried, every day. They used go up in shifts to be fed. She was a great woman."

Sandra, daughter of an Italian mother and Irish father, became part of the Fusciardi clan when she married Ernaldo in 1968. Their daughter Michelle, like sons Renato and Guido, is also in the business — married and living in Wexford, she runs a fish-and-chip shop with her Irish husband.

We sat at the back of the eating area, with the midday trade building to a lunchtime rush and

Frank Sinatra crooning "I've Got You under My Skin" on the jukebox, while she told me the Fusciardi story.

When Elio and Louisa Fusciardi arrived, they first ran an ice-cream parlour in the building next door to the present Fusciardi's. "After a short while they sold to the Morelli family," Sandra explains, "and moved into this building to run a fish-and-chip shop. It had been a fish-and-chip shop as far back as 1890, and next door had always been an ice-cream parlour. These days, next door is Romano's Italian Restaurant. Elio and Louisa reared their family and built up the business here in number 10 over the years."

The accommodation over the shop has four bedrooms, as large as many a suburban home. "When Ernaldo was growing up in Capel Street he used be able to play football on the road," Sandra says, "but it's changed a lot since then."

In the mid-sixties, Elio and Louisa Fusciardi retired and handed over to their offspring. Silvio, Ernaldo, Lorenzo, Norma and Eda ran the business together until, in the way of things, they one by one branched out and Ernaldo was left running things in Capel Street.

Silvio opened his own place in Abbey Street in 1990; Lorenzo opened in Bray in the early 1980s; Norma married and now helps in Abbey Street; Eda went to the US.

"The shop always did take-away," Sandra explains, "and until 1970, when we extended this far back, there was only the front part of the shop. We can seat about 120 people now. In the earlier days it used be terribly busy and stay open until 1 a.m. We close now at 7 p.m. There were a lot of people living on Capel Street in those days. It was a very different place, with lots of clothes shops, butchers, grocers, chemists and a Johnson Mooney and O'Brien bakery.

"Our customers were people who came to shop in the street, but now we're mostly reliant for customers on people working in the area. It's much more a daytime business now. With all the building work going on we've a lot of builder customers. And of course there are the children who come from around Strand Street, whose parents before them would have been customers too."

Change continues and a sort of reversal is under way. "There are a lot of apartments being built around the area," Sandra explains, "and people say the Luas will revive Capel Street. We all hope so. Ernaldo is treasurer of the Capel Street Committee, which works for the good of the street. We all want to see it build up again."

Running a fish-and-chip shop is hard work but the Fusciardis, past and present, aren't work-shy and, anyway, it's what they want to do. "We did in the past try to venture into other things, like serving spaghetti," Sandra says, "but it didn't work. People want fish and chips. It's passing over to the boys now, to Renato and Guido. They've a working day which begins at 9 a.m. and ends about 7 p.m. They get the potatoes in the market, then peel and chip them themselves. The same with the fish. They cut and fillet it and make the batter. It's hard work but it's always been that way, all done in the family."

The Ernaldo and Sandra Fusciardi family home is in Goatstown but Renato and Guido have decided to live in the accommodation above the Capel Street shop and to keep it open until later at night. As well as Renato and Guido Fusciardi, the shop gives employment to Margaret, whom Sandra calls "a sort of general manageress", who has worked for the family for more than 30 years, and a number of casual staff. Time was when inter-marrying was the way in the Italian community in Ireland. This too has changed with the present generation. "Young people now marry into the wider Irish community," Sandra says, "which is a good thing. When I was young I spent a lot of time around this area, with my Italian cousins. I met Ernaldo in Portrush, though. I was visiting my sister who had married a Morelli and Ernaldo was visiting his aunt and uncle. We knew each other to see around Capel Street and we'd meet at weddings and such.

"We met in November, got engaged in January and were married in May. A lot of my generation have homes in Italy but Ernaldo's parents let the family home go. No one was interested in owning it at the time but of course we're sorry now. We still have relatives in Italy and go to see them often. They visit us here too."

Fusciardi's, 10 Capel Street, has attracted the odd celebrity customer and been a film location. When it played the part of the café in *The Most Fertile Man in Ireland* a great rush of business followed. Bob Geldof gets his chips there when in Dublin and actor Donald Sutherland called for a take-away and chat a few years ago when going through the antique shops in the area.

The Fusciardis will be staying in Capel Street and continuing in the fish-and-chip shop business, Sandra Fusciardi is adamant. "The boys have it now; it's work and it's for them and they like it. It will go on with them, definitely."

Gerry (right) and Rowland Griffin, Oil and Gas Services Ltd, Sandymount. *Photograph: Eric Luke*

Oil and Gas Services Ltd

13 Gilford Road, Sandymount, Dublin 4

The problems and undeniable traumas of house heating are perennial and certainly not new. They are changing however – and with more speed and efficiency over the last 40-odd years than ever in the history of home comforts before that.

Oil and Gas Services Ltd, who've been in the heating business since 1968, are better positioned than most to tell the story of the hot and the cold of it.

To begin in the middle, there's a story from the winter of 1981 which spotlights the uniquely central role a heating company plays in our needy lives.

Gerry Griffin, the one-time accountant who set up the company in 1967 and who, though retired, is still its managing director, tells it like it was.

"The freezing winter of 1980–81 was one of our most difficult periods," he says, memories of the event still clear and detailed. "On New Year's Eve the temperatures plummeted to between -8 and -12 and on New Year's Day the heating of huge numbers of people failed. We came in to work on 2 January at 7 a.m., fully manned and ready, to find no heating in the offices, about 50 calls on the answering machine and more coming in.

"We were washed out with calls and, by 9 a.m., we'd swarms of people almost knocking the door down too. The problem lay with the effects of the freezing temperatures on the oil and I'd to demonstrate this to the droves of people who were blaming us.

"I got on to RTÉ and they made an announcement explaining the blame lay with the oil and the *Evening Press* appeared with similar headlines and that saved our lives! Suddenly those who'd been blaming us and going berserk laid off. RTÉ sent round a crew and we demonstrated for them how boilers could be got up and going. That cold period lasted to the end of February. We were continually awash with calls but we survived!"

Gerry might be MD but the day-to-day running of the company is in the safe, second-generation hands of his general manager son, Rowland Griffin. These days, too, Oil and Gas Services operate from relaxed offices attached to the granite-built one-time Church and Quaker Meeting Hall on Gilford Road in Sandymount.

They moved there in 1971 from beginnings in much more crowded conditions. Gerry Griffin, helped along by the odd good-humoured interjection from Rowland, tells that bit of the story too.

"The beginning! Oh, God help us ..." He laughs, then settles to the story. "The company was conceived in November 1967 and born on 1 February 1968. I was the accountant with a company in Synge Street which serviced garage-forecourt equipment all over the country. This meant we'd close links with the petrol companies, especially Esso.

"It was Esso which rang the company one day and asked if it was interested in taking on the servicing of central-heating boilers. They weren't but one of the directors and myself went to see Esso and it was agreed we'd set it up as a sideline of the main company.

"Oil Fired Services, as it was then, was up and running by 1 February with three Mini-vans and three heating engineers. It was a sideline which got bigger and bigger, faster and faster, and eventually ran out of space in Synge Street."

Central-heating service engineers were a rare breed in the early 1960s, a time when houses were kept warm with the imaginative use of storage, mobile gas and solid-fuel heaters, accompanied by the wearing of woolly vests. By the late 1960s, when Oil Fired Services began to take off, oil heating had begun to mushroom too.

"We thought, when we got the vans fitted out with shelves, that we were really ahead of the posse," Gerry remembers. "The opposition didn't have shelves! We'd a key tool too in the nozzle spanner. We thought we were the cat's pyjamas with two engineers for Dublin and the third in Cork."

The heating service business was very different then. "Customers' supply and service agreements entitled them to routine and unlimited breakdown calls. We worked 365 days of the year, 7 days a week and had to guarantee to provide service within 24 hours of being called out. We operated like that for a large number of years. Boilers were installed in sheds and lean-tos, in all sorts of places. My own was in the kitchen and lasted 30 years!"

By July 1971, and the move to Sandymount, Oil Fired Services had become a separate company owned and run by Gerry Griffin and other shareholders. "It was a very, very sensible move," Gerry remembers. "It gave us space and parking – something which even then was difficult in Synge Street."

Rowland joins in with a piece of earlier history. "This had been a church, a Quaker Meeting Hall built in 1876, but in use as a store and offices by the time we came along. There was an elderly customer used come to us to have her boiler fixed and she'd met her husband at a dance here."

His father recalls landmark times in the company, and oil crises. "Initially we used Mini-Austins but moved on to Ford Escorts. The high point was when we had three vans in Cork, two in Limerick, one in Waterford and about 13 in Dublin. During one of the oil crises, in the mid-1970s, we were on our way to Northern Ireland in a van for petrol when an Esso station in Dundalk filled us up. That kept us going for a couple of months."

By the time the next oil crisis arrived they'd converted the vans to liquid petroleum gas so that they could switch between it and petrol.

"That absolutely saved us when there was a long period during which we couldn't get any petrol at all," Gerry says. "Those were very hairy times! Because of the crises people became wary of oil, and solid-fuel ranges and backboilers became popular. Fuel merchants in Dublin combined together and formed a co-operative which provided back-up and know-how and called itself Coal Information Services. It became a dominant force in heating services for many a year and we became installers of dual-purpose backboilers."

He laughs. "You had to be imaginative, resilient and flexible to survive! It's wasn't just us, it was the same for everyone in the business!"

Solid fuel/oil combinations went on for about 10 years until, in the late 1970s, gas arrived. "Dublin Gas had been supplying town gas to a limited number of customers but when natural gas came that was the really big change," Gerry explains, "with a completely new set of problems for us to become acquainted with. In 1989 we changed the name of the company to Oil and Gas Services Ltd."

Oil and Gas Services is one of very few companies who still service oil boilers. "The average age of an oil boiler is 15 years but there are some aged 30 out there and we're still looking after them," Gerry says.

Rowland, who joined the company in 1992, talks about the gas end of things. "It's a lot more complicated and EU regulations require you to be highly efficient. They see pilot lights as wasteful, for instance. Things are becoming totally electronic and more efficient while parts are becoming more expensive and harder to get. The gas boiler is more or less silent, and cleaner."

What about solar or wind power? Rowland shakes his head, says he thinks it's a long way off, especially in Ireland. "The heating future's with gas, as far as I can see," he says.

Today's company is smaller and runs a fleet of seven Peugeot Partner vans. "Back in the oil-fired days we were installing boilers," Rowland says, "but we're not installing any more. At the height of the 'tiger economy' we couldn't get service engineers for love nor money and were turning work away in the winter of 2001. Now we've got seven excellent engineers and a services manager, Colm O'Connor. We've two full-time and two part-time workers in the office. We built an extension in 1997 and got new computers. You have to keep ahead."

Tony Reinhardt (left) and John Behan in the reception area of Leary's Photo Lab in Ranelagh.
Photograph: Cyril Byrne

Leary's Photo Lab

15 Chelmsford Road, Ranelagh, Dublin 6

The world of the photography lab used to be a black and white one. Then a little colour crept in; then a little more. Now it's all colour. It used to be too that chemicals did the job of developing; now most images appear via the magic of digital.

Tim Leary has lived and worked through all of the changes. He's retired now and doesn't take pictures anymore. "I worked with them for too long, since I was a young child, working in the Raglan Lane business with my father. Sometimes I miss it, but not often."

Leary's Photo Lab is still there, no longer Leary-owned but continuing to process and finish film, as well as taking photographs. Tim Leary bowed out in 1999, handing over to the man who'd worked with him in the business for 28 years, Tony Reinhardt. "It's in good hands," Tim Leary assures — and remembers his own time.

Tim Leary's father, Albert, worked in photography for the United Drug Company in the 1920s and 1930s. In 1946, he started his own photographic laboratory and photo-finishing business in Parnell Square. Four years later he moved things to 31 Raglan Lane. "It was just a coach-house," Tim remembers, "but those were the best of times. It was all hand-printing then, one print at a time, and all black and white. We used 48-gallon tanks of chemicals. We did the same for a long time after we moved to Ranelagh, only going into colour about 1975–6. The earlier cameras were mostly old 120 and 127 Brownies, and the prints mostly small ones. My father used to stamp numbers on the back of his work and I still come across small black and white prints from time to time with his stamp on them. They're in houses everywhere."

Albert Leary worked hard and ran his small business in the thorough way of his times. "He had messenger boys going round on bikes to collect film from the chemists'," Tim says, "collecting, collecting — they were always collecting. My father would work all night; he had to. It was a very tiny business then and he had to keep it going. Customers would give their film into the chemist and expect it back, developed, before 10 a.m. next morning. So my father would have it collected, then develop and have it delivered back early next day. There were a lot of small photographic finishers in Dublin in the sixties and seventies"

He recalls some of them – Crann Helm of Mount Street Crescent, Ryan's of Parkgate Street, Lyall Smith in Rathgar and, biggest of all, Kodak in Rathmines, in whose black and white laboratory he himself trained. "They were old-fashioned businesses," he says, "all gone now. As is Hodges Lab, a bigger company which was very competitive and put a lot of smaller people out of business. Gone themselves now."

Tim Leary joined his father in the business in 1957 and nine years later the company moved to 15 Chelmsford Road in Ranelagh. "We needed more facilities and more space and in Ranelagh we could have a shop, lab and studio," Tim points out. "We started doing photographic work when we moved to Ranelagh too, as well as running the shop and lab. My family, wife and children, were always involved. My father died in 1981; my mother and I ran things together until 1986, when she died. In 1999 I decided it was time to get out myself. It was a nice business to be in, but I don't miss it. I especially like seeing pictures taken by my father."

Tony Reinhardt, a working part of the Leary business since 1971, took over when Tim Leary retired. He runs things these days with John Behan, from a premises of more modest aspect than they'd like. "This is an AI listed building," John explains, "so we've had to take down all signs and advertising."

The pair have been friends since they first went to school together in St Mary's in Haddington Road and later to Westland Row CBS. They've been working together since the late nineties. "People call us Laurel and Hardy," John says.

Tony Reinhardt joined the company as a lab assistant, which meant, he says, that he was a "general dogsbody". He grew up in Sandymount but knew the older Ranelagh fairly well. "It was like a village in the 1970s," he says, "not as hectic as it is now. You can't move today without tripping over parking-disc and clearway signs, none of which have anything to do with traffic management. Every other shop, too, is a take-away food place."

And these are just the environmental changes. The business side of things has changed dramatically too since the seventies. And not all for the best either.

When celebrated pop artist David Hockney condemned digital manipulation for heralding the death of photography as an art form, he was echoed by Tony Reinhardt. "There's a lot of technology around photography today but very little knowledge. The colleges are producing photographers to beat the band who go out, take pictures and then try to fix them on their computers when they go home – all instead of taking a good picture in the first place."

Still, he's convinced analogue photography "will always have a niche market. Not like in the 1970s, though, when business was flying and I would collect film from 50 or 60 chemists'. We developed, enlarged — the whole gamut. At the height of the season we'd have 600 black and white films to be done per day and about 80 colour. Now true black and white is rare. We get a fair amount of old prints to make into new negatives or prints and the quality of the originals is second to none. You'd never get it today."

Leary's greatest ever amount of business came from the Pope's 1979 visit; their lowest ever time was during the foot and mouth scare. Tony Reinhardt says that, these days, Holy Communion and Christmas business has "fallen off. It's all videos and digital now, though people still like to get special photos developed. Summertime is still our busiest time. Business is very quiet from mid-January to mid-March, until St Patrick's Day."

John Behan agrees with all of this, adding that "summer is always hectic, go, go go. It's holiday shots and professionals too coming in with their work. Then there are portraits and weddings and graduations to be done. And of course we do digital too." With another 35-year lease signed in the last few years, Leary's Photo Lab will be developing with the business for a few years yet to come.

Making sausages for over fifty years: Tony Molloy at Olhausen on the Malahide Road.
Photograph: Matt Kavanagh

Olhausens

Sausage making in Dublin was for years in the hands of a number of venerable butchering families. Still is, in that the experience and traditional methods of several of the families are these days found in the Olhausens brand, a name which crops up as often and affectionately in early twentieth-century tales of the city as does the Howth tram. The two are not unconnected.

When Leopold Bloom emerged from Olhausens on the June day he spent wandering around Dublin in 1904, he was holding a parcel in each hand, one of which contained a lukewarm, pepper-sprinkled pig's crubeen. Bloom would have known Olhausens well: the pork butchers had by then been trading for eight years at number 72 Talbot Street.

They're still well known. In 2003, according to managing director Denis Murphy, Olhausens "sold 40 sausages to every man, woman and child on this island". But Olhausens Ltd, Pork and Bacon Producers, have long left Talbot Street, together with many other Dublin city centre traders, for the space and facilities of the suburbs. The company is these days found in Unit 3, Malahide Road Industrial Park, Dublin 17.

Other things, too, have changed. The shops have gone (the company is now a supplier to supermarkets, catering companies and the like) and Olhausens is bigger than ever it was (230 people on the payroll, 2 production plants, 28 vehicles on the road), has diversified (5 different product lines) and is now owned by a group of wholly Irish private investors.

What hasn't changed is the emphasis on quality pork and bacon products and the steadfast input of those who know the business. When Olhausens Ltd took over Kearns and Byrnes, it took on the nous and experience of two other sausage-making family businesses. Before that, in 1977, when Freddie Olhausen sold the original company to butchers Terence Gormley and Thomas le Blanc, the new/old Olhausens gained the priceless knowledge of people like Tony Molloy, still making the loose, naturally cased, sausages today in Coolock that he first made as an apprentice in Gormley's in 1948.

The company has the expertise too of Declan Williamson, vigorously looking after what is probably one of the biggest sausage rooms in the country and who has been more than 30 years in the business. He began serving his time in the Talbot Street shop when he was 14 years old.

What hasn't changed at all is the name. Olhausens it was in 1896 when William Olhausen, a butcher newly arrived in Dublin from central Europe/Germany, set up the business, and Olhausens it still is.

Denis Murphy says they kept the name "because of brand recognition. Olhausens has been known and regarded since the days it was advertised across the front of the number 31 tram going to Howth." The company has another spot in advertising history: when 1927 legislation allowed for advertising on Radio Éireann, Olhausens was the first to take a slot. The company paid £5 for five minutes: a lot of money and a lot of time in radio terms then, and now.

The company's origins are clear, but the Olhausen family story through the early years of the twentieth century are not so accessible. Denis Murphy, only with Olhausens since the late nineties but a working lifetime in the food industry, tells it as he has heard it.

"Back in the late nineteenth century, a lot of central Europeans/Germans arrived in Dublin. There were Olhausens, Reinhardts and Hafners. They all established butcher shops in various parts of Dublin."

William Olhausen, in Talbot Street, butchered behind the shop, primarily pigs. All of his sausages and puddings were made by hand; sausages would have been made of pork, rusk and his own specialised seasonings.

The natural casing then was made of sheep gut – these days, with a healthy 15 per cent of the company's sausages still made *au naturel*, the casing is manufactured collagen. The early Olhausens company, according to Denis Murphy, "went from father to son" and in the 1970s was being run by Freddy Olhausen, son of William.

Denis Murphy here digresses from the Olhausen story to outline the parallel story of the Gormley and le Blanc sausage-making families. Both of these, in the mid-twentieth century, were running traditional butcher shops and making sausages in Dorset Street. "Through the 1950s and 1960s, they developed a chain of such shops under the Gormley name. There were 10 in all, in the newer estates and in the city centre. In 1977, these two families bought Olhausen from Freddie, the son of the original William Olhausen. In 1981 all of the butchering and processing moved out to Coolock."

In time the shops all closed and the Olhausens' manufacturing side grew as a supplier of supermarkets, catering food outlets and the like. In time, too, the company took over Best Food

Services, which were producing Kearns and Byrnes, two other notable and old Dublin sausage brands.

Bernard Gormley is the company chairman and four of the le Blanc family work in the company but there is no longer any Olhausen, Byrnes or Kearns family involvement. Since February 1999, the company has been owned by a group of private investors, all Irish.

Many of today's employees are from central and eastern Europe, completing the circle begun when a central European immigrant started the business in 1896.

Tony Molloy tells how it was when he started in the business in 1948, as an apprentice in Gormleys in Dorset Street. "Gormleys was a small business, more like a family, with everyone on first name terms. Most butchers were like that at the time.

"To make the suasages you used lean meat, fat meat and some beef to give it the pinky colour. Each shop had its own seasoning, basically pepper, salt, nutmeg and mace. The seasoning for the puddings was much the same, with pimento added. You had to keep tasting to make sure it was all right; it's all measured now and more consistent. We did a great trade too in pressed beef."

His colleague, Declan Williamson, remembers the original Olhausens at 72 Talbot Street as "one of the bigger shops in Dublin at the time. There were about 16 or 17 girls working there, with about five of them working in the factory at the back three days a week. We did everything ourselves: boning, cooking hams, making sausages, puddings and brawn. Customers would come in for pigs' legs and feet and eat them with a pint in the pub next door."

Olhausens in Talbot Street was a "very, very busy shop. The guards from Store Street used come in for their rashers and sausages, big country men, as well as tourists and everyone else getting off the train. Back then you worked, and you learned, and if you got it wrong you got a kick in the arse. It's a great trade and I've no regrets about spending all of my time in it."

Denis Murphy adds that the company has tried hard to keep expertise on board and ensure that its product is both traditional and one of quality. "We distribute nationwide, from Letterkenny to Killorglin. Food quality and hygiene standards are so high now we need to produce and sell in volume to keep going." Denis Williamson says he "still wouldn't eat anyone else's product. I take pride in what we do," he grins, "and, at the end of the day, the proof of the pudding's in the eating."

Pat Carthy, pawnbroker, Marlborough Street. *Photograph: Matt Kavanagh*

Carthy Pawnbrokers
85 Marlborough Street, Dublin 1

Pat Carthy is a special case. "There are only four pawnbrokers left in the Republic of Ireland and I'm one of them. The others are Kilbrides at Leonard's Corner, Breretons in Capel Street and Kearns in Green Street. There's two in Belfast, to the best of my knowledge."

Things weren't always thus. Change has been coming in the pawnbroking business for longer than most realise — and not all to do with the marauding Celtic Tiger either. "We gave up taking in clothes about 40 years ago," Mr Carthy says. "That's all gone."

A third-generation pawnbroker, he's laconic and laughing when he adds that "you meet all kinds of people in this business. It's interesting, not the sort of work many would go into, but it definitely gets into your life."

His premises at 85 Marlborough Street in Dublin city centre is both jewellery shop and pawnbroker's, with business these days divided fairly evenly between the two. He remembers livelier pawnbroking times in the 1960s.

"There were three pawnbrokers in Marlborough Street then," he says, "as well as two in Buckingham Street, one in Amiens Street and one in Talbot Street. And that was just this area. With all those shops around, we were still taking in 1,500 pledges on a Monday morning, taking in shoes, everything. The number of articles being pawned was colossal but it's been dropping every year since then. Nowadays we take in mostly jewellery — but also cameras, electrical goods, golf clubs." And guitars, naturally. Some things never change.

The three balls outside, a centuries-old symbol of the business, haven't changed either. They hang from their wrought-iron support, gold plated and shining, as we stand fearlessly admiring beneath them.

"They're more than 100 years old," says their owner, "and they're peeling, even though I had them gold-plated five years ago. It's the pollution, eats right through the gold."

Closer inspection shows him to be right. Closer inspection also reveals a small hole in the sign carrying the shop's number — a bullet hole put there in 1916.

The building is Georgian and some 250 years old. Originally a town residence, the ground floor later became a drapery shop and, more than 100 years ago, a pawnbroker's. In those earlier pawnbroking days, the staff used to live above the shop and pawned bikes were stored an unbelievable four storeys above the ground on the top floor.

Mr Carthy's grandfather was a pawnbroker in North King Street, so his son, Pat's father, knew what he was letting himself in for when he bought the Marlborough Street shop in 1954.

"Weldons owned it before," Mr Carthy explains. "They had three shops and sold my father this one. They still have a shop in Clarendon Street but it's an antique jeweller's now. I've been here myself since the late seventies."

The pawnbroking part of things is separate, entered through a discreet door to the left of the shop. Customers have the privacy of hatches; business is conducted through iron bars and goods taken in are stored on the floors above. "We lend hundreds of euro now," says Pat, "whereas it would have been shillings before. Mostly people come back for their goods. It's just a loan we give, after all. We're particular about what we take in and about what jewellery we buy in the shop too. Customers come in every day of the week. They'd come on a Sunday too if we were open and they needed money."

Goods not reclaimed are auctioned off, either in O'Reillys in Francis Street or Herman Wilkinson in Rathmines.

It's sad, surely, people parting with things held dear because of a desperate need of money? Not so, says Mr Carthy. "We give people loans," he stresses, "and give them back their goods when they reclaim them. If they went to an auctioneer, their goods would be gone forever, sold. No one says auctioneering is a sad business. Or that banks are, although they charge huge interest and take everything a person owns if they don't get their money."

He's in no way aggrieved saying this. A quarter of a century in the business has shown and taught Mr Carthy a lot about people and life.

The shop is busy, a constant stream of customers interrupting his tale. Proving his point about not accepting everything, a boy in school uniform arrives and casually offers a ring for sale. Mr Carthy isn't interested. The boy mooches about a bit, then leaves. "Probably his mother's," Mr Carthy observes.

He has stories aplenty. Like the one told by the receipts found at the back of an old safe when they were dismantling it a few years ago. "They were for binoculars and were made out to the Commander of the Dublin Brigade of the Dublin Fusiliers in 1922. Seems he'd come and taken the stock of binoculars for the IRA's fight in the Civil War. They were never returned so those using them may have been shot."

He tells another story, this one more contemporary. "A fellow came into the pawn office about five years ago with a huge, really huge, gold bangle he wanted me to melt down. He'd been digging the foundations for his bungalow when he found it. He knew it was a Viking bangle and so did I, but he didn't want archaeological digs or the museum people on the land, which belonged to his father-in-law.

"This bangle was the real thing, an artefact with the clay still on it. Well, it took a long time and a lot of persuading but he did the right thing in the end and it went to the museum."

Upstairs, above the selling and lending activity on the ground floor, there are dusty old rooms with elaborately decorative plaster ceilings and old doors with carved wood surroundings. This is where the electrical goods, golf clubs and binoculars are stored, along with old ledgers recording transactions through the years.

It's also where Mr Carthy keeps some framed treasures. Like the 1890 pawn ticket for money lent on stocks and shares, and the smoke-damaged invitation to a party sent by Mary Carthy, who owned the house in 1760. "My mother's name is Mary Carthy. We found it behind a fireplace when we were doing work. I think it's more than a coincidence that a Mary Carthy should have owned the house in 1760 and now we own it."

He owns both number 85 and the building next door and has planning permission for apartments, with retail outlets on the ground floor. There are preservation orders on both buildings and Mr Carthy is adamant that their nature and ornate beauty will be carefully conserved.

Coupled with the changing use of the building is the fact that neither of his children will be going into the business – one is an engineer; the other is in showjumping. So is the end of his and the family's time in pawnbroking in sight?

"I suppose it might be. But if the business dies here the English crowd will move in and they charge far higher interest rates. They lend to royalty and Arabs over there." He considers the question again. "I suppose I'd regret going out of the business. But then whatever happens, happens."

Maureen Gelletlie at Hunter's Hotel, Co. Wicklow. *Photograph: Bryan O'Brien*

Hunter's Hotel

Rathnew, Co. Wicklow

"There is nothing," wrote Dr Samuel Johnson, "which has yet been contrived by man by which so much happiness is produced as by a good inn."

He was right, of course, and Hunter's Hotel, Rathnew, Co. Wicklow — a good inn for almost a decade before the wise doctor was born — has had the wit to inscribe his wisdom on its menu. Hunter's has for so long been a place of retreat and escape for Dubliners that it seemed a good idea to include it in this book.

The legendary, as well as the famous, have stayed in Hunter's over the years. Bram Stoker did, as did the king and queen of Sweden and Liza Minelli. Joyce Grenfell, Peter Ustinov, Walter Osborne, Jack Lynch, Bryan Ferry and Paul Simon have stayed. Daniel Day Lewis visits with his father-in-law, Arthur Miller. Barry Fitzgerald of "Dublin and Hollywood" stayed in 1953 and so did Laurel Hardy of "Hollywood".

On a sunny Sunday, the dining-room in Hunter's is as convivial as a family at dinner, the rambling rooms with low ceilings inviting intimacy, the gardens all around ablaze and a-bloom. Much as it's always been in fact.

Hunter's, unarguably one of the country's better known hotels, began life as a coaching inn around 1700, serving the main Dublin to Wexford road. (Dr Johnson was born in 1709.) It was called the Newry Bridge Inn and had been well mentioned in guidebooks and the like before the Hunter family, in the shape of John Hunter, a butler in nearby Ballycurry, took it over with his wife Elizabeth in 1825.

In time one of their sons, Robert, took over while their other son, George, moved on to the Wooden Bridge Hotel. A generation later and Sarah, daughter of Robert, took over Hunter's.

By then, an institution had been established and the scene set for the family which owns and runs today's hotel to move in.

Tom Gelletlie tells the story of life's turns and fascinating ways with laconic ease. His mother, Maureen, who has given most of her years to Hunter's, comes and goes with anecdote and fact. Her other son, Richard, continues with the business of running the hotel.

The first Gelletlie, Tom says, was also a Thomas, a farm labourer who came from Scotland and worked as a gardener in Castlepollard, Co. Westmeath. When he married Jane Nicholl, daughter of the steward of nearby Tullynally Castle, they moved to Inistioge, Co. Kilkenny, where Thomas worked in Woodstock House demesne. They had four children: Thomas, Jane, James and Adam, who died. Their mother remarried a Mr Ruxton, a man she'd known in the Tullynally Castle days, after her husband died and the family moved back to Co. Westmeath.

The young Thomas Gelletlie learned the trade of watchmaking from his stepfather – and set in motion the family's second business in south Wicklow, that of watch and jewellery making.

Jane Gelletlie-Ruxton kept up her Wicklow links and in time her son Thomas returned to work for Barton's Watchmaker and Jewellery shop in Wicklow town, where he met the extraordinarily named Francina Dorcas Tuke. Francina was a watchmaker too and older than her suitor by seven or eight years. Love had its way and they married. They had one son, named Thomas.

Francina and her son Thomas went on running the shop, now named T.J. Gelletlie Jewellers, when Thomas Gelletlie senior died. Thomas grew to manhood and a friendship with Fanny Hunter, which led to marriage in 1897. The Gelletlie-Hunter connection was established.

"Fanny had about 12 brothers and sisters," today's Tom Gelletlie explains. "Some died, some were killed in the Boer and Great Wars. The hotel was being run by her sister Sarah and brother Charles Parnell Hunter, whose godfather was Charles Stewart Parnell, who used come and play cards in the hotel with a revolver on the table beside him for fear of assassination. Neither Charles nor Sarah married. Charles, a great fishin' and shootin' man, died in 1935. Sarah ran the hotel and lived to become a 91-year-old fascinating relic of the Victorian age."

Thomas and Fanny Gelletlie, meanwhile, were living over the jeweller's shop and rearing their children, Francie, Cecil and Lillie. Cecil, the only boy, became the favoured fishing and shooting companion of his uncle Charles.

A life being lived elsewhere was heading their way. Maureen Murtagh of Cootehill, Co. Cavan, was born to a farming family but had an aunt who decided her life for her. "She said to my mother that I should go into the hotel business," Maureen explains, "because then I'd at least be well fed and have a clean room and bath. It's given me those but I've given it my life too. It's been a way of life – but I wanted to be in the hotel business anyway because I liked meeting people and liked the buzz."

Maureen Murtagh arrived in the area in the late 1930s to work first in Kilmacurragh Hotel, near Redcross, Co. Wicklow. From there she moved to Hunter's as a trainee manager.

Maureen and Sarah Gelletlie got on famously. Maureen got on even more famously with Cecil

Gelletlie. None of this cordiality prevented her taking off for a stint managing the Bundoran Great Northern – but it did bring her back. In 1944 she married Cecil.

Maureen was Catholic, Cecil Protestant, "a thorny issue in those days", Tom says. They lived over the shop in Wicklow town and had five children – Joan, Helen, Ruth, Richard and Tom. "As Aunt Sarah grew older, my mother helped more and more with the running of the hotel," Tom says. "Cecil, my father, died in 1964. Aunt Sarah, who died in 1966, left the hotel to my mother, Maureen."

Maureen runs today's hotel with Richard as hotel manager and Tom, who modestly says he "helps out". The Gelletlie daughters all opted for lives outside the family business: Joan lives locally, Helen in Dublin and Ruth in Leeds.

Maureen Gelletlie remembers vividly how "the pattern of business has changed. In earlier days, when Aunt Sarah was running things, husbands home on leave from the services would bring wife, children and nanny and stay for three to four weeks. They'd go off in the middle of the day with wine and baskets of food to picnic. In the evening they would have high tea.

"Later on, when bicycles came into vogue, cycling parties would cycle from Dublin to stay. Then literary groups would come down from Trinity College, go on walking tours, make a note of the first spring flowers and such. There was no radio and no TV and, until the end of the 1940s, no telephone from midday on Saturday to Monday morning. The advent of the car meant more people came and went for short stays."

Hunter's 16 bedrooms are "completely as they were in terms of their sense of time", Maureen says, "though they've all modern comforts. A few years ago we installed phones – but everyone has their own phone now so we needn't have done so!"

They don't do weddings and functions in Hunter's, just a very steady restaurant and return visitors trade. The continuity of ownership is important and reassuring for guests, Maureen says, though a newer Ireland is reflected in the 30 staff members. Most are local but others come from Belarus, China and Hungary. Chef Martin Barry is from Waterford and is aided and abetted by Jeys Warren, from Surinam via Sri Lanka. Bernie Smullen has been with Hunter's since the early seventies; Margaret Thompson is assistant manager to Richard.

Richard Gelletlie, proving that history really does repeat itself, married Joan Kavanagh, a goldsmith and jeweller who runs the Wicklow shop. Tom travels to work in Hunter's from his south Dublin home; Maureen Gelletlie lives with the job in Hunter's Hotel. The hotel's future, Tom says, lies safely within the family, with Richard's children. "It's an all-absorbing thing," he understates, "running a hotel." Or a way of life, as Maureen Gelletlie would have it.

Acknowledgements

There wouldn't have been a *Trade Names* but for Jack Fagan, who started me writing the series and kept me at it when I might have skived off.

There wouldn't have been a book but for Frances O'Rourke, who edited the series, kept insisting there was a book in it and then worked tirelessly to bring it about.

If it hadn't been for Mary Hetherington's genius some of the pieces might have been lost forever to technology's filing system.

And in the most generous way possible everyone else in the Property Department in *The Irish Times* kept me and the series going, not least by coming up with new names when I flagged. Thanks to Orna, to Kate and to Justin, who also edited. Thanks too to Lorraine.

And, of course, great and many thanks to Peter Thursfield and *The Irish Times* photographers, without whom the words would have no pictures.

To the companies who make up Trade Names, my heartfelt thanks for your time and patience — and for being so generous with your memories.